For the Bride

Demetrios Presents

For the Bride

By Deborah McCoy

JE HOUSE PUBLISHING Ltd.
222 West 37th Street
New York, New York 10018

Contemporary wedding photography (unless otherwise noted) by:

Tim Roberts
Roberts Photographics, Inc.
Boca Raton, Florida

All floral centerpieces and bridal party flowers (Flower chapter)
designed by:

Tim Berry
Floral Concepts
Boca Raton, Florida

Published by: JE HOUSE PUBLISHING Ltd.
222 West 37th Street, New York, New York 10018

Copyright © 1993 by Deborah McCoy
Library of Congress Catalog Card Number: 93-080141
ISBN: 0-9638939-0-4
Selections from "The Passionate Palate" reprinted with permission of McIntosh and Otis,
Inc. Copyright © 1972 by Jeanine Lamoth and Roberta Wolfe Smoler.
Selections from "The New Jewish Wedding" copyright © 1985 Anita Diamant, reprinted
by permission of Simon & Schuster, Inc.
Manufactured in the United States of America.
First printing

Color Separations & Final Film by Studio Colour Group Inc., 105-6 Gurdwara Road,
Nepean, Ontario, K2E 8A3, Canada

For the Bride
is dedicated first and foremost
to Dino
forever my love...

and to
Millie and Donald... since birth my support group
and to
Poopsey... my pal
and to
Pam ...who made it possible

and to
Jimmy...who made it happen

Table of Contents

Part 1

Part 2

Part 3

Part 1

A radiant bride and groom exit their ceremony under a shower of rice.

Introduction

emetrios James Elias is the President of Ilissa, the *world's* largest manufacturer of bridal gowns. Brides know him better as Demetrios, that incredible, innovative designer whose magnificent gowns grace the pages of national bridal magazines.

I, Deborah McCoy, own Elva's Bridals, Floral Concepts and Ambiance Wedding & Party Planning in Boca Raton, Florida, and am a member of the Association of Bridal Consultants. When first inspired to do a bridal book, I called Demetrios. I wanted to work with the best.

After years in the bridal business I had discovered that most brides share a common problem: they're lost when it comes to planning their weddings. They would come to my store, sit down with me and take copious notes on everything I said about wedding planning. I failed to understand why this was happening with such frequency, until I went to the library and bookstores.

I found many bridal books but most were archaic and filled with erroneous information. To buy one, in my opinion, is like purchasing a passport to a nervous breakdown. Most of these *revised* guides are well over ten years old, and today's weddings simply are *not* the same as they were then. Some books recommend a short engagement because it only takes four to six months to "comfortably" plan a wedding. That may have been true in 1980, but if you follow this advice today, I guarantee you'll be anything but comfortable.

In the contents of a popular book it's stated that you can budget a formal wedding for up to 300 guests at a club or hotel for $4,000, including food and liquor, flowers, invitations, music and photography. When I read this I wondered if the author and I were living on the same planet. Then I realized the book was 30 years old.

The most disturbing thing to me, however, was the fact that these authors simply were not in the bridal business — not one of them planned weddings for a living.

Demetrios and I discussed this in detail. We spent much time researching the market, statistics on marriage and today's woman. We also noted that during the past 10 years our society has gone through dramatic change.

For one, the cost of a wedding has increased by 400 percent. Women now make up half the work force in the United States, and close to 50 percent of those who marry have attended or graduated from college. According to the last census, young people are waiting longer to marry than ever before because they want to finish their educations and establish their careers. This also means they have more money. A survey in *BRIDE'S* showed that newlyweds had a combined income that was 35 percent above the national average.

Demetrios and I also talked about the needs of today's bride. She still wants the fairy tale. Her wedding day is the most romantic, important day of her life and because it is, it must be perfect. A bride today wants romance but she realizes that it needs to be tempered by realism. And for that reason, we created *For the Bride* — a book designed to answer her questions and give her a logical approach to wedding planning. But more than that, it's beautiful!

We also know that planning a wedding can be exasperating and at times frustrating. A bride and her family must interview countless business people to evaluate their goods and services. Then a decision must be made — which is the hardest part of all. I have seen brides and their mothers agonize over their decisions. Is her gown the most beautiful, did they choose the right hotel, the band with the best sound, the most fabulous florist?

If you plan your wedding with the same foresight with which you purchase a new car (the average cost of a wedding exceeds the average price of a new car), chances are you don't have to worry. This means reading, shopping, interviewing and researching; all the things you do when you're about to make a major investment. *A wedding is an investment in memories*, whether you make a good or bad investment is up to you.

Demetrios and I also recognize the value of tradition — that beautiful bridge to our history that must be treasured and passed on to our children. But we also know that certain traditions require modification. In *For the Bride,* we stress the need for the groom and his family to become more involved in the wedding planning process both

emotionally and financially. A wedding can be too heavy a burden to place on the bride's family alone.

Throughout the book we're also going to emphasize the importance of being practical and using common sense (who was it who said, "Common sense isn't so common?"), and exercising good taste when it comes to planning *your* wedding. Your head may be in the clouds but it's essential to keep your feet on the ground.

Moreover, we also are concerned about what happens after... A beautiful wedding and a beautiful marriage should go hand in hand, yet the divorce rate in the United States has soared during the past few years. There are, however, premarital counseling programs available that effectively cut the divorce rate among participants. We have featured a chapter on them in *For the Bride.* We urge all engaged couples to participate.

We sincerely hope the experience and success Ilissa has had in the bridal industry, combined with the experience and success I've had planning hundreds of weddings, will make planning *your* wedding the most romantic, beautiful, and happiest time of your life.

For the Bride is the culmination of our experience. It was conceived to be a beautiful book with fabulous illustrations and pictures. But it also was written to be the most complete, factual and realistic reference book you'll need to plan the wedding of your dreams. Read. Enjoy. Refer to it often. *For the Bride* was written for you.

Debbie & Demetrios

A romantic centerpiece of Livia roses and baby's breath is the highlight of this reception table.

How to Use This Book

At the beginning of *For the Bride* are the WEDDING TIME TABLES. These charts are based on your particular time frame — the months you have available to plan your wedding. They schedule your entire wedding for you, A to Z. Consult them often. Whether you have one year to plan your wedding or five months, these charts will tell you what to do and when. Proper scheduling is the key to planning a stress-free wedding.

For the Bride is divided into three parts:

PART I gives you general information about the complexity of wedding planning. It's designed to get you thinking logically and rationally. Planning a wedding is something you must take seriously. It's not easy — but it can be fun — if you go about it in the right way.

PART II of *For the Bride* is entitled *The Plan*. These chapters follow the planning sequence of a wedding — from the first step to the last. Read these chapters carefully. They're the format for your wedding. Refer to them often.

PART III of *For the Bride* gives you general information and addresses any last minute questions you might have concerning your ceremony and reception. It also offers tips on how to avoid disaster and a final check list to ensure everything runs smoothly.

Read *For the Bride* in its entirety, then refer to it often. It's *your* guide to *your* wedding.

A romantic, afternoon wedding on the beach.

Wedding Time Tables

The *Wedding Time Tables* are planning schedules that are based on the months you have available to plan your wedding. If you had 12 months or more to plan, for example, you would consult the time table on the next page. This advises you on the best time to reserve your ceremony site (12 months before), order your wedding gown (eight months before), and reserve your formal wear (three months before). Each time table is a schedule that relates to your particular time — the months you have available to plan your wedding. Find *your* time table and schedule your wedding accordingly — then refer to it often. Proper scheduling will help alleviate stress.

I realize that the time tables may have to be adjusted to meet your particular needs. In some areas around the country, reception and ceremony sites must be reserved two years in advance. If you're getting married near prom time, for example, it's necessary to book a limousine much earlier than the three months provided by the *Wedding Time Tables.*

Use the *Wedding Time Tables* as your guide. Once you complete the tasks specified by the *Wedding Time Tables* cross them off the list. This will be a good indicator of what you've accomplished and what's left to be done.

Happy Planning!

These are *suggested* schedules. It may be necessary to adjust them to meet your particular needs.

Wedding Time Tables

If you have 12 months or more to plan

	12	11	10	9	8	7	6	5	4	3	2	1	Wedding Day
Reserve ceremony place	●												
Reserve reception place or caterer	●												
Reserve entertainment	●												
Plan honeymoon	●												
Premarital counseling, religious						●							
Premarital counseling, non-religious						●							
Announce engagement, newspaper					●								
Reserve photographer/videographer		●											
Reserve florist		●											
Order wedding gown					●								
Order headpiece and veil					●								
Order bridesmaids dresses							●						
Order invitations			●										
Order wedding cake				●									
Order men's formal wear										●			
Reserve makeup artist, hairstylist, nail technician										●			
*Reserve limousines or other transportation									●				
Get a marriage license, including												●	
blood tests if applicable											●		
Do final check — last chapter												●	

*Reserve early if your wedding falls near prom time.

These are *suggested* schedules. It may be necessary to adjust them to meet your particular needs.

Wedding Time Tables

If you have 11 months or more to plan

	12	11	10	9	8	7	6	5	4	3	2	1	Wedding Day
Reserve ceremony place		•											
Reserve reception place or caterer		•											
Reserve entertainment		•											
Plan honeymoon		•											
Premarital counseling, religious							•						
Premarital counseling, non-religious						•							
Announce engagement, newspaper						•							
Reserve photographer/videographer			•										
Reserve florist			•										
Order wedding gown					•								
Order headpiece and veil					•								
Order bridesmaids dresses							•						
Order invitations				•									
Order wedding cake				•									
Order men's formal wear										•			
Reserve makeup artist, hairstylist, nail technician										•			
*Reserve limousines or other transportation									•				
Get a marriage license, including												•	
blood tests if applicable											•		
Do final check — last chapter												•	

*Reserve early if your wedding falls near prom time.

18

These are *suggested* schedules. It may be necessary to adjust them to meet your particular needs.

Wedding Time Tables

If you have **10** months or more to plan

	12	11	10	9	8	7	6	5	4	3	2	1	Wedding Day
Reserve ceremony place			•										
Reserve reception place or caterer			•										
Reserve entertainment			•										
Plan honeymoon			•										
Premarital counseling, religious							•						
Premarital counseling, non-religious						•							
Announce engagement, newspaper						•							
Reserve photographer/videographer			•										
Reserve florist				•									
Order wedding gown					•								
Order headpiece and veil					•								
Order bridesmaids dresses							•						
Order invitations				•									
Order wedding cake				•									
Order men's formal wear										•			
Reserve makeup artist, hairstylist, nail technician										•			
*Reserve limousines or other transportation									•				
Get a marriage license, including												•	
blood tests if applicable											•		
Do final check — last chapter												•	

*Reserve early if your wedding falls near prom time.

These are *suggested* schedules. It may be necessary to adjust them to meet your particular needs.

Wedding Time Tables

If you have 9 months or more to plan

	12	11	10	9	8	7	6	5	4	3	2	1	Wedding Day
Reserve ceremony place				•									
Reserve reception place or caterer				•									
Reserve entertainment				•									
Plan honeymoon				•									
Premarital counseling, religious							•						
Premarital counseling, non-religious						•							
Announce engagement, newspaper						•							
Reserve photographer/videographer				•									
Reserve florist				•									
Order wedding gown					•								
Order headpiece and veil					•								
Order bridesmaids dresses							•						
Order invitations						•							
Order wedding cake								•					
Order men's formal wear									•				
Reserve makeup artist, hairstylist, nail technician										•			
*Reserve limousines or other transportation									•				
Get a marriage license, including												•	
blood tests if applicable											•		
Do final check — last chapter												•	

*Reserve early if your wedding falls near prom time.

These are *suggested* schedules. It may be necessary to adjust them to meet your particular needs.

Wedding Time Tables
If you have 8 months or more to plan

	12	11	10	9	8	7	6	5	4	3	2	1	Wedding Day
Reserve ceremony place					•								
Reserve reception place or caterer					•								
Reserve entertainment					•								
Plan honeymoon					•								
Premarital counseling, religious							•						
Premarital counseling, non-religious						•							
Announce engagement, newspaper								•					
Reserve photographer/videographer					•								
Reserve florist					•								
Order wedding gown						•							
Order headpiece and veil						•							
Order bridesmaids dresses							•						
Order invitations								•					
Order wedding cake							•						
Order men's formal wear										•			
Reserve makeup artist, hairstylist, nail technician										•			
*Reserve limousines or other transportation									•				
Get a marriage license, including												•	
blood tests if applicable											•		
Do final check — last chapter												•	

*Reserve early if your wedding falls near prom time.

These are *suggested* schedules. It may be necessary to adjust them to meet your particular needs.

Wedding Time Tables
If you have 7 months or more to plan

	12	11	10	9	8	7	6	5	4	3	2	1	Wedding Day
Reserve ceremony place						●							
Reserve reception place or caterer						●							
Reserve entertainment						●							
Plan honeymoon						●							
Premarital counseling, religious								●					
Premarital counseling, non-religious							●						
Announce engagement, newspaper									●				
Reserve photographer/videographer						●							
Reserve florist						●							
Order wedding gown								●					
Order headpiece and veil								●					
Order bridesmaids dresses								●					
Order invitations									●				
Order wedding cake									●				
Order men's formal wear										●			
Reserve makeup artist, hairstylist, nail technician										●			
*Reserve limousines or other transportation									●				
Get a marriage license, including												●	
blood tests if applicable											●		
Do final check — last chapter												●	

*Reserve early if your wedding falls near prom time.

These are *suggested* schedules. It may be necessary to adjust them to meet your particular needs.

Wedding Time Tables

If you have 6 months or more to plan

	12	11	10	9	8	7	6	5	4	3	2	1	Wedding Day
Reserve ceremony place							•						
Reserve reception place or caterer							•						
Reserve entertainment							•						
Plan honeymoon							•						
Premarital counseling, religious								•					
Premarital counseling, non-religious								•					
Announce engagement, newspaper									•				
Reserve photographer/videographer							•						
Reserve florist							•						
Order wedding gown							•						
Order headpiece and veil							•						
Order bridesmaids dresses							•						
Order invitations									•				
Order wedding cake								•					
Order men's formal wear										•			
Reserve makeup artist, hairstylist, nail technician										•			
*Reserve limousines or other transportation									•				
Get a marriage license, including												•	
blood tests if applicable											•		
Do final check — last chapter												•	

*Reserve early if your wedding falls near prom time.

These are *suggested* schedules. It may be necessary to adjust them to meet your particular needs.

Wedding Time Tables

If you have 5 months or more to plan

	12	11	10	9	8	7	6	5	4	3	2	1	Wedding Day
Reserve ceremony place								●					
Reserve reception place or caterer								●					
Reserve entertainment								●					
Plan honeymoon								●					
Premarital counseling, religious									●				
Premarital counseling, non-religious									●				
Announce engagement, newspaper										●			
Reserve photographer/videographer								●					
Reserve florist								●					
Order wedding gown								●					
Order headpiece and veil								●					
Order bridesmaids dresses								●					
Order invitations									●				
Order wedding cake									●				
Order men's formal wear										●			
Reserve makeup artist, hairstylist, nail technician										●			
*Reserve limousines or other transportation									●				
Get a marriage license, including blood tests if applicable											●	●	
Do final check — last chapter												●	

*Reserve early if your wedding falls near prom time.

These are *suggested* schedules. It may be necessary to adjust them to meet your particular needs.

Wedding Time Tables

If you have 4 months or more to plan

	12	11	10	9	8	7	6	5	4	3	2	1	Wedding Day
Reserve ceremony place									•				
Reserve reception place or caterer									•				
Reserve entertainment									•				
Plan honeymoon									•				
Premarital counseling, religious									•				
Premarital counseling, non-religious													
Announce engagement, newspaper										•			
Reserve photographer/videographer									•				
Reserve florist									•				
Order wedding gown									• *Rush Cut!*				
Order headpiece and veil									•				
Order bridesmaids dresses									• *Rush Cut!*				
Order invitations										•			
Order wedding cake										•			
Order men's formal wear											•		
Reserve makeup artist, hairstylist, nail technician											•		
*Reserve limousines or other transportation									•				
Get a marriage license, including												•	
blood tests if applicable											•		
Do final check — last chapter												•	

*Reserve early if your wedding falls near prom time.

A tall hurricane globe and romantic bow make this centerpiece unique.

Thinking of the Wedding
An Overview

efore the announcement of your engagement, think about your wedding day and envision what you want. Whether you are dreaming of a large, formal affair at a grand hotel or a small gathering on a wind-swept day at a beach, one factor that will turn your wedding dreams into reality is money. To determine if your dreams are feasible and affordable, it's important to discuss *all* aspects of your wedding with your fiancé and families. I suggest you do this *before* you announce your engagement, so there will be no hard feelings or misunderstandings once the wedding preparation begins.

What Makes Weddings so Difficult?

The wedding industry as a whole is unique because it's dominated by small businesses. I like to think of it as a pie, with each slice representing a different business (caterers, florists, photographers, etc.) that will provide goods and services for

your wedding day. Your goal is to bring these businesses harmoniously together — on the same day, at the same time, in the same place. This is what makes wedding coordination so time consuming and difficult.

It doesn't matter if your wedding is a small catered affair at home, or a reception for 500 at a grand hotel. The same elements are common to both. Rings must be purchased along with dresses, flowers, photography, food and liquor. This list seems endless, yet no bride wants to sacrifice those special touches that make up a romantic, traditional wedding. This means riding to the ceremony in a limo, cutting a fabulous cake, and sailing off into the sunset with Prince Charming. It's every woman's dream, as well it should be.

Modifying Tradition

Through the centuries and even today, tradition has dictated that the bride's family pay for her wedding. This tradition has its roots in ancient

The bride exits the limousine with the aid of the groom.

27

custom, where a man had so many daughters, it behooved him to pay for the celebrations if he was lucky enough to marry them off. He also provided a handsome dowry to further entice the groom. The dowry has become obsolete, and so must the practice of the bride's family paying for the entire wedding celebration.

While many bridal books and magazines still uphold this tradition, I believe it's time for tradition to be *modified*. It's not fair to saddle the bride's family with the total expense of a wedding — unless her name is Rockefeller. This is one time when tradition must be put aside for what's fair, since both parties share and benefit from a wedding. A wedding is a celebration that should be

regarded as a *joint venture*. Both families should pool their resources for the benefit of the young couple beginning their life together. Bitterness and resentment harbored by one family against another, especially over money, is no way to start a marriage.

In the nineties, the *average* cost of a wedding will exceed $20,000. This is a far cry from the $5,000 weddings that were the average a decade ago. In the past ten years, wedding costs have increased 400 percent, and for this reason the financial responsibility *must* shift from the bride's parents. They can no longer be expected to shoulder the whole burden. It's time for the groom's parents and the bride and groom themselves to contribute — if they're financially able.

Timing Makes a Difference

Whether your wedding is large or small, formal, informal or semi-formal, remember that planning takes time. If you become engaged in January, for example, and plan on being married in April, you may have difficulty buying a wedding gown or bridesmaids dresses from a bridal shop, where you can't buy a dress off the rack unless you are buying a *sample* or *discontinued* style. Wedding gowns and bridesmaids dresses are *ordered* and take at least three months to be delivered.

If you allowed yourself three months to plan your wedding, you might also have a rough time finding a place for your ceremony and reception, or finding entertainment. The best rule of thumb is to give yourself 10 months to a year to plan your wedding. If you happen to live in a densely populated area such as New York or Los Angeles, be aware that reception places must be booked sometimes as far as two years in advance.

By giving yourself enough time, you'll be able

The bride and groom share a few fun moments together.

International Stock Photography

The bride, groom, and bridal party posed after the wedding.

to plan your wedding in an orderly, scheduled fashion. If you don't, things may snowball and you may end up feeling lost and totally out of control.

Holidays - A Word of Advice

If you plan on having your wedding near a holiday, make inquiries early. Most places are heavily booked around holidays, so give yourself at least a year to plan your wedding and reserve your choice.

And don't forget Mother's Day. This is one of the biggest days for restaurants, private clubs, and hotels. The last thing you need is to have your wedding crammed into the schedule the week before Mother's Day (or Easter, or Christmas) when their sole preoccupation is how many hams they should glaze and turkeys they should stuff. Also avoid the week after, when

everyone, including management and staff, are exhausted.

It's best to choose a date three weeks before the holiday, or three weeks afterward. Many brides, for example, like the idea of marrying close to Valentine's Day. But if flowers are important to you on your wedding day — and you don't have unlimited funds — don't do it. Wholesale florists stockpile flowers before holidays. Easter, Mother's Day, Valentine's Day and Christmas are the biggest floral days of the year for wholesalers as well as retailers. This means that flowers can cost 100 percent more (wholesale and retail) before holidays. It also means flowers stockpiled for long periods of time, in anticipation of the seasonal high sales volume, are not fresh. I don't like to do weddings before holidays. It is frustrating to work with flowers that are half dead and to pay an exorbitant price for them.

Rule: Set the date for your wedding three weeks before a holiday or three weeks after to avoid mayhem, and to save yourself time, aggravation and money.

This rule also applies to entertainment, limos, caterers, etc. It seems that all businesses are affected by holidays. If you're planning your wedding near a holiday, make inquiries to see that all merchants and service people have your wedding date available, and that their rates are reasonable. If you experience trouble, consider a date change.

How to Shop

The best way to find quality vendors and service people for your wedding is through referral. I can't stress this enough. Ask recently married friends, relatives and co-workers what businesses they used for their weddings and receptions. Were they happy with the companies and service personnel they employed? If not, what were their complaints? I think you'll find that the same names keep popping up over and over. Reputation — good or bad — spreads like wildfire in the bridal industry. When clients ask me about a certain hotel for their reception or a bakery for their cake, I tell them what I know from experience, or what I've heard from other clients. Listen and learn from others' experiences and mistakes. It will save you time, legwork and money.

Many brides turn to *The Yellow Pages* for assistance, but it's my opinion that the phone book should be your last source for reference when choosing vendors for your wedding and reception. Your most reliable source remains *word of mouth*.

A wedding is one of the most personal, beautiful, but stressful experiences you will ever go through, and you must employ the most experienced, honest and caring people to take you through it. *The Yellow Pages* can't tell you how honest, experienced, or caring a business is, but a recently married bride can.

Ceremonies and Receptions

Now is the time to think about possible ceremony and reception sites — before the announcement of your engagement. Be sure to give yourself plenty of options for the ceremony and reception. The more options you have, the less aggravated you'll be. You'll be able to sit down with your families and comfortably make choices without feeling so pressured. If you must change the date to accommodate the type of wedding you've always envisioned, or change the time to coordinate the ceremony to the reception, no one will be the wiser. Do not etch a date in stone.

Never assume your church will be able to marry you in June, as you've always dreamed. Don't assume your club will be available for the reception. Many unhappy brides have done just that, only to have their ceremonies and receptions in places forced upon them by availability. Don't let this happen to you.

Religious Ceremonies

If you want to be married in a particular church or synagogue but are not a member of the congregation, you may run into difficulty. If you fit this description, call the minister, priest or rabbi and arrange a meeting as soon as possible.

Non-denominational churches will marry non-members for a fee (which may be exorbitant). So will many Protestant churches. The best thing to do if you are not a member of a congregation is to ask friends and family members if they are familiar with any churches that are flexible in their marriage requirements and have reasonable fees.

Many religions also insist that engaged couples take premarital religious instruction and marriage training. The Catholic Church, for example, can be very explicit in its requirements.

Also be aware that you may run into difficulty if one person has been previously married, or you share different religions. Be sure to call your clergy to check on *all* religious requirements before setting a date.

Atypical Ceremony Sites

If you plan on being married on a beach, in a park, museum or any atypical place, make inquiries immediately. Call the institution or city hall. Ask about availability and requirements for weddings. Find out what rules you must follow, and if you need a license. Ask about fees, deposits, and when the balance is due.

RECEPTIONS

Afternoon weddings, or those held on Friday or Sunday, are usually less expensive than those held on Saturday night, which is the first choice of most brides. Buffets are usually more expensive than sit-down dinners because food is charged "per item." Sit-down dinners are *packaged* to provide more for your money. Contrary to popular opinion, weddings held at home are not necessarily less expensive than those taking place at private clubs, restaurants, or hotels (unless you're doing your own cooking). Party rentals and caterers are expensive. By the time you estimate the price of an "at-home" wedding, you might find

that a wedding at a private club, or hotel, costs about the same without the headaches.

Thinking of a June wedding? You may want to reconsider. June has always been *the* traditional month for weddings. In 1990, the last Saturday in June was the biggest wedding day of the year with 44,000 weddings. More than half of all weddings take place on Saturday, and any month's total of weddings depends on the number of Saturdays in that time period. June is usually followed in popularity by the other summer months, with the fifth most popular month being September.

Take a hard look at these facts when planning your wedding. If you live in a place where winters are severe, you don't have much choice but to have a summer wedding. But if it's possible to marry in the spring or fall, consider doing so. Every bride needs a little tender loving care when she plans her wedding, and sometimes that's hard to get if a business has 30 other weddings the same month as yours. Try to bypass the summer when restaurants, hotels and clubs are popping out weddings like cars off an assembly line.

Scheduling Ceremonies and Receptions

If your ceremony and reception are not at the same location, it's essential that the two events be coordinated, preferably one right after the other. I do not like weddings where there are two, three or more hours between the ceremony and reception. Guests do not like to get dressed up, or drive a long distance to attend a wedding, knowing they're going to have to wait a few boring hours in uncomfortable clothes for the reception to begin. Many in this position don't attend the ceremony, and opt only to attend the reception. And who can blame them? This arrangement is partic-

The bride and groom, seated at a love dais, share a few intimate moments.

ularly unfair to out-of-town guests who are unfamiliar with the area and don't know where to go, or what to do to keep themselves entertained.

I recall one wedding where the bridal party (having nowhere to go after the ceremony) went back to the hotel lounge to wait for the celebration to begin. When I arrived two hours later to deliver the reception flowers, they were hugging the barstools.

It is up to the bride to make arrangements for the bridal party and out-of-town family and guests if there's dead time between the ceremony and reception. To avoid this problem, schedule your reception immediately following your ceremony. Don't inconvenience your guests, who are your first consideration.

A long wait between the ceremony and reception is even more tiring for a bride and groom, already stressed on their wedding day. A few hours with nothing to do can really put a damper on things, and having a few drinks before the party starts can be disastrous. Photographers frown on this. One mentioned to me, "The camera doesn't lie. If you're tipsy, you'll show up tipsy in photos." While this makes for funny brides, it doesn't make for pretty ones.

Ceremony and Reception - Two in One

If you're thinking of having your ceremony in the same place as the reception, make sure the club, restaurant or hotel has the facilities to handle both affairs. If you're considering an "at-home" wedding, check to see if the home is equipped. This means large enough rooms or grounds (if you're contemplating a tent, run to the nearest video store and rent *Betsy's Wedding*) and a kitchen that a caterer can make use of with large enough ovens and refrigeration equipment, etc. Make sure there's room for a dance floor, band, orchestra or disc jockey, if you're providing entertainment.

Your guests should be your first consideration, however, no matter where the festivities are held. You must make sure they're not inconvenienced in any way, so that they enjoy your day as much as you do.

ENTERTAINMENT

Start to think about entertainment. Give yourself enough time to reserve it, because bands and disc jockeys sometimes book a year or more in advance. Ask recently married friends, relatives and business associates *what* entertainment they had at their receptions, and *who* they had. Maybe some preferred a band to a disc jockey, or a "one man band" for an informal wedding. Maybe one D.J. was found to be mediocre, another outstanding. Referral is once again the key to finding good entertainment at a price you can afford.

A Word of Advice

Many brides and their families don't feel dance

A harpist plays before the ceremony.

music is important at morning or early afternoon weddings. They employ a harpist, strolling violinist, or a guitarist. Is it any wonder that their guests leave early?

Don't expect guests to have a few drinks and hors d'oeuvres, lunch or brunch, and then sit around and listen to violins for the remainder of the party. It just doesn't work that way. If your budget doesn't allow for a band or orchestra, get a disc jockey. Dancing has always been an integral part of a wedding. Even if you have to play music on a compact disc, or a tape player, you'll be glad you did.

PRECAUTIONARY MEASURES

Wedding Cancellation Insurance

Many times weddings are canceled or postponed because of unforeseen circumstances like a death in the family. It's important to be aware that most vendors, no matter what the reason, will be reluctant to return your deposits. This is usually backed up by their contracts.

Fireman's Fund Insurance Company in Novato, California, has come to the rescue, offering insurance to protect your deposits with added extras like coverage for your wedding attire and wedding gifts if they are damaged, coverage to retake photographs if they don't turn out, and liability coverage for your wedding and reception. The cost of this "weddingsurance" is minimal.

It is also important to note that this insurance can be upgraded to cover your total losses — not just the loss of your deposits. Many times if a wedding is canceled the vendor may turn around and sue you for the full amount of the contract. For that reason, it's advisable to consider weddingsurance to cover the full cost of your wedding and reception expenses. For more information, consult the Appendix.

Make Follow Up Part of the Plan

Everyone has seen a talk show featuring brides and grooms who have experienced terrible wedding-day trauma: the dress that didn't come in on time, the caterer who got the date mixed up, the flowers that never made it to the ceremony, the cake that wasn't delivered.

Take it from me, these disasters need not happen. Often they occur because the bride did not follow up properly. This is a must when planning a wedding. It's up to you to stay in contact with the people you've hired. You have one wedding to plan, they might have 40 bookings. Speak with them regularly during the wedding planning process. Make sure they get to know you. *Follow up on a regular basis.* There are factors you can't control — a hotel fire, for instance, or a traffic accident that sends your cake flying. But trust me, if you employ good people, they'll do everything in their power to rectify the situation, even at the last minute.

In Part III of *For the Bride*, there's a final checklist that you should complete the week before your wedding. Follow it to help ensure that everything runs smoothly on your wedding day.

IN SUMMARY

Reserving the place for the ceremony and reception and booking entertainment are the toughest hurdles to clear when planning a wedding. Start making inquiries — now. Do your own legwork, and research and analyze all possibilities. Then make and reserve your choices.

The bride and her father, a moment to treasure.

A formal, evening wedding at the Boca Raton Resort and Club.

Budget and Finance

After your engagement, get together with your families. The courteous thing to do is meet with the bride's family first. Find out what they feel their obligations are — what "type" of wedding they're envisioning. You might find what *they* want and what *you* want are two entirely different things. The mother of one of my clients almost fell from her chair when her daughter told me she wanted a traditional wedding. Her mother thought she wanted a small ceremony followed by a cocktail party.

After you meet with the bride's family, the groom should meet with his family. He must stress that a wedding is too much of a financial burden to place on one family, and that he as well as the bride will benefit. He might ask his parents to help pay for part of the wedding expenses in lieu of a gift. He also should stress that their emotional and financial support will be greatly appreciated by him, his future bride and her family. He might then suggest they meet with the bride's family to discuss the wedding.

At this meeting, the bride, groom and their families should determine the total budget for the wedding. If possible, expenses should be divided proportionately. If the bride's family is paying for

ceremony and reception flowers, then the groom's family should pay for the liquor. If the groom's family is paying for the entertainment, then the bride's family should pay for the food, etc. Decide what each family will contribute. But don't assign monetary amounts to wedding components at this time. Don't say, "I'm going to spend $1,000 for my wedding gown, and $500 for flowers," because you haven't yet surveyed the market. Once you do, you'll be able to decide where you want to concentrate your time, effort and dollars.

Financial Guidelines

Once you establish financial guidelines — who'll pay for what, how much they're able to pay and how much you and your fiancé will contribute — you can begin to budget your total wedding dollars. Do this before the announcement of your engagement so you can make plans and cope with possible disappointments. Maybe Uncle Harry lost his business and can't give you the $5,000 he's promised you for your wedding since you were a toddler. Maybe, after much thought, you and your fiancé will have to secure a loan to have the wedding of your dreams. Now is the time to make plans. Don't wait until the stress of

A formal, evening reception.

wedding planning makes you think you've bought a one-way ticket to a loony bin. Don't let money woes put a damper on what should be a happy time.

Address money problems from the start. Many of my clients tell me, "I cut back my guest list, because it was very important to me that I do my wedding my way. I didn't want less expensive centerpieces. I didn't want to serve chicken." The guest list is the first thing to pare down if you want to save money, or you want a smaller but more elegant wedding.

Compromise Your Way to Happiness

As the future bride and groom, you should act as mediators at family meetings to avoid letting one family dominate. You also should be willing to pitch in and help financially if possible. If you want that Grand Tradition gown, or printed menus for the guests, or a "Viennese Dessert Table" — things your families find extravagant — pay for them yourselves. The important thing is to make your families comfortable and happy while planning your wedding. *The key is to compromise.*

Be courteous to family members, and thank them on a regular basis for time and effort they're putting forth on your behalf. Make sure everyone takes the project seriously because today's wedding is a business venture — a major investment.

As mentioned earlier, the average cost of a wedding in the nineties will exceed $20,000 (which is more than half the average American's income). This is a lot of money to lose if something goes wrong. That's why it's crucial that those who contribute hard-earned dollars to your wedding think of it as a business project. Hard work and attention to detail will make your wedding day a beautiful, happy experience for all involved. A wedding is an investment in memories. Whether you make a good or bad investment is up to you.

If You Live Together - Who Pays?

I, personally, believe it unfair of a couple to ask families to pay for their wedding if they're living together. A wedding is a celebration that marks a woman leaving the home of her parents to begin a new life with her husband. In Jewish ceremonies, the couple stands under a "chuppa" or canopy, that many say symbolically marks the beginning of a new home. If you and your fiancé live together, the wedding takes on a different significance. It makes your cohabitation legal and binding.

According to the last census, more than half the people who married had cohabited. Most women who are living with their fiancés, tell me they'd be too embarrassed to ask their families to pay for their weddings. Many ask for, and accept, contributions to the affair in lieu of gifts. One bride's grandmother, for example, bought her gown, another's parents paid for the liquor at the reception, with the groom's parents paying for flowers. But this might not happen. If you host your own wedding, which you should do if you're living together, be prepared to handle it all yourself, both emotionally and financially.

A Word of Advice

More and more couples today are hosting and paying for their own weddings and can well afford to do it. A *BRIDE'S* magazine survey found that newlyweds had a combined income that was 35 percent above the national average household income in the United States. This affluence is the result of young people waiting to marry until their educations are completed and their careers established.

The bandleader gets the party hopping!

If you are a career couple hosting your own wedding, try to put things in perspective and remember that $20,000 is a lot of money to spend on a wedding. That tidy sum could buy a new car or could become a down-payment on a house. With your fiancé, examine your priorities and your budget, then decide on the type of wedding that's best for you. And don't go into debt. A wedding can end up like a hangover. After it's all said and done, you might not feel so good when you wake up in the morning.

How to Budget

I can't tell you how many times clients have told me, "Wow! I just had a meeting with the caterer and florist, and I had no idea how much this was going to cost!" To avoid the sticker shock of a wedding, I advise doing preliminary legwork. Armed with your list of referred businesses — hotels, clubs, catering halls, bands, D.J.s, florists, bakers, bridal shops, stationery stores, etc.— call upon them. Most businesses offer price brochures for weddings. If they don't have them get a feel for their prices and note them.

Once you get home, *average* the prices for each item but compare apples to apples. For example one disc jockey charges $300, one charges $500, and another $450. The average is about $420. Bands, on the other hand, may range from $1,500, to $3,500, or more. Average the cost, but don't average bands and D.J.s together.

You should next compare hotels or clubs and their reception *packages* for value as well as price. You might note that the hotel you loved is $25 per head higher for a sit-down chicken dinner than the country club, but the country club is giving you more for the money. If you were thinking of inviting one hundred guests, that's a $2,500

difference. Um! Maybe that honeymoon in Hawaii is possible after all.

Next, think of the number of people you want to invite (include bridal party and spouses or dates), for example 150 or 175. Base your estimates on the higher number. Assume everyone will show up, which proportionately will affect the cost. More people require more centerpieces, food, liquor, invitations, etc.

Once you survey the market and know the costs (this is going to take a lot of time on the phone and legwork), and have an estimate of the number of guests you plan to invite — you can begin to realistically plan a budget, *and make choices.* Maybe floral centerpieces aren't as important to you as good entertainment, or maybe you'll have to settle for thermographed invitations rather than engraved ones. Look at the following Preliminary Budget. After you've done your legwork, mark down the *averaged* prices for the items on the list. Once again, be sure to average apples to apples. Under reception costs, for example, you should have averages for sit-down dinners, buffets, and cocktail-hors d'oeuvre receptions. Also, mark down who will pay for each item, or how much they'll contribute. Once you complete this, total all items and add on 15% to cover contingencies, then add applicable sales tax. Once your Preliminary Budget is complete you'll know whether or not your wedding is affordable. If it's not, cut back your guest list, or tone down various aspects of the wedding — less expensive invitations, a D.J. instead of a band, chicken instead of surf-and-turf. You have plenty of options. Once you decide on the amount you intend to spend on each item, mark it in the "Amount Budgeted" column of the Preliminary Budget and stick to it!

The structuring of a reasonable, practical budget — one that everyone can work with — is the most important thing you can do to ensure your happiness, and the happiness of everyone involved in planning your wedding.

The bride and groom share a kiss and a toast.

Sisters make special bridesmaids.

Preliminary Budget

	Average Price or Cost	Contributor and Amount Contributed	Amount Budgeted
Engagement Costs:			
Engagement Ring			
Engagement Photos			
Engagement Parties (if applicable)			
Ceremony Costs:			
Rental of Facility			
Officiant's Fee			
Coordinator's Fee (if applicable)			
Organists and Musicians			
Flowers and Decorations			
Guest Book			
Wedding Programs			
Reception Costs:			
Estimated Number of Guests:			
a. Food			
b. Liquor			
c. Extras (valet parking, linens, rental fees, etc.)			
d. Tax, Service Charges or Gratuities			
Flowers/Decorations			
Entertainment			
Favors for Guests			
Wedding Cake			
Bridal Wear:			
Wedding Gown			
Headpiece and Veil			
Alterations			
Accessories (shoes, slips, bras, etc.)			
Jewelry			
Hair, Makeup, Nails, Facial, Massage, etc.			
Groom's Wear:			
Rent or Buy Formal Wear			
Accessories (shoes, studs, etc.)			

Preliminary Budget

	Average Price or Cost	Contributor and Amount Contributed	Amount Budgeted
Gift Expenses:			
Gifts for Bridal Party Members			
Gifts for Hosts of the Wedding			
Gifts Bride and Groom Give Each Other			
Rehearsal Dinner:			
Estimated Number of Guests:			
Invitations			
Caterer and/or Restaurant Cost			
Flowers and Decorations			
The Other Essentials:			
Flowers for Bridal Party			
Photography			
Videography			
Invitations (including thank-you notes)			
Invitation Accessories (printed napkins, etc.)			
Rented Transportation			
Wedding Rings			
Honeymoon (include costs of trip, clothes, etc.)			
Blood Tests, Premarital Physicals			
Marriage License			
Wedding Cancellation Insurance			
Premarital Agreement (lawyers' fees)			
Premarital Counseling (non-religious)			
Preservation of Gown and Veil			
Preservation of Bridal Bouquet			
TOTALS			

ADD A 15% CONTINGENCY FACTOR: _____

ADD APPLICABLE SALES TAX: _____

TOTAL OF ESTIMATED EXPENSES: _____

A Word of Advice

Weddings are paid for up-front, usually the week before. Many vendors will not accept credit cards or checks, so prepare to pay cash. If you budgeted realistically and stayed within your limits, you should have few problems. I've seen many hysterical brides, however, who didn't have the money when it came time to pay the bill. The stress they put themselves under — not to mention their fiancés and families — is no way to start a marriage. What should have been the happiest time of their lives became the most miserable.

The groom takes a much needed break.

The Basics

Get together with your families to decide when your wedding should take place. I would advise giving yourself a minimum of 10 months to one year to plan your wedding. Allow even more time if you live in one of those highly populated areas where wedding and reception sites are often reserved two years in advance. Decide on a month you think would be best, then consider:

Your work schedules

Are they flexible? Will you be able to take time off?

Be sure to schedule your time so that you're able to take three days off prior to your wedding for last minute preparations. This will also give you some time to relax and enjoy yourself — have a massage, or spend a day at the beach. This isn't as important for the groom, but I advise that he skip work the day before the wedding to assist the bride. *Stress levels are at their highest the week before the wedding.* Don't burden yourself unduly.

Will you have time for a honeymoon?

Many of my clients plan huge weddings without allowing a few days for a honeymoon. Their wedding is Saturday night and they're back to work on Monday. A honeymoon is as much a part of your wedding as the ceremony. It was designed to give newly married people time to relax and enjoy one another before returning to the stress of everyday life. Even if you're living together, you'll need rest and relaxation after going through the rigors of a wedding. Don't deny yourself a honeymoon. Build it into the budget from the beginning. You'll be glad you did.

Is weather or season a factor?

Is traveling in winter difficult for your out-of-town family and guests if a Christmas wedding has been your dream? Do you live in a summer or winter resort town that makes it difficult and expensive to book rooms for your guests? If so, consider changing the date.

Are you planning a June wedding?

Avoid the "hottest" wedding months, June, July, and August, for example, when clubs, restaurants and hotels are up to their ears in weddings. Every bride needs a little tender loving care when she plans her wedding. If you can, it's better to have a

Beautiful flowers make an elegant table.

wedding off-season when things are slower and more relaxed. Don't get caught in a rat race.

Is your planned ceremony site appropriate for the type of wedding you're envisioning?

Many brides wish to be married in their church or temple, which is appropriate for any wedding type — formal, semi-formal or informal. Other brides, however, wish to be married in hotels, restaurants, parks, museums, even on the beach. Take time to consider if the place is equal to the formality of your wedding. You would not have a formal wedding in a park, for example.

Is the date you're considering on or near a holiday?

Try to avoid this if possible. *Reserve your wedding three weeks before the holiday or three weeks after* to avoid stress, aggravation and elevated prices. For more information, read Chapter 3, "Thinking of the Wedding: An Overview" and follow the three-week rule.

RESERVING THE CEREMONY SITE

Call places you're considering for your ceremony. Ask if your tentative *month* is available, what *days* are open in that month, and what *times* are

CEREMONY CHART

St. Joan's Church or Temple Beth El, or the Holiday Inn, etc. in July.

	Fri. night	Sat. morning	Sat. afternoon	Sat. night	Sun. afternoon	Sun. night
1st weekend		10	1 or 2			
2nd weekend						
3rd weekend			3			
4th weekend					3	

available on those days. Make yourself a chart like the one above for each place you're contemplating. It lists ceremony times on weekends in July.

Look at the chart. On the first Saturday in July, the ceremony must take place at 10 a.m., or 1 p.m. or 2 p.m. On the third weekend, the wedding would take place at 3 p.m. Saturday, and on the fourth weekend, 3 p.m. Sunday. What are your options?

The *time* you choose for your ceremony is a key factor in determining the *type* of wedding you want to have. For example, if you had your ceremony at 10 a.m., you would have no choice but to have a semi-formal or informal wedding followed by a brunch. Morning ceremonies are not appropriate for formal, "black tie" affairs, if that's been your dream. Nothing looks more ridiculous than the wedding party and immediate families arriving at the ceremony in tails and formal gowns in the morning.

Many brides consider having an early-afternoon ceremony followed by an evening reception so they can have a "formal" wedding. This is inadvisable for a couple of reasons. First, the *time of the ceremony* designates the formality of the wedding *not the time of the reception*. Dress that's appropriate for an afternoon ceremony is *not* appropriate for an elegant, formal, evening affair. Nothing looks sillier than the bridal party and guests showing up in the middle of the afternoon in tails, or tuxes and long formal gowns. That type of garb is only for evening receptions.

Second, a ceremony and reception that is not timed sequentially means that guests have nowhere to go between the ceremony and reception. This is especially unfair to out-of-town guests unfamiliar with the area.

If you find you have problems reserving the *time* you want for your ceremony, or the date is unavailable, consider changing the place for your ceremony. Or you can change the date to accommodate your wedding, whether it's informal, semi-formal or formal. (In the next chapter, I'm going to discuss in detail the necessity of properly structuring a wedding for beauty and cohesiveness.)

The Reception — How to Narrow the Field

Once you have possible ceremony sites in mind, it's time to consider reception locations. Give yourself plenty of options so you won't be discouraged if your first choice is booked.

When speaking to the person in charge of catering, whether it be the catering director or manager, be sure to:

Tell them the number of people you expect. Rooms hold only so many guests. Also inform them of the type of entertainment you're contemplating. An orchestra or a band takes more space than a disc jockey, and along with your guest list will determine the size room you'll need.

Ask if they have facilities to handle both a ceremony and reception if you'd like to have them both in the same place. Make sure they have separate quarters for a cocktail hour if you're planning one. Many clubs in our area don't have separate facilities for a cocktail hour, and offer guests cocktails and hors d'oeuvres by the pool. This is fine if

you live in a tropical climate and winter doesn't pose a problem, but a rainy day can put a damper on things no matter where you live.

Ask how many weddings will take place on the same day, at the same time as yours. More than one wedding going on at once at a small hotel or club is distracting. At a large facility, this shouldn't matter.

Once you have researched reception possibilities, log them on a chart like the one following. Now compare your Ceremony Chart to your Reception Chart. Coordinate ceremony times to reception times. Plan the two sequentially so your guests won't be inconvenienced. And don't rule out Friday night if Saturday or Sunday isn't available.

Look at your Ceremony Chart. Let's say you

Reception Chart

July	Fri. night	Sat. morning	Sat. afternoon	Sat. night	Sun. afternoon	Sun. night
The Marriott						
1st weekend	x				x	
2nd weekend		x				
3rd weekend				x		
4th weekend			x			
Boca Pointe Country Club						
1st weekend		x				
2nd weekend				x		
3rd weekend						
4th weekend						x
Sea Farer Restaurant						
1st weekend			x			
2nd weekend				x		
3rd weekend	x					
4th weekend						x

want to have a semi-formal wedding on Saturday. You'd like the ceremony to start at 3 p.m., with cocktails and hors d'oeuvres served from 4:30 p.m. to 5:30 p.m., followed by dinner. According to the Ceremony Chart, the third Saturday in the month is the only one available.

Now look at your Reception Chart. The Marriott is the only place that has the third Saturday night available, but it's 45 minutes from your ceremony site. You notice, however, that the following Sunday night is available at Boca Pointe and the Sea Farer. Now look at your Ceremony Chart, and see if it's available for the following Sunday afternoon. It is! What's wrong with Sunday? Your family and guests will get home at a reasonable hour, and besides, from a catering standpoint, Sunday is usually less expensive than Saturday night (which is the choice of most brides). At this point, you have two viable alternatives before calling out-of-town family and friends.

Notifying Family and Friends

Next, call your family and friends, especially those who live out-of-town, to see if your tentative wedding date suits them. If it doesn't, consider changing the date. After all, what's a wedding without the ones who've been closest to you throughout your life?

How accessible is your wedding to your out-of-town family and friends? Airline reservations must be made weeks in advance to get seats and the best fares. Hotels and motels must be booked to guarantee rooms. Call them to inquire about rates for your out-of-town guests. Ask what discounts they offer if a block of rooms is reserved and what extras they offer such as free breakfast, happy hour, limo service to and from the airport,

etc. Think of motels and hotels in terms of their walking accessibility to restaurants, shops and things to do. Some guests on limited budgets may not be able to rent cars once they're in town.

Once you have a couple of options for your ceremony and reception, call out-of-town family and friends. Say, "John and I are thinking of being married in July, either the third Saturday or the fourth Sunday. What's best for you?"

Make a chart like the one below. Log their answers on the chart.

GUEST CHART

July

	3rd Saturday	4th Sunday
Uncle Harry	x	
Susan James		x
Grandpa Joe		x
Bill Jones	x	
Howard Smith		x

After you've called your out-of-town guests, schedule your wedding. In this case, the majority like Sunday. Uncle Harry and Bill Jones will have to change their plans if they want to attend.

CEREMONIES AND RECEPTIONS - RESERVE YOUR CHOICES

Once you've decided where to have your ceremony and reception — reserve them — with the least amount of deposit money possible. Be aware that no matter what has transpired, *your date is not reserved until you leave a deposit and obtain a receipt.*

Churches and synagogues usually don't require deposits, but be sure to ask. Public places — parks, museums, etc. — will, as will the restaurant, club or hotel where you plan to have your reception. When talking to the person in charge of catering you might say, "My parents are coming to town in a couple of weeks to give you a deposit. In the meantime, let me give you this token amount to hold the date." Hopefully, they'll be too busy to call for the rest of the money until final planning gets underway.

Deposits usually are not refundable, so be careful. No one knows what will happen in eight to 10 months that could cancel or postpone the affair. Don't make deposits haphazardly or agree to exorbitant amounts. Bargain to get the amount as low as possible.

Don't sign a contract at this time. Get price brochures, a receipt for your deposit (have it put in writing that this is completely refundable within 48 hours if you change your mind), and go home to think about your decision. There's plenty of time to sign a contract later (see Receptions chapter).

OTHER CONSIDERATIONS
The "At Home" Ceremony and Reception

If you're considering Aunt Meg's fabulous backyard for your ceremony and reception, make sure Aunt Meg has the facilities to handle a wedding (unless you're having an informal affair with a small number of guests). Interview caterers. Be guided by their expertise and decide with them if an "at-home" wedding is a feasible and affordable choice. Be sure Aunt Meg's house meets the caterer's needs (large enough rooms, fully equipped kitchen, etc.). If you're planning on having a large, traditional wedding at home, you should employ a wedding consultant.

Wedding Consultants

Professional wedding consultants plan your wedding and reception for a fee. They design your wedding and reception to meet your specifications within your budget. They may plan part of it, or all of it — that's up to you. They formulate a plan, carry out the plan, and follow up to make sure everything runs smoothly. Their fee may be a flat amount, or it may be a certain percentage of the total cost of the wedding and reception. Some are paid solely by the vendors they contract for your wedding — photographers, florists, caterers...

Referral is the key to finding a competent wedding consultant. Ask friends, relatives, neighbors and business associates. Don't ask anyone who is likely to gain monetarily from their suggestions, a business, for example. (Chances are they'll be paid a referral fee [kickback] from the wedding consultant they suggest to you).

Here are the advantages:
— If you have the money, but not the time to plan a wedding, a wedding consultant may be for you. Your family may live out-of-town and not be able to help you. Or you might have a demanding career and a wedding consultant may be the answer to your prayers.

A wedding consultant alleviates all headaches (or should). All you do is write the checks and leave the rest to them.
— If you are having a large wedding — 150 or more guests — and you've never planned one before, it might be wise to hire a wedding consultant.
— If you are having a semi-formal or formal traditional wedding at home, you should hire a wedding consultant. The reason is simple. At-home weddings require a lot of planning and work. This means caterers, dance floors, linens, silverware, entertainment, decorations... The list

A happy bridesmaid makes the day.

is endless. I recommend you never attempt this type of wedding singlehandedly without plenty of experience.

— A wedding consultant offers you *experience,* answers your questions and plans the wedding logically and rationally.

Here are the disadvantages:

— A wedding consultant can be expensive.

— A wedding consultant may be incompetent and or inexperienced.

— A wedding consultant denies you the opportunity of having a hands-on approach to planning your wedding.

— A wedding consultant may employ the same vendors and service people, denying you the opportunity of seeing goods and services better suited to your needs, tastes and budget.

— You will pay more for the goods and services acquired by a wedding consultant. Most wedding planners are paid referral fees from those vendors whose goods and services they book for your wedding and reception.

If you opt for a wedding consultant, don't think you're out of the woods. Hiring a wedding consultant doesn't mean you can forget about the wedding and show up 10 months later — "while sounds of wedding bells dance in your head..." — and walk down that glorious aisle. Here's a more realistic approach:

— Interview wedding consultants before hiring one. Make sure they acquiesce to what *you* want for your wedding, not what they want.

— Test them to see how well they follow up before you hire them. Leave messages to see how fast they return your calls.

— Once you hire one, do "follow ups" on a weekly basis. Leave nothing to chance.

— Know all the names and phone numbers of the suppliers and business people the wedding consultant is using, from florists to photographers. Make occasional checks with these people to ensure that the wedding consultant is following through.

An elegant Jewish wedding.

The Proper Structure

What does "style" mean? According to the dictionary, it is a "distinctive and characteristic manner." Apply "style" to a wedding and what does the formula equal? It equals YOU!

STYLE + WEDDING = YOU

Your wedding day should reflect *your personality,* your tastes, likes and dislikes — your way of doing things. Your budget might limit your dreams, but it has nothing to do with plain good taste and common sense. These two intangibles — not money — applied liberally to your wedding will make it beautiful, meaningful and elegant.

Let's begin by looking at wedding "types" and how they relate to the personalities of you and your fiancé.

The Informal Wedding

This wedding can be the most fun and the least expensive. It's for people who are more comfortable wearing casual clothes, relaxing at bistros with friends they've known for years, than they are attending the ballet followed by a late night supper at Maxim's. Many of my clients plan informal weddings because they're not stiff or pretentious. This wedding is a warm, fun way to celebrate.

The informal wedding may be a ceremony at church with a party following at your house, or that of family or friends. It might be a ceremony in the early morning by the ocean, celebrated with a beach party or picnic. Your choices are virtually limitless. The only rule to follow is to *keep it informal* from start to finish.

Send invitations reflecting the mood of the wedding — something simple that may be handwritten. There only should be one attendant each for bride and groom, and their dress should reflect the mood of the wedding. You would not put your bridesmaid in a satin, ruffled gown, for example, nor would the best man wear a tux. Your wedding gown may be short in length, even a mini with a wrap-skirt, or it might be the kind of dress you'd wear to a party or to the club for dinner. If you are being married on the beach, you might wear a bathing suit with a floral wrap and put fresh flowers in your hair. Your fiancé might wear Hawaiian garb, and your invitations might say "Luau, Beach Dress Only."

The Formal Wedding

If it's formal you want, keep it formal and go by the book because no wedding can get as out of hand as this one. I have attended formal weddings where videotapes of the couple played on monitors around the room, and huge poster-type portraits of the bride stood on easels near the reception entrance. The reaction I overheard was, "Do you believe this?" I also have been at so-called formal weddings where guests paid for their own liquor. At weddings, guests are simply not asked to foot the bill for their own drinks. How would you feel if a close friend invited you to a party, then asked you to pay for each libation?

Brides like those mentioned above spent so much on themselves that their guests suffered. They went way over budget on their photography, for example, which left them no choice but to cut back their reception budget. *The reception is an integral part of your wedding.* It is a life-celebration that you are hosting. Your guests' enjoyment should be your first priority.

It's their opinion of "your day" that will shape the success of your wedding. If you must choose a less expensive photographer, or cut back on flowers — so that your reception will be the gracious kind of party your guests will remember with enjoyment — then do it.

If you opt for a formal wedding and have the money to spend, remember — more does not mean better. Garishness and vulgarity have nothing to do with good taste and common sense. The formal, traditional wedding was never meant to be overdone or ostentatious. It was meant to be tasteful, understated and supremely elegant. Keep it that way.

The Semi-Formal Wedding

The semi-formal wedding is a middle-of-the-road affair for those who want the tradition of a formal wedding without its rigidity. The males of the wedding party, for example, do not have to wear tuxedos and neither do male guests. The bridesmaids may wear short dresses if the bride chooses. But the hardest part of planning a semi-formal wedding is keeping it semi-formal.

Most brides don't know what distinguishes a formal wedding from a semi-formal wedding. Virtually 99 percent of the time, they mix the formal with the semi-formal, making their weddings look unstructured and haphazard. The semi-formal wedding is not formal so gear your thinking accordingly. This must be reflected in the invitations you send, the gown you select, the dress for your wedding party and guests, and the time of day you choose for your ceremony.

It's not easy to structure the formal, semi-formal or informal wedding. All are made up of *components* — flowers, music, gowns, invitations, etc. — that must relate harmoniously in style. All have certain standards that must be upheld. If you meet the standards and relate your wedding components to one another, your wedding will be well-structured and beautiful. If you don't, your wedding will look haphazard, confused and sloppy.

To ensure that your wedding is properly structured, ask yourself these important questions: "What makes my wedding informal, semi-formal or formal — what are the standards?" And, "How can I correctly relate the components to make sure my wedding is properly structured?" Read this scenario:

It's 9:45 a.m. You've always wanted a *formal* wedding (but couldn't get the church at 5 p.m., because it was booked). You put "Black Tie optional" on the invitations. Guests begin

3. Would you like them to wear an elegant tea-length or mid-calf dress or suit, or a simple cocktail dress, with or without hat or headpiece?

4. Would you like them to wear elegant, beaded, ornate gowns or suits, long or tea-length, or an elegant cocktail dress?

VI. GUESTS' ATTIRE:

1. Would you like your female guests in pretty day-suits or dresses? The male guests in suits?

2. Would you like your female guests in elegant day-dresses or suits? Your male guests in suits?

3. Would you like your female guests in elegant, tea-length, or mid-calf, dresses or suits, or cocktail dresses, the male guests in either suits or tuxedos?

4. Would you like your female guests in elegant, long, or tea-length gowns or suits, or elaborate cocktail dresses, the male guests in tuxedos?

VII. TYPE OF INVITATIONS:

1. Are you thinking of phoning your guests or handwriting them an invitation?

2. Are you going to have them printed?

3. Are they going to be printed by thermography?   Have raised lettering .

4. Are you thinking of engraved or custom invitations?

VIII. TYPE OF MUSIC - ENTERTAINMENT:

1. Are you planning not to have music at the ceremony, but perhaps a guitar player at the reception, or maybe you'll just play records, tapes or discs?

2. Are you planning on a harpist, organist or soloist for the ceremony with a disc jockey or small band for the reception?

3. Are you planning to have a choir sing at the ceremony, or have trumpets, an organist, soloist or harpist, maybe all of them, and a band or orchestra for the reception?

IX. FLOWERS - DECORATIONS

1. Are you thinking of bridal-party flowers only?

2. Are you thinking of bridal-party flowers and decorations for the ceremony site?

3. Are you considering bridal-party flowers and decorations for the ceremony site, as well as center-pieces for the reception?

4. Are you considering bridal-party flowers, and flowers and decorations for the ceremony site, and floral centerpieces and decorations for the reception?

Log Sheet

Circle the number you chose for each question

WEDDING COMPONENTS:

	I		S		F	
1. Bride's Attire	1		2		3	4
2. Number of Bridesmaids and Groom's Attendants	1					
3. Bridesmaids' Attire	1	2		3		
4. Groom and Attendants' Attire	1		2		3	
5. Mothers' Attire	1		2	3		4
6. Guests' Attire	(1)		2	3		4
7. Invitations	1	2		3		4
8. Music-Entertainment	1		2		3	
9. Flowers-Decorations	1	2		3		4
	I = _____		**S =** _____		**F=** _____	

TOTAL the *number* of circled answers in each category.

If the majority of your answers (at least five of nine) fell within CATEGORY **I**, you're envisioning an *informal wedding*.

If the majority of your answers fell within CATEGORY **S**, you're envisioning a *semi-formal wedding*.

If the majority of your answers fell within CATEGORY **F**, you're envisioning a *formal wedding*.

LET'S ANALYZE YOUR ANSWERS:

If the majority (at least five of nine) of the answers on your log sheet fell within one category you're thinking correctly. Your wedding will be well-structured, cohesive and beautiful — whether formal, semi-formal or informal. If your answers fell within one category, but the wrong category (your answers indicate you're having an informal wedding, but you thought it was semi-formal?), read on to learn the proper criteria for each wedding type. See where your answers differ. Then re-evaluate your thinking and make the necessary changes so that your wedding will be correctly structured.

For your wedding to be well-planned, the majority of the answers on your log sheet must fall within one category. Read the proper criteria on the next pages for each wedding type. Compare this information to your answers.

COMPONENT I: BRIDE'S ATTIRE

CATEGORY I:

An informal wedding gown may be a pretty dress, or suit, if the bride is being married in church or temple. It may be elegant or simple, depending on the reception that follows. The dress will not have a train. A veil and blusher are not appropriate, although a hat or simple headpiece is suitable. If the wedding is on a beach or a ranch, for example, the bride's dress should reflect the mood of the occasion.

CATEGORY S:

A semi-formal wedding gown is a traditional gown, either sheath or full skirt. If the wedding is in the morning or early afternoon the beading or fabrics should not be elaborate. This should be saved for the bride marrying late afternoon or evening. Whatever the time, the veil can be either short or fingertip length. The train can be either short or medium length.

CATEGORY F:

A formal wedding gown is the most elaborate and should be saved for late-afternoon and evening weddings. The gown is traditional, either sheath or full skirt. It may be heavily beaded, or it might be a designer gown, simple in its elegance but made of fine silk. The train should be either medium or long. The veil should be fingertip or longer.

COMPONENT II: BRIDESMAIDS AND MALE ATTENDANTS

CATEGORY I:

For an informal wedding, the bride chooses one attendant, as does the groom.

CATEGORY S:

For a semi-formal wedding, the bride chooses two or three attendants, as does the groom (numbers need not match because you should have one usher for every 50 guests).

CATEGORY F:

For a formal wedding, the bride chooses four or more attendants, as does the groom. Again, numbers don't have to match.

COMPONENT III: BRIDESMAIDS' ATTIRE

CATEGORY I:

For an informal wedding, the maid or matron of honor (there is only one attendant) should be dressed in pretty street clothes — a dress or suit — for example, if the ceremony is in church or temple. If the ceremony is in a park, or on the beach, the "dress" should reflect the mood of the wedding and the party afterward.

CATEGORY S:

For a semi-formal wedding in the morning or early afternoon, the bridesmaids may wear matching street-length, or mid-calf dresses or suits. They may even wear them tea-length. The dresses or suits, however, should not be made of ornate fabrics, nor should they be beaded or glitzy. Floral prints are acceptable, as are taffeta, polished cotton or shantung (raw silk). The color depends on the season. Hats or simple headpieces are appropriate. Black or black-and-white dresses are not acceptable for morning or afternoon weddings.

For a semi-formal wedding in the late afternoon, with a late-afternoon or evening reception, dresses should be satin, taffeta, iridescent taffeta or shantung (raw silk). They may have some beading and colors may be dark depending on the season. The gowns may be long, tea-length or mid-calf. Light cotton floral prints and polished cotton, or cotton dresses are unacceptable. Hats or simple headpieces are permitted. Black or black-and-white dresses are not advisable for semi-formal weddings.

CATEGORY F:

For a formal, late-afternoon wedding, bridesmaids dresses should be satin, taffeta, iridescent taffeta or shantung (raw silk). They may be lightly beaded, and colors may be dark depending on the season of the year. They may be worn long, tea-length or mid-calf. Black or black-and-white dresses are inadvisable for afternoon weddings.

For the formal, evening wedding, bridesmaids may wear dresses or suits, long or tea-length. They may be beaded or made of ornate fabrics. They may be black or black and any combination of color.

COMPONENT IV: GROOM AND ATTENDANTS' ATTIRE
CATEGORY I:

For an informal wedding held in temple or church, the groom and his best man should wear business suits. They also may dress according to the occasion. If they're having a wedding on a ranch, for example, western wear would be appropriate.

CATEGORY S:

For the semi-formal wedding held late morning or early afternoon, suits are appropriate, although everyone seems to wear tuxedos these days, *which are NOT appropriate for a morning or early-afternoon wedding.* "Strollers," that look similar to tuxedos but don't have satin trim, are appropriate for these weddings, as are "cutaways." NO TAILS, please, for morning or afternoon weddings.

CATEGORY F:

For the formal wedding, tuxedos are appropriate, along with white dinner jackets in tropical climates or summer. After six, you may wear tails.

And at no time are tuxedo cummerbunds to match the bridesmaids dresses. They should match the color of the tuxedo, or be black. A wedding is not a prom.

COMPONENT V: MOTHERS' ATTIRE
CATEGORY I:

For an informal wedding in church or temple, mothers may wear pretty dresses or suits, with or without hats. Or, they may dress according to the occasion — remember the wedding on the ranch?

CATEGORY S:

For a semi-formal wedding in the morning or afternoon (before 4 p.m.), mothers may wear elegant day-dresses or suits, mid-calf, or street length — not long. The dress or suit she chooses should not be heavily beaded or glitzy. Black is not appropriate. A hat or small headpiece may be worn.

For a semi-formal wedding in late afternoon, mothers should wear a tea-length or mid-calf dress or suit, or simple cocktail dress. Beading should be minimal, fabrics not too ornate. Black is not appropriate.

For a semi-formal wedding in the evening, beading and glitz may be more elaborate, lengths remain the same.

TIP: For those of you in the early afternoon ceremony-evening reception dilemma, there's not much you can do but change from a suit or day-dress for the ceremony to a cocktail dress or evening suit for the reception. All the more reason to coordinate your ceremony as close as to your reception as possible.

CATEGORY F:

For a formal wedding (after 5 p.m.) mothers should wear gowns or suits that are long or tea-length, heavily beaded, or made from ornate fabrics. Styling may be simple or elaborate. An elegant cocktail dress also may be appropriate. Black is suitable.

COMPONENT VI: GUEST ATTIRE
CATEGORY I:

For an informal wedding in church or temple, female guests may wear pretty street-length dresses or suits. Men may wear dark suits, or light ones in tropical climates. Or they may wear anything that reflects the mood of your wedding and reception. You might put on your invitation "Luau — Hawaiian Dress Required."

CATEGORY S:

For a semi-formal wedding in the late morning or early afternoon, female guests may wear street-length or mid-calf elegant day-dresses or suits. (No glitz!) Men may wear dark suits, or light ones in tropical climates. For a semi-formal wedding in late afternoon, female guests may wear tea-length or mid-calf dresses and suits, or a simple cocktail dress. Beading should be minimal; fabrics, not too ornate.

Dress for a semi-formal, evening wedding may be more elaborate but lengths should remain the same. Men may wear dark suits, or tuxedos if the invitation states, "Black Tie optional" or "Black Tie invited or preferred."

CATEGORY F:

For a formal wedding, female guests may wear long or tea-length gowns or suits. They may be heavily beaded or ornate. An elaborate cocktail dress is also appropriate. Men must wear tuxedos only if the invitation states "Black Tie," otherwise a dark suit will do.

COMPONENT VII: INVITATIONS
CATEGORY I:

For an informal wedding, it is appropriate to call guests by phone or to send handwritten invitations, or simple printed ones. They should reflect the mood of the wedding and party following.

CATEGORY S:

For a semi-formal wedding, invitations must be thermographed or engraved. They may be decorative or plain. Invitations stating "Black Tie optional, preferred, or invited" are for semi-formal weddings held at 4 p.m. or later.

CATEGORY F:

For a formal wedding, invitations must be engraved or thermographed (if money is a concern). These run the gamut from the plain, simple and elegant to the flashy and ornate. Invitations to a formal wedding should say, "Black Tie."

COMPONENT VIII: MUSIC AND ENTERTAINMENT
CATEGORY I:

For an informal wedding, it's not necessary to have entertainment. If you choose, you may have an organist, harpist or soloist at the ceremony, with guitarist or pianist for the reception, but even music played on a compact disc or tape player will do.

CATEGORY S:

Entertainment for a semi-formal wedding may be a band or disc jockey at the reception, with a harpist, organist or vocalist for the ceremony.

CATEGORY F:

For a formal wedding only a band or orchestra will do for the reception. Music at the ceremony should consist of an organist, harpist, vocalist, choir, or all four. It can be as elaborate as you would like.

COMPONENT IX: FLOWERS AND DECORATIONS
CATEGORY I:

For an informal wedding, you may choose not to have flowers or decorations at all. Most brides, however, like to carry a bouquet and the groom should have a boutonniere if being married in temple or church. You may even have arrangements on either side of the altar.

For a theme wedding like a luau on the beach, you may decide to present guests with leis and wear one yourself. You may decorate the tables with hurricane lamps and exotic silk flowers. Your choices are endless.

CATEGORY S:

Flowers for the semi-formal wedding should include a minimum of fresh flowers for the bridal party, ceremony site and centerpieces — floral or otherwise — for the reception tables. Although, you may decorate and have as many flowers as you like.

CATEGORY F:

For a formal wedding, the sky's the limit. You may decorate and have as many flowers as you wish. The minimal acceptable for the formal wedding is fresh flowers for the bridal party and ceremony site, and fresh floral centerpieces for the reception.

By now you should understand that there isn't any one factor that constitutes the informal, semi-formal or formal wedding. Each type of wedding has *standards* to uphold, and parts or components that must relate harmoniously to one another. It's up to you to uphold these standards. This will make your wedding well-structured and beautiful.

Part 2

A special moment.

Diamonds
and Wedding Bands

iamonds. Mention the word and my eyes dance. I don't think anything is more divine than the fire and brilliance of a beautiful diamond. When *Modern Bride* conducted a survey, brides said the most exciting thing about wedding planning was shopping for their gowns. But what about the search for that special diamond ring?

PART I:
A Romantic History

Found thousands of years ago in India, diamonds were first mentioned in a Sanskrit document called *The Lesson of Profit*, dating from the 4th century B.C. In India, diamonds were valued as items of trade and a source of income for the royal family. Until diamonds were discovered in South America in the 18th century, India remained the world's only source.

Ancient cultures were intrigued by the diamond's exceptional hardness. A diamond crystal, that looks like two pyramids joined at the base is *not* brilliant, but thousands of years ago diamonds weren't valued for their beauty. The ancients felt that diamonds had mystic powers to keep away evil spirits and repel poisons. They were regarded more as talismans than jewelry and were placed in elaborate settings to make them more attractive.

The Italians were the first to "cut" diamonds in the fifteenth century, a milestone in its history. For the first time, the beauty, fire, brilliance and color of these lifeless gems were released. Never again would they be regarded as objects of mysticism. From here on, diamonds would be treasured as objects of rarity and great beauty.

By the Middle Ages, the wealthy sported diamonds and other gems in their wedding jewelry. The ruby — the color of the heart — was particularly valued along with the sapphire, which was symbolic of the heavens.

Colored gemstones are still popular for engagement rings, especially in England. It came as no surprise to the British when Diana Spencer chose a sapphire engagement ring. It did, however, cause embarrassment for the Queen. Charles and Diana had chosen the ring from a selection brought to the palace by the Crown Jewelers, Garrard. When the ring was submitted to the Queen for approval, she reportedly was under the impression that it had been designed specifically for the future Princess of Wales. In reality, it was a stock ring that was featured in Garrard's catalogue, and anyone with the equivalent of about $50,000 could buy one. The Queen was not amused.

The English own their share of historic diamonds including the Koh-i-Nur and the Regent — that are part of the Crown Jewels kept in the Tower of London. Queen Victoria, who ruled in the 19th century, was the greatest promoter of these rare gems. She loved them, wore them and was an avid collector. She spent a fortune with the same Crown Jewelers, who, more than a century later, would provide Diana Spencer with her engagement ring.

The Koh-i-Nur "Mountain of Light" is an historic Indian diamond — the largest one in the world at the time — whose history goes as far back as 1304, when it was owned by the Rajahs of Malwa. In time, it came into the hands of the East India Company, who presented it to Queen Victoria in 1850. The Queen, disappointed with the dull look of the diamond, decided to have it re-cut, and the Koh-i-Nur went from 186 carats to about 109.

Legend has it that the Koh-i-Nur brought harm to men who owned it, so Queen Victoria specified in her will that only the *wife* of a male sovereign could wear it. It was later set in the State Crown and worn by Queen Alexandra and Queen Mary. The Queen Mother, mother of Queen Elizabeth II, was the last to wear it at her coronation, thus honoring Queen Victoria's will.

By 1850, when Queen Victoria accepted the Koh-i-Nur, diamonds were becoming scarce. But sixteen years later in South Africa, vast diamond fields were discovered, and diamonds became available to more people than ever before. For the first time, ownership did not require immense wealth. By 1884, diamonds were mined in Australia, which today leads the world in production.

In 1954, diamonds were also found in Russia. Russia's output now exceeds South Africa's, and they rank fourth in the world.

Although India (along with Israel, Antwerp and New York) remains one of the world's top diamond cutting centers, it no longer occupies the position it held for 2,000 years as a top producer. Even so, the majority of the world's historic diamonds — including the blue Hope — came from India.

The cursed Hope, the only historic diamond on display in America, was stolen from the French monarchy during the revolution. Marie Antoinette supposedly wore it. In 1830, it was bought by Henry Hope. Legend has it that Mr. Hope and his family died in poverty, and those families who acquired the stone afterward purportedly suffered bankruptcy and death. The famous New York jeweler Harry Winston bought the Hope in 1949.

On November 8, 1958, a package was delivered by mail to the Smithsonian Institution. It had $2.44 in postage and was insured for $151. Inside was the Hope Diamond, a gift from Harry Winston. It was placed in a bulletproof case, where it's been on display ever since.

Today, "diamonds are a girl's best friend," and 20th century diamond cutting has brought the gems to new heights. There are princess cuts, trilliants, and heart-shaped diamonds, made all the more dazzling by today's creative settings. But let's not forget Mr. Tiffany, that famed New York jeweler, who in the late 1800s invented a remarkable, but simple, setting for a diamond. He suspended the stone from the band of the ring by prongs. This enabled light to pass through the diamond, making it come alive with color and brilliance. The Tiffany setting is classic, elegant and timeless. It and a diamond go together like... "love and marriage."

PART II - THE PARTICULARS
What about the Four Cs?

Not many people can afford to buy investment-quality diamonds — those that are near flawless, close to colorless and cut to excellent proportions. When a woman becomes engaged, she wants a beautiful ring. And most likely she wants a gorgeous, fiery, bright, white diamond to grace her finger. If you're a bride-to-be who first and foremost wants a *beautiful* diamond, read this.

Chances are you've heard about the 4 Cs—Color, Cut, Clarity and Carat weight. These are important components to consider when acquiring a diamond. But there's more to it than that, factors you should be aware of before you purchase.

There's so much emphasis placed on flaws (clarity) and color, that we sometimes forget the most important factor in determining a diamond's *beauty*. This factor is called the *make*, which is *the cut, proportioning and finish* of a diamond. If the make is bad, the diamond won't be beautiful — it's as simple as that. If you want a beautiful diamond engagement ring, you should learn if it has a good make.

Don't Be Fooled by Flaws

I'm forever frustrated when I hear clients say, "My fiancé wants a VS1 (minimal flaws), with J (near white) color." That sounds great, but the diamond won't look like a VS1 with J color if the make is bad.

A diamond is created by nature, which determines its size, how free it is from flaws and its color. What nature can't influence is how the

stone is cut, proportioned and finished. That's left to man. Throughout the centuries, diamond cutting — which began as a crude process — has evolved into a precise art following certain scientific standards. To ensure beauty and value, it's important that you choose a diamond that is as close to these standards as you can afford.

If a diamond is cut wrong, its brilliance (a combination of fire and life) is diminished. The stone may appear lifeless and even dull. In 1919, Marcel Tolkowsky mathematically calculated *ideal* dimensions for a brilliant (round) cut diamond that established a standard for cut and proportioning. The closer the stone is cut to this *ideal,* the more fire and life it will have. To most people a diamond's beauty is its most valuable asset. It's important, therefore, to understand why the make is so critical, and why flaws aren't all they're cracked up to be (unless you are buying an investment-quality diamond).

People admiring your engagement ring don't usually pull a loupe (jeweler's magnifying glass) from their pockets for an internal inspection. They look at the size, the color — whether it's yellow (undesirable), or white (preferable) — and how it *sparkles!*

If you walk around with a dull, lifeless, pasty-looking diamond on your finger, the fact that it's practically flawless with white color won't mean a thing. What really counts is that you have a beautiful, fiery, bright diamond that everyone will admire regardless of its invisible flaws.

In Jay Feder's book *The Practical Guide to Buying Diamonds,* he states, "It is not uncommon for a diamond merchant to push color and clarity and almost disregard the quality of the cut. This sometimes results in the purchase of a diamond that is really worth 20, 30, or 40 percent less than what

Diamond grading report

GIA GEM TRADE LABORATORY

A Wholly Owned Subsidiary of the Gemological Institute of America.

580 Fifth Avenue	550 South Hill Street	1630 Stewart Street
New York, New York 10036	Los Angeles, California 90013	Santa Monica, California 90404
(212) 221-5858	(213) 629-5435	(213) 828-3148

DIAMOND GRADING REPORT   0123456   3/07/89

THE ABOVE REPORT NUMBER HAS BEEN INSCRIBED ON THE GIRDLE OF THIS DIAMOND

THE FOLLOWING WERE, AT THE TIME OF THE EXAMINATION, THE CHARACTERISTICS OF THE DIAMOND DESCRIBED HEREIN BASED UPON 10X BINOCULAR MAGNIFICATION. DIAMONDLITE AND MASTER COLOR DIAMONDS, ULTRA-VIOLET, MILLIMETER GAUGE, DIAMOND BALANCE, PROPORTIONSCOPE.

RED SYMBOLS DENOTE INTERNAL CHARACTERISTICS. GREEN SYMBOLS DENOTE EXTERNAL CHARACTERISTICS. SYMBOLS INDICATE NATURE AND POSITION OF CHARACTERISTICS, NOT NECESSARILY THEIR SIZE. MINOR DETAILS OF FINISH NOT SHOWN. DIAGRAM MAY BE APPROXIMATE.

KEY TO SYMBOLS
- ° CRYSTAL
- ⌣ FEATHER
- · PINPOINT
- EXTRA FACET SHOWN IN BLACK

SHAPE AND CUT ROUND BRILLIANT
Measurements 6.50 - 6.58 X 3.90 MM.
Weight   1.01 CARATS

PROPORTIONS
Depth   59.6%
Table   62%
Girdle   THIN TO MEDIUM, FACETED
Culet   SMALL
FINISH
  Polish   VERY GOOD
Symmetry   GOOD

CLARITY GRADE   VS1

COLOR GRADE   H
Fluorescence   NONE

COMMENTS:

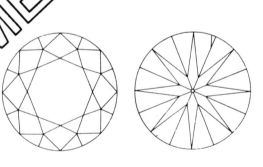

GIA GEM TRADE LABORATORY

GIA Gem Trade Laboratory

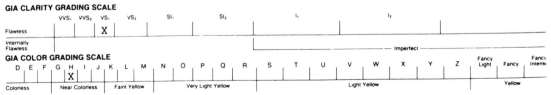

GIA CLARITY GRADING SCALE

	VVS₁	VVS₂	VS₁	VS₂	SI₁	SI₂	I₁	I₂
Flawless			X					
Internally Flawless							Imperfect	

GIA COLOR GRADING SCALE

D	E	F	G	H	I	J	K	L	M	N	O	P	Q	R	S	T	U	V	W	X	Y	Z	Fancy Light	Fancy	Fancy Intense
				X																					

Colorless	Near Colorless	Faint Yellow	Very Light Yellow	Light Yellow	Yellow

This report is not a guarantee, valuation or appraisal. The recipient of the report may wish to consult a jeweler or gemologist about information contained herein.

NOTICE: IMPORTANT LIMITATIONS ON REVERSE

Diagram courtesy of the Gemological Institute of America.

the merchant is charging you, just because of the poor cut."* Tiffany's, in its *HOW TO BUY A DIA-MOND* brochure, also notes that cut is the most important factor when evaluating a stone for beauty and brilliance. So how do you know if the stones you're looking at are correctly cut?

The Diamond Grading Report

On the opposite page is a sample diamond grading report from the Gemological Institute of America, one of the world's most respected gemological institutions, providing education and gem testing to the public as well as the jewelry trade. The GIA grades diamonds according to a system recognized worldwide. There are other respected grading laboratories, however. A list is provided in the back of this book.

Some diamonds of a carat or more come with grading reports, so be sure to ask for one if you're considering a diamond of this size. If it doesn't, and you're thinking of buying a fine diamond, you should insist that the jeweler send the diamond to a respected laboratory for testing. If the diamond has a grading report from a laboratory that isn't listed in this book, it might be wise to have the stone re-evaluated.

Many jewelers say these reports aren't always accurate and are a waste of time and money. But it should be noted that an accurate standard of grading, recognized worldwide, has been developed by the GIA and other laboratories. While mistakes are made when grading diamonds, it's better to have a report from a respected laboratory than no report at all.

To make it easy for you to read a grading report, I've color-coded it for your convenience. But first, some advice. Diamonds can be damaged through

carelessness, and it's important that the stone is in the same condition as when it was graded. It's also critical to make sure you're looking at the same diamond described in the report. If the diamond grading report indicates that the report number is inscribed on the girdle (the small rim that surrounds the diamond), have the jeweler show it to you. Otherwise, have the jeweler measure the diamond to ensure that the dimensions of the diamond match those on the report. (See sample report.) Also, on most grading reports the position of the flaws in the diamond are shown on the diagram. Match the flaws on the diagram to the ones in the diamond you're examining to ensure they are one and the same. If your diamond doesn't come with a grading report, I've provided tips and information to help you make the right choice.

Unmounted Diamonds - Look at No Other

It is essential to look at *all* diamonds unmounted. It's impossible to determine a diamond's true color or to see its flaws if the stone is mounted. The diamond's setting can enhance its color, and you might be deceived into paying hundreds, even thousands of dollars more than if you had seen the stone without the setting. The same holds true for flaws. Diamonds are set to hide obvious flaws, flaws that you'll never see if the stone is mounted. It should be no problem for a good jeweler to remove a diamond from its setting for your inspection.

The Parts of a Diamond

In order to better understand a diamond and properly purchase one, you should be familiar with its parts.

* Footnote see page 356.

The Parts of a Diamond.

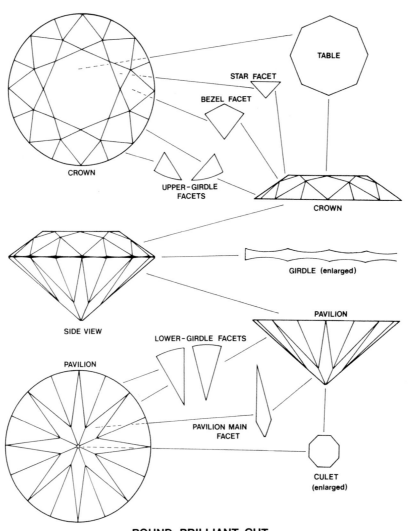

**FACET ARRANGEMENT OF A
STANDARD ROUND BRILLIANT**

TABLE

STAR FACET

BEZEL FACET

CROWN

UPPER-GIRDLE
FACETS

CROWN

GIRDLE (enlarged)

SIDE VIEW

PAVILION

LOWER-GIRDLE FACETS

PAVILION

PAVILION MAIN
FACET

CULET
(enlarged)

ROUND BRILLIANT CUT

Diagram courtesy of the Gemological Institute of America

It's important to be able to recognize the parts of a diamond, because the way a diamond is cut, proportioned and finished will mean more to its beauty than any other factor.

The First Step - Determining Proper Make for Round Stones

To determine if a diamond has proper make, let's look at the grading report and start with the color aqua — *depth percentage.*

Study the following illustrations relating to depth percentage (expressed as a percentage of the diamond's diameter at the girdle). The stone on the left is cut to the *ideal*. Look how much light is refracted back to the eye. This diamond will have the greatest amount of fire and life, or brilliance. The stone in the middle is cut too shallow, and therefore only part of the light is refracted back to the eye. This diamond will appear dull. The last diamond is cut too deep and refracts the light back to the center. This stone will look dark in the middle. These illustrations demonstrate the importance of good depth percentage.

A diamond with a good depth percentage should fall within the range of 53 percent to 63 percent on your diamond grading report, although some jewelers feel that 63 percent is a little deep. To ensure that you're buying a diamond that's not too shallow or too deep, try to stay close to 60 percent.

TIP: If your diamond does not come with a grading report, have the jeweler measure the total depth of the diamond, from the top of the table to the culet, and the width of the diamond, edge to edge at its widest point. Then divide the depth by the width, which will give you the depth percentage.

The Table Percentage

The illustrations on the next page relate to the table percentage (also in aqua on the grading report), which is the size of the table in relation to the diamond's diameter. In the illustrations, the diamond on the left has a table cut to excellent proportions. The stone on the right has a

Depth Percentage

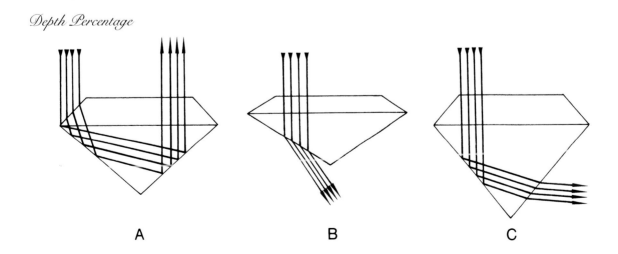

A   B   C

Diagram courtesy of the Gemological Institute of America.

table that's too large, while the diamond in the middle has a table cut to good proportions. A diamond that displays a lot of brilliance will have a table cut to good or better proportions.

According to the Diamond Dictionary, a table percentage of up to 60 percent is passable, with the best considered to be 57 percent, although many jewelers disagree, and feel that a table percentage of up to 64 percent is passable. Don't go over 64 percent, however, or the brilliance of your diamond will be affected.

TIP: Table percentages are extremely hard to determine if you don't have a grading report. The best rule of thumb — look at the illustrations on this page. Notice the two squares (formed by the facets) that cross one another. They are outlined in black. If the sides of the two squares bow in, just like in the first illustration, you've got a diamond with a great table percentage. If they look like perfect squares (illustration two), the table percentage is passable. If the squares start to bow out, you're looking at a diamond with a poor table percentage.

Make and Fancy Shapes

Tolkowsky calculated the ideal for round diamonds only. For that reason it's more difficult to

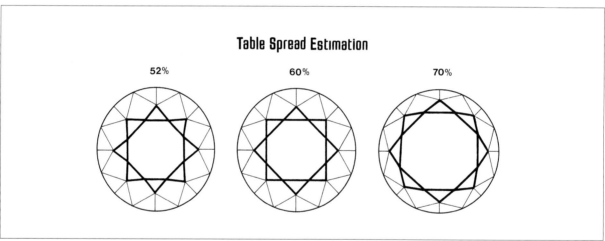

Table Spread Estimation

52% 60% 70%

Diagram and photos courtesy of the Gemological Institute of America.

Bow-tie effect in a marquise and pear-shaped diamond.

determine the proper make of fancy-shaped diamonds — any that are other than round — with only a grading report.

The depth percentage on the grading report should fall within the 53 percent to 63 percent range just like a round stone. Even if the proportions are within the acceptable range, however, you should examine the diamond to see how strongly it exhibits the "bow tie effect" pictured opposite. This occurs in marquise, pear-shaped, or oval diamonds. Stones with a prominent bow tie should cost less per carat.

If you're interested in a fancy shaped diamond, compare many of them so you learn to note the difference in their brilliance. The more fire and life they have, the better the make.

Is the Diamond Round?

Next look at the diamond's measurements (chartreuse). The first two measurements represent the widest and narrowest diameters of the girdle. If the stone on this grading report were perfectly round, the dimensions would be 6.5 x 6.5. But because diamonds are never *perfectly* round, two dimensions are used.

The greater the difference between these two figures, the more *out-of-round* the diamond. There should not be more than two-tenths of a millimeter difference between the two dimensions. If there is, the diamond is out-of-round and should cost less.

A very out-of-round diamond is easy to see with the naked eye because it occurs when the girdle is not round. Look at the picture above. If the diamond is visibly out-of-round, the stone should cost much less.

TIP: If your diamond does not have a grading report, ask the jeweler to measure it with an A.D.

The out-of-round diamond.

Leveridge gauge. He will turn the diamond in the gauge, looking for the maximum and minimum measurements of the diameter. The difference between these two numbers will tell you whether it's a round diamond.

Proper Measurements for Fancy Cuts

Fancy cuts may be cut too narrow or too thin, although this may be a matter of preference. Some people like fatter pear-shaped diamonds, others like them thinner. It's important, however, that they fall as close to industry standards as possible. Look at the following illustrations. To determine if your fancy shape falls within the correct length-to-width ratios, divide the length measurement by the width. The figure you come up with should fall within these ratios.

Try to stay as close to these figures as you can. They ensure that your diamond has not been cut

LENGTH-TO-WIDTH PREFERENCES

Shape		Preferred	Too long	Too short
Emerald		1.50-1.75	2.00 + Lean	1.25-1.10 Squarish
Heart		1.00	1.25 + Indented pear	1.00 − Stubby
Marquise		1.75-2.25	2.50 + Sliver	1.50 − Stubby
Oval		1.33-1.66	1.75 + Thin	1.25-1.10 Fat
Pear		1.50-1.75	2.00 + Gaunt	1.50 − Stubby

From the GIA Jeweler's Manual © 1992 Gemological Institute of America. Reprinted with permission.

too wide or too long. Don't consider a diamond that falls far from the preferred ratios.

TIP: If your diamond does not come with a grading report, have the jeweler measure the diamond for you. Then check the information above to ensure that your diamond falls within the appropriate ratios.

How Many Carats?

Next (orange) on the grading report is the *weight* of the diamond. Notice that I said *weight*, not size. The *weight* of a diamond is measured by carats. One metric carat = .200 gram.

A one-carat diamond is divided into 100 points. If a stone is 25 points, for example, it's one-quarter of a carat. If it were 33 points, it would be one-third of a carat. A 2.50 ct. diamond means it's two carats and 50 points. The abbreviation for carat is "ct."

In the world of diamonds the value increases with specific increments of weight, i.e. .25, .50, .75, and one carat, etc. That's why diamonds slightly less than one carat are much less expensive than one-carat stones of the same quality. If value is important to you, it's better to buy a one-carat diamond that's the same quality as one that's 98 points. This is why it's essential that you know the *exact* weight of the diamond you're considering. As Mr. Feder states, "A perfect .99 ct. diamond is currently worth 40 percent less than a full 1.00 ct. With medium-grade stones of the same weight, value will vary 20 to 30 percent."

If you're on a budget, buy a stone slightly less than one carat, because it will look bigger when it's set. Most fancy shapes also look bigger than their round counterparts.

TIP: If the diamond does not have a grading report, be sure to have the jeweler accurately weigh the stone. He does this by simply putting it on a scale.

Spread Table and Carat Weight

A *spread* table occurs when the table is cut larger than it should be, which decreases the size of the crown. This in turn reduces size of the crown facets, which lessens the amount of fire a stone displays. This is why spread diamonds often look flat and lifeless. What a spread table does, however, is make the stone look bigger.

Although a spread table actually relates to how a diamond's been cut, or its make, I mention it here since so many jewelers refer to how a diamond "spreads" rather than its true carat weight. "It spreads just like a one-carat diamond!", they'll say. Whether it spreads like one or not, it isn't. So be careful. Spread diamonds are easy to recognize so be on the lookout for them. The Tiffany HOW TO BUY A DIAMOND brochure says most diamonds are spread, which negatively affects the beauty and brilliance of the diamond. Most

consumers are unaware of this problem.

When you visit a jeweler, ask what the stone weighs. He should answer you in carats, which must correlate to the weight listed on the grading report. Be careful of any jeweler who characterizes the diamond's size by spread or by the way it *appears,* instead of by its true weight.

Check the table percentage on the grading report to safeguard against buying a spread diamond. Don't go over 64 percent. If you don't have a grading report, follow the TIP under Table Percentages.

The Girdle

The girdle is the rim that separates the crown facets (top of the diamond), from the pavilion facets (bottom of the diamond). Girdles may be faceted or plain, and are extremely important in determining the fragility of the diamond. A girdle that is too thin, called knife-edged, may break or chip, but a girdle that is too heavy will detract from the stone's beauty and make it look smaller. Look on the grading report for the description of the girdle (yellow). Notice the report describes how thick it is and if it's faceted or not.

According to the Diamond Dictionary, the girdle should appear like a fine white line in diamonds up to two carats. It also may appear to be scalloped. Anything that looks heavier than a fine white line, however, is classified by varying degrees of thickness. A thick girdle will make a diamond look smaller and is undesirable. The ideal girdle is one that's medium in thickness. It should also be noted in fancy shapes (particularly pear, marquise, and heart), that the girdle should be thicker near the points. This protects them from chipping or breaking.

TIP: If your diamond doesn't have a grading

report, the girdle is the easiest component to judge with the naked eye. Follow the information above to insure that the girdle has been cut correctly.

The Culet

Look at your grading report for a description of the *culet* (blue). The culet is that little point at the end of the diamond, but it's actually not a point, but a flat, polished facet. A culet should be small, not large, because if it's large (open) you can see it by looking into the stone. It should not be polished into a point, either, because then it's easily breakable. Check to see if the culet is chipped, broken, or off-center, which would reduce the price. A culet on the grading report should be described as small (optimum) to medium (passable). Next, look at a round stone from the top, and make sure the culet is dead center.

TIP: If you do not have a diamond grading report, it's easy to determine the quality of the culet with a loupe.

How to Use a Loupe

By now you may be wailing, "How am I supposed to see these things?" Enter the *loupe* — the jeweler's magnifying glass. Loupes are 10x power, which is an international standard that prevents improper grading. If one jeweler looked at a diamond with higher magnification, revealing more flaws, he would downgrade it. If another jeweler looked at the same stone with less magnification, and flaws were missed, he would upgrade it. Hence a standard was established. When you go

Photos courtesy of the Gemological Institute of America.

A knife edge girdle.

A thick girdle.

A girdle cut to good proportions.

An extra large culet.

to a jewelry store, you may ask to use a loupe, but make sure it's 10x *only*.

Loupes are important, because just like a microscope they enable you to examine diamonds closely on the outside as well as the inside. Learn to use a loupe before visiting a jeweler. Call a jeweler's supply store (listed in the phone book), and buy one — they're not expensive. Then practice with it. Hold the loupe between the thumb and index finger about one inch from the eye. Borrow your mother's diamond engagement ring, hold it in your opposite hand and bring it within one or two inches of the loupe, moving it backward and forward until the diamond is in focus. To steady the ring, make sure your palms touch one another. Once you practice a while, you should be able to clearly see the diamond both inside and out. Many jewelry stores also have microscopes to view diamonds. These have an advantage over the loupe because they provide background light to clearly see the stone. If you examine a diamond with a microscope, make sure you focus it yourself. That way there's less of a chance of missing inclusions in the diamond, which might happen if the microscope is focused for you. The optimum condition is to use both a loupe and a microscope.

Polish + Symmetry = Finish

According to the dictionary, symmetry means "Exact correspondence in size and position of opposite parts." When referring to a diamond, symmetry means the facets on one side must match the facets on the other side.

The *quality* of the polish and the symmetry of the facets is called the *finish*. Finish, polish and symmetry are found on the grading report (red).

Polish and symmetry relate to the skills of the diamond cutter and are important in determining the value and price of a stone. The finish, whether good or bad, also affects the diamond's brilliance. That's why the diamond you're considering should have "good" polish. If it's listed as fair or poor, the cost of the diamond should be less.

The most common faults found in diamonds with improper symmetry are found in the following diagram. Look for them when examining a round diamond. If a diamond has any of these characteristics, it should sell for less.

TIP: For those without a diamond grading report look at the chart, and with a loupe, evaluate your diamond to see if it has any of the same characteristics. If it does, it should sell for less.

Clarity Grade (Flaws)

The vast majority of diamonds have flaws. It's important to assess the flaws (clarity) in a stone to determine its value — not its beauty. The evaluation of flaws in a diamond is found on the grading report under CLARITY GRADE (pink).

All I hear from clients contemplating the purchase of a diamond is VVS, VS, SI, — but do they even know what those letters mean? VVS means very, very slightly included; VS means very slightly included; and SI means slightly included. (An inclusion is a flaw appearing inside the diamond.) After the SI grades, we progress downward to the imperfect grades, or those diamonds with inclusions that you can see with the naked eye.

If a flaw appears on the surface of a diamond, it's called a *blemish*. If a stone has no flaws, either inclusions or blemishes, under 10x magnification, it is given a grade of FL. If it has no inclusions and minor blemishes, it is given the

SYMMETRY CHARACTERISTICS IN ROUNDS

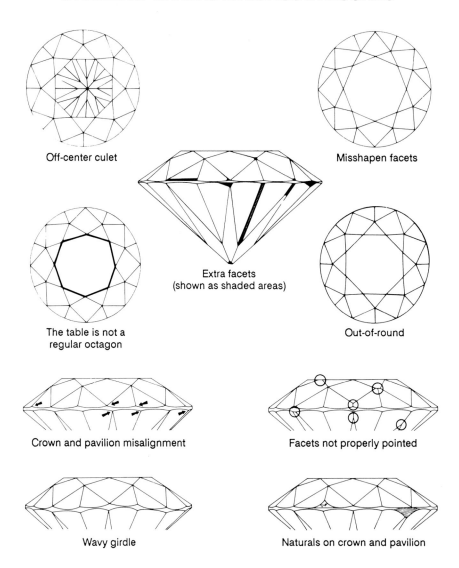

Off-center culet

Misshapen facets

Extra facets
(shown as shaded areas)

The table is not a
regular octagon

Out-of-round

Crown and pavilion misalignment

Facets not properly pointed

Wavy girdle

Naturals on crown and pavilion

grade IF. VVS1 and VVS2 are grades given to diamonds with inclusions (that an expert has trouble finding with a loupe) and minor blemishes. These are premium grades. VS1 and VS2 are grades given to stones with tiny inclusions that are difficult to see with magnification. If you can afford them (and everything else looks good), they're terrific diamonds.

SI1 and SI2 are grades given to stones that have inclusions that are easily seen under 10x power. If you're on a budget and their make and color is good, they're good diamonds to buy. I1, I2, and I3 are the imperfect grades — the inclusions are often visible without the use of a loupe. It should be noted that the I1 grade, if well cut and of good color, will make a nice looking ring.

The Rapaport Diamond Report is to diamonds what the "blue book" is to cars. It recently recognized a new classification for diamonds called SI3. This grade is slightly above the imperfect grades. If you're on a budget, and the make and color is good, these might not be a bad buy. But take note that the GIA does not yet recognize this grade.

The Other Factor - Where's the Flaw?

Also influencing the clarity grade is the position of the inclusions within the diamond. This has a direct impact on grading and value.

The worst place for a flaw to be is under the *table*, because it's so recognizable (position 1). Nor is it good to have a flaw under the *star facet* or *crown facet*, because they're readily noticeable (positions 2 and 3 respectively). Flaws in these positions will downgrade the value of your diamond. The best place for flaws to be (if you must have them), is near the *girdle* — (position 4). The optimum is a flaw seen from *the pavilion side only* — (position 5). Flaws in these positions are

hardly noticeable and may be hidden by the mounting. In the industry, these flaws are sometimes called "prongable" — flaws that may be covered by the prongs. Remember that dark spots, in terms of grading, are worse than light ones.

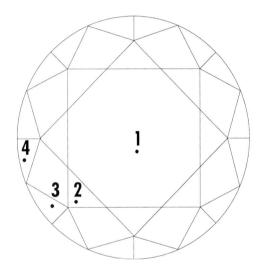

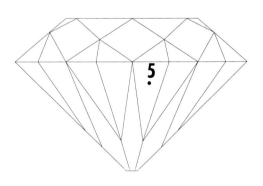

The position of flaws in a diamond.

Photos courtesy of the Gemological Institute of America

A natural at the girdle.

A bearded girdle.

Looking for Flaws with a Loupe

The ideal way to look at a diamond is *unset* against a *white* background. When looking at an unset diamond, turn it over so that it rests on its table. With a pair of tweezers (actually jeweler's tongs) pick up the stone. Be very careful that it doesn't slip and examine the diamond through the *pavilion* side. Look deep into the stone for flaws that may be tiny white spots, or black spots, or may even look like bubbles. You may even see cracks. Look also for small cracks penetrating the diamond from the girdle. Then put the stone down, turn it clockwise, pick it up once again with the tweezers, and look at it again so that none of the stone is missed. Next, turn the stone over, pick it up, and look at it through the table and under the surrounding facets for flaws. Look at the surface of the diamond for blemishes including polishing lines (a groove or scratch left by the polishing wheel), a rough or wavy girdle, or a *natural* (a part of the original diamond left on the girdle), or an extra facet along the girdle that is caused by the cutter removing a natural. If it's small, the cutter will leave it. It's considered a minor defect. But if it extends over another facet,

it's considered a cutting flaw. If the diamond has a natural, make sure you can't see it from the top and that it doesn't affect the stone's roundness.

There is also another flaw common to girdles — a *bearded* girdle, which looks like small lines, or hairs, emanating from the girdle.

Check to see that the facets are symmetrical. If they're not, you may have either a missing or extra facet. Brilliant diamonds have 58 facets, so do marquise, pear-shaped, heart-shaped, and oval diamonds. Trilliants have 44 facets, and quad-rillions (squares) have 49 facets.

Look for *laser lines.* Lasers are now being used to vaporize dark spots in diamonds. The result is fine white lines that can be seen with a loupe. Watch for them. You will normally see them if looking at the diamond from the side. The jeweler should tell you if the diamond has been laser treated.

Laser treating is a mixed blessing. If you buy a lesser-quality diamond, the laser treatment will make it cleaner and prettier. But if you're buying a fine quality stone, it should not be laser treated. It should be naturally clean — that's what you're paying for. And, of course, look for the obvious.

This includes nicks, pits, chips, scratches and cracks that should not break the surface. Any of these flaws can severely devalue a diamond.

The purchase of a loupe won't turn you into Mr. Tiffany. Using a loupe is like using a stethoscope. Put it in your ears and you hear your heart beat. Put it in your doctor's ears and he knows how well it's beating.

The GIA's Color Scale goes from "D" (no color) to "Z" (light yellow). Optimum color grades are D, E and F, which are considered colorless and are expensive. The next grades considered near colorless are G, H, I and J. The next grades down are faint yellow — K, L, M.

By the time you reach M, however, you should notice the yellow tint in the diamond (although it

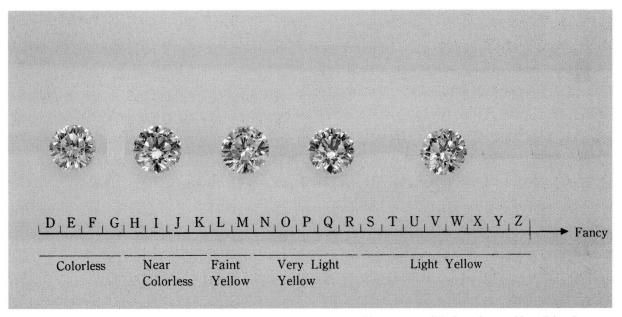

Color grades in diamonds.

Photo courtesy of Mr. Suwa, Suwa and Sons, Tokyo, Japan.

The Color Grades - What to Look For

Look on the grading report for the color grade (lilac). Many people think the whiter the diamond the better the color, and they're right. But color grading takes this a step further. According to the GIA, the diamond with the finest color actually has *no color*. A diamond with no color is like looking into a limpid pool of the cleanest, purest water imaginable. The GIA gives this diamond a grade of "D". It's the finest color grade for a diamond. Water is transparent, and so is a "D" color diamond.

may be less evident if the diamond is well cut). As the diamond progresses down the color grading scale, it decreases in value.

Because some people will not notice the subtle differences in mounted stones until they reach K color or beyond, it's a must to see diamonds unmounted. Beware that the difference between a diamond with D color and K color can mean thousands of dollars.

Color is the second most important factor in determining the beauty of a diamond. As mentioned previously, I don't advise buying a fine diamond unless it has a grading report. If the diamond you're considering doesn't have one, have the jeweler send it to the GIA Laboratory to be graded.

Tips for Evaluating Color in Unmounted Diamonds

The way to look at an unmounted diamond is against a *white* background *only*, table down, under *natural light or white fluorescent light*. I can't stress this enough. Jay Feder in his book, *The Practical Guide to Buying Diamonds,* says, "Most jewelry stores have very strong lighting that specifically distorts the color and makes everything look similar."* This, he says, confuses the buyer.

If the jeweler does not have a grading tray (a white trough with sides used to grade diamonds for color), take a piece of white cardboard, bend it in half, and put the diamond, table down, against the fold, then with the jeweler, go outside to look at the diamond in daylight. Turn the diamond around and move the cardboard so you can examine the stone at varying angles. See how much yellow you can see in the diamond. The optimum, of course, is no color like a glass of mountain-spring water. The more yellow you see, the less the cost of the diamond.

Many jewelers have "diamond lights" simulating daylight. If your jeweler has one, examine your diamond under it. If not, go outside.

Many jewelers also use *master* stones that are a set of small diamonds or cubic zirconia (CZs) that represent the color grades of diamonds. When a much larger stone is compared to these, however, the larger stone may look darker than the master stone leading to a false evaluation of the color. That's why it's best to evaluate the color of a diamond by comparing it to the color of different stones of about the same size. With practice, you should be able to pick up the slight variations in color.

Fluorescence

Fluorescence is so important to a diamond's color that it is listed in the grading report. Under color grade (lilac), you will see the word *fluorescence*. But what is it? In the Oxford Universal Dictionary, fluorescence is defined this way:

"The colored luminosity produced in some transparent bodies by the direct action of light, especially of the violet and ultra violet rays; the property, in certain substances, of rendering the ultra-violet rays visible, so as to produce this phenomenon." In daylight, when subjected to ultra-violet rays, or in any place that features fluorescent lighting, the diamond may appear to have a blue or yellow color, although blue by far is the most prevalent. Under normal lighting conditions, however, the diamond's true color will be evident. To check a diamond's fluorescence, look at it under a "black" light.

A diamond that fluoresces blue will make the stone look whiter than it is, a plus for a diamond that doesn't have terrific color. And, these stones aren't more expensive than diamonds that don't fluoresce. But be aware that fluorescence is frowned upon in stones with fine color, because it masks the exceptional color of the diamond.

Look at your diamond grading report. Each one lists the degree of the stone's fluorescence (if any) and the color it fluoresces. This is important to know because it's estimated that 50 percent of all diamonds fluoresce. If a stone fluoresces, its degree of fluorescence may affect the price you pay.

* Footnote see page 356.

TIP: If your diamond doesn't have a grading report, look at it outside or under a white fluorescent light, or if possible, a black light. If you see a blue tint, the diamond fluoresces. If the diamond has good brilliance, there's nothing to be concerned about. If the stone appears hazy or waxy, however, the fluorescence may be affecting its brilliance which means it should cost less.

Be aware of *Premiers* — diamonds so-called because of their unique properties of fluorescence, most of which come from the Premier or Williamson mines in Africa. If the color of the diamond you're considering has white or yellow color, but exhibits a high degree of blue fluorescence, you may be looking at a premier — a yellow, or white stone that looks bluish in daylight or under fluorescent bulbs. The difference is that while the diamond appears blue, it's brilliance is severely affected. These stones may have a dim, greasy, hazy, or milky appearance. Be sure to check this thoroughly. You should pay considerably less for a premier.

If You Have Questions?

If you would like further information about how to buy a diamond, or information about a diamond you're considering, call Jay Feder, author of *The Practical Guide to Buying Diamonds* (see Appendix). Mr. Feder is a strong promoter of diamond education for the public.

Tips for Buying that Diamond Ring

It's always good to be referred to a jeweler. Once again, ask recently married friends, family or business associates where they bought their rings, and if they were happy with the jeweler. Don't buy your ring at the first jewelry store you go to. Shop around. Make sure the jeweler gives you *all* the information about the diamond you're considering — in writing. Be leery if he refuses. If you're buying a fine stone, be sure to see the grading report. If the diamond doesn't have one, ask for one from a respected laboratory. If the jeweler balks, go elsewhere. Go to small respected jewelers and the big guys (often found in shopping malls). By now you should be armed with all the information you need to buy the right diamond. Copy the list on page 89. When you shop for diamonds, take it with you, fill it in, then go home and evaluate which diamond is the best for you.

SETTINGS
Selecting the Setting

Now that you've selected a diamond, how should you set it? The best setting is the one that looks the most attractive on your hand and feels the most comfortable. Settings range from the simple to the elaborate. It's all a matter of taste and budget.

Prong settings suspend the diamond from the band of the ring. They're the most common setting for solitaire (single) diamonds, and the best setting because they allow the most light to enter the stone. They also are the easiest to clean, but don't offer much protection for the girdle, especially if it happens to be thin. The Tiffany setting is the best example of a prong setting.

White diamonds should be suspended from white prongs. If you set them in yellow, they'll reflect the yellow of the gold and look more yellow than they are. That's the last thing you want. So what's the solution if you're a yellow-gold person? Set the stone in white prongs, but keep the band yellow. It's as easy as that.

If you're extremely active in work or play, the

prong setting may not be a good choice. Prongs wear down after a time and may loosen. (Active people should have their settings checked every six months.) If you swim a lot, or your hands frequently come in contact with bleach, check your ring often, because chlorine may damage the setting.

If you're active, a round or oval diamond might be a better choice than a heart-shaped, marquise or pear, which are more fragile. A bump the wrong way may cause the points to break or chip. Also, get a prong setting with six prongs instead of four, even if you have a small diamond. If one of the four prongs gives way, the diamond may slip out. (If your diamond is insured, your worries are reduced.)

Bezel and *channel* settings are often preferable for active people. A bezel setting encases the girdle in metal, while a channel setting holds the diamond(s) at opposite ends, with no metal touching its sides. The "anniversary ring" is an example of a channel setting. Either setting prevents the diamond from chipping. Set white diamonds in a white bezel or channel.

If you're purchasing a diamond with yellow color, set it in yellow-gold prongs, bezel or channel. Believe it or not, the gold setting will blend with the yellow color of the diamond. A white setting, on the other hand, will emphasize the diamond's yellow color. Choose a coordinating yellow gold band.

Gold and Platinum - Their Color and Strength

White gold is stronger than yellow — and platinum is stronger than both. The color of yellow gold depends on its karat. The more gold it contains, the richer the color and the softer it becomes. Look at the chart.

24K = 100 percent gold

18K = 75 percent gold

14K = 58.5 percent gold

If you are active, choose a 14K gold setting. It's strong. If you have a desk job and can afford it, 18K gold — white or yellow — would be appropriate. White gold no matter the karat, however, is more brittle than yellow gold or platinum, so have the setting checked at least once a year. Look at the ring inside the band and make sure it's stamped 14K (585 if the ring came from Europe) or 18K (750 if the ring is European). This will help ensure that the gold content in the ring is true. Don't buy a new ring that isn't stamped.

If you are active, prefer white gold and money is no object, you might choose a platinum setting (that is also white in color). It's more expensive, but it's strong and doesn't wear down as gold does. A platinum ring should be stamped on the inside "plat" or "PT." If the ring is European, it should be stamped "PT950."

The Side Stones

A diamond solitaire may be flanked with other diamonds, or colored gems called "side stones." Side stones are a matter of taste and budget.

Everyone is familiar with baguettes (named after those long loaves of French bread) that are either narrow and straight, or narrow and tapered little gems that flank the center diamond. They're beautiful and expensive.

Other stones that serve well as side stones are round diamonds and trilliants. Trilliants are expensive, but gorgeous. If you have a slightly yellow stone that you want to make look whiter, flank it on either side with blue sapphires. The contrast will enhance the color of the diamond considerably.

TIP: If you want trilliant side stones but can't afford them, take three round diamonds and set them in a white gold triangle. This will accomplish the look you want for less money.

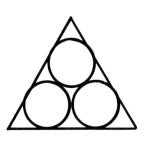

If you use side stones (other than one baguette on each side of the center stone), your engagement ring will require a custom made wedding band to match. A gold or gold and diamond wedding band will not sit flush against this ring. A custom ring will have to be made to go with it. This can be more expensive than buying a *set* of rings, in which the wedding band is part of the package, or buying a plain gold band for a simple solitaire.

Be Aware - Single Cuts

Many times smaller diamonds, the kind used for side stones or in wedding bands, will be *single cut*. They only have 17 facets — not 58. This is extremely important because single-cut stones aren't as flashy. How could they be? Make sure *all* the diamonds in your rings are *full* cut, with 58 facets. If they are single cut, the ring(s) should cost much less.

Insurance - Protect Your Investment

It's not a bad idea to have your diamond insured against loss, breakage and theft. You may insure your diamond on your homeowner's policy. Check with your insurance agent.

The Wedding Band

The wedding band — like endless love — has no beginning or end. It's a symbol worn by a woman and her husband as a visible reminder of the eternal hope, faith, love and joy they've placed in one another. Today wedding bands come in all shapes and sizes, from the simple to the elaborate. They may be adorned with gems, or without.

Choosing Your Wedding Band

A wedding band may be worn with an engagement ring or without. If worn with your engagement ring, it should match or complement it. It shouldn't be too big for your finger. Try different size bands with your ring. It's a matter of taste and budget.

Many women switch their engagement rings to the fourth finger of their right hand after the ceremony and wear their wedding band on the fourth finger of their left hand. If you decide to do this, you might opt for a thicker wedding band with some gems to give it importance. Some brides don't like the idea of two rings, on the other hand, and will wear one that's a combination engagement ring and wedding band. The choice is yours.

Tips for Buying that Plain Gold Band

Shop price when you buy a plain gold band. Bands come flat, or half-round, with milgrained (serrated) edge or without. They also come *comfort fit.*

The factors that influence the cost of a plain gold band are the width or millimeter size, weight of the ring, ring size, and karat weight — for example, 14K or 18K. When you shop for one, it's important to compare oranges to oranges. For example, let's say your ring size is a six and you want a flat, 14K gold band, plain-edge, four-millimeters in width. Go from store to store and see who offers the best value. Have the store weigh the ring, for example five pennyweight, or 7.775 grams. (Gold is weighed in pennyweights and grams. There are 1.555 grams to one pennyweight.) After you shop a few stores, you might notice a big difference in the price. As long as the rings you're considering are marked 14K, are four-millimeters in width with a plain edge, are a size six, and weigh the same — *the rings are identical.* Buy the one with the best price.

A size eight band will be more expensive than a six, and a nine millimeter will be more expensive than a four, because they're larger and require more gold. A milgrained edge is more expensive than a plain edge. 18K bands will be more expensive than 14K.

Comfort-fit bands are the most expensive gold bands. Instead of being concave on the inside — or flat — they are made convex. In order to do this, more gold is added to the bands to round them on the inside. This supposedly makes them more comfortable. It also makes them heavier and

more expensive. Once again, shop price and compare apples to apples. "I want a size 10, comfort fit, 14K yellow-gold band with milgrained edge, eight-millimeters." Prices may vary greatly store to store. To be sure the rings you're considering are identical, have them weighed, then buy the one with the best price.

Make sure your band is stamped 14K or 18K. Don't buy a new ring that doesn't have a stamp.

In Summary - Have Fun, and Don't Go Over Budget

No matter how much money you have to spend, it's important to follow these guidelines to ensure you're buying the most beautiful diamond for your money. Copy the checklist on the next page and take it with you when shopping. It will eliminate guesswork. I hope I've impressed upon you that there's more to buying a *beautiful* diamond than flaws and color.

Don't go over budget. Many of the big guys in this industry offer financing — at a hefty 18 percent or more. Interest can end up costing much more than the ring, so be careful. Spend what you can afford, and be happy!

Diamond Comparison Checklist

Name of Store:_____

Address:_____

Phone Number:_____

Clerk/Jeweler's Name:_____

Diamond Grading Report:	Stone 1	Stone 2	Stone 3	Stone 4
Laboratory Name:				
Date Issued:				
Certificate Number:				
Shape & Cut:				
Measurements:				
Weight (carats):				
Depth and Table %:				
Girdle:				
Culet:				
Finish: Polish & Symmetry:				
Clarity (flaws):				
Color & Fluorescence:				
Setting (Gold, etc.):				
Price:				

Additional Comments:

A pre-wedding photo taken on the beach. Notice the birds in the background.

The Engagement

If a gentleman asks you to be his wife, even if he doesn't offer you a ring, and you accept — you are engaged. You are the fiancée, the future groom is the fiancé. Both are pronounced the same.

Rings have been symbolic of betrothal throughout the centuries. Diamonds were worn in wedding jewelry as far back as the Middle Ages, and today the diamond is the choice of most brides in the United States.

Today, many brides skip the engagement ring and wear only a wedding band. The choice is yours.

The First Step

After you become engaged, notify both sets of parents with the good news and your children (if you have them) from previous marriages. Traditionally, the groom's parents called the bride's, and invited them and the newly engaged couple to cocktails or dinner. Today, either set of parents may make the call, but the idea is to get everyone together as soon as possible. If younger children are involved, it's my advice that everyone meet in more casual circumstances, perhaps at a picnic. Your decision should be based on what you feel is best for your situation.

After your immediate families are told of your engagement, you should inform your friends and business associates. *Do not send printed engagement announcements.* This is tacky — the implication being, "Send a gift!" You may announce your engagement, however, with a party that may be as formal or informal as you wish. Traditionally, the parents of the bride hosted both the engagement party and the wedding, but times have changed. If both families are sharing the cost of the wedding, then they should split the cost of the engagement party. If you and your fiancé are hosting your own wedding, then *both* sets of parents may host an engagement party for you. Your choices are limitless based on your preferences and finances, but don't invite anyone who will *not* be invited to the wedding.

Many brides skip engagement parties altogether, because the wedding itself is so expensive.

TYPES OF ENGAGEMENT PARTIES AND INVITATIONS

The Informal Engagement Party

This party may be a beach party, picnic, or cookout at your mom's house. The guests may dress informally — or wear whatever suits the mood. You may do your own cooking or have it catered — anything goes. Call your guests to invite them to the party, or send funny invitations. Once again, gifts should not be expected.

Sample Invitation - Informal Engagement

Please celebrate
our engagement with us
at a barbecue at the home of
Sheila and Allan Mogel
June 10th — 5:00
38 Guest Drive, Morganville
Sue Smith and Don Jones
Regrets only: 864-9865

The Semi-Formal Engagement Party

The semi-formal engagement party may be, for example, a luncheon or cocktail party. It may be hosted at your parents' home, a friend or relative's home, or even at a restaurant or club. Entertainment is not required nor is formal dress, and there's no need for centerpieces or decorations on the tables, although they add a nice touch. Printed invitations should be sent, but they should be decorative and light. Once again, guests aren't expected to bring gifts.

Sample Engagement Invitation - Semi-Formal

If both sets of parents are hosting the party:

Mr. and Mrs. James Michael Rudden
and
Mr. and Mrs. John Dudley Finch
invite you for cocktails and hors d'oeuvres
to celebrate the engagement of their children
Maria Suzanne
and
Paul Adam
on Saturday, the second of November
at eight o'clock
at the home of Mr. and Mrs. Finch
3432 Northwest Fifth Avenue
Parkersberg, Vermont

Regrets only — 456-321-4567

The Formal Engagement Party

A *formal* engagement party normally precedes a *formal* wedding. They take place at private clubs, hotels, or restaurants and are usually evening affairs where dinner is served, and entertainment and dancing are featured. Fresh flowers decorate the tables.

Just like a wedding, formal, engraved invitations (or thermographed) are sent out by the hosts, (they may even specify "black tie"), and response cards are returned by the guests. Guests, however, aren't expected to bring gifts to an engagement party.

Sample Engagement Invitation - Formal

If the bride's parents are hosting the party:

Mr. and Mrs. Robert Scott Harmon
request the pleasure of your company
at dinner
in honour of the engagement of their daughter
Susan Louise
to
Donald Hudson Limone
son of
Mr. and Mrs. Donald Weston Limone
on Sunday, the ninth of December
at seven o'clock
Rolling Hills Country Club
Warren, Michigan

Black Tie

"Surprise" Parties

Many brides like to surprise family and friends with their engagements. They host a party (reason unspecified) and spring the news on their guests. This honor goes to the father of the bride who rises and announces the good news with a toast. "There's a reason I called you all here —- because this is a joyous occasion. At this time, I'd like to announce the engagement of my daughter Anne to Bob Smith. Let's all stand and drink to their happiness!" A surprise party is a fun way to announce your engagement.

Engagement Gifts

If you should receive gifts at engagement parties, or people send them once the engagement has been formally announced, be sure to reply immediately (within three weeks) with a hand-written thank-you note.

The Newspaper Announcement

An engagement should be announced within 12 months of the wedding, but at least two months before the date. If you're having a party, announce the engagement afterward.

Engagement and wedding announcements appear in either the *society* or *life-style* section of the newspaper. If you are planning on announcing your engagement, call the paper's society or life-style editor to find out about its policy (each one may be different). Ask which days the newspaper prints announcements and about submission deadlines. Chances are, you'll be asked to fill out a form that they'll send you. It's best to type your answers, and always use full names — no nicknames. If they don't have a standard form, you'll need to make your own. Type your name, address, and home and work phone numbers at the top of an 8 1/2 x 11 page, so the newspaper can contact you if necessary. See examples in this chapter. Then word your announcement like the following examples. Put a RELEASE DATE at the top of the page, informing the newspaper when you'd like the announcement to appear, although there are no guarantees.

Many newspapers also accept photographs. These may be of the future bride, or of the engaged couple. When you call the newspaper, ask if they accept photos and how they should be submitted. Always put your name and phone numbers on the back of the photograph, and the name of the photographer. Most newspapers require good quality, glossy, black-and-white prints, either 8 x 10s, or 5 x 7s.

If you're no longer living in the same town where you grew up, you should send an announcement to both town newspapers — the same with your fiance, although *only* the parents of the bride announce the engagement.

Here are a few examples. Notice the parents of the bride (or just the mother) make the announcement.

— Classic:

Mr. and Mrs. Peter Jones of Boca Raton announce the engagement of their daughter, Jennifer Alice, to Walter Berry, the son of Mr. and Mrs. Sean Berry, of Indianapolis, Indiana. The wedding will take place in June.

I don't advise putting street addresses in announcements, nor do I advise specifying the wedding date. You might be inviting thieves into your home. You don't even need to name the town, if you're from the same one in which the announcement appears.

Some newspapers also will include the educational background of the bride and groom and where they're employed. It depends on the newspaper.

— Announcing the engagement yourself:

Lynn Swanson, a teacher with the Black Forrest School District, and David Sweeney, a florist with Ardmore Floral Design, are planning a July wedding. Ms. Swanson is the daughter of Mr. and Mrs. Harry Swanson of Pittsburgh, Pennsylvania. Mr. Sweeney is the son of Mr. and Mrs. Bradford Sweeney of Brattleberg, Rhode Island.

—- If your parents are amicably divorced: (mother remarried).

Mrs. Linda Anne (or Dillford) Thompson of Denver and Mr. Dudley James Dillford of Santa Fe, wish to announce the engagement of their daughter, Susan Louise, to Frank Pinstone, son of Mr. and Mrs. David Pinstone of Atlanta.

— If they're not amicably divorced: (mother remarried).

Mrs. Linda Anne (or Dillford) Thompson of Denver wishes to announce the engagement of her daughter, Susan Louise Dillford, to Frank Pinstone, son of Mr. and Mrs. David Pinstone of Atlanta. Ms. (or Miss) Dillford is also the daughter of Mr. Dudley James Dillford of Santa Fe.

— Or, if the mother is remarried, she and her husband may make the announcement:

Mr. and Mrs. Leonard Thompson of Denver wish to announce the engagement of Mrs. Thompson's daughter, Susan Louise Dillford, to Frank Pinstone, son of Mr. and Mrs. David Pinstone of Atlanta. Ms. (or Miss) Dillford is also the daughter of Mr. Dudley James Dillford of Santa Fe.

— If the groom's parents are divorced:

Mr. and Mrs. James Roston of Los Angeles wish to announce the engagement of their daughter, Ruth Marie, to Mr. David Lawrence of Cleveland, Ohio. Mr. Lawrence is the son of Mrs. Dolores London of Albany, New York, and Mr. Charles Lawrence of Atlanta, Georgia.

— If one of the bride's parent's is deceased:

The engagement of Susan Smith, daughter of Mr. Robert Smith (or Mrs.) and the late Mrs. (or Mr.) Smith, to Mark O'Meara of Fort Lauderdale, son of Mr. and Mrs. Harrold O'Meara of New York City, is announced by the bride's father (or mother).

— If both of the bride's parents are deceased, a close relative may announce the engagement:

Mr. and Mrs. George Jones would like to announce the engagement of their niece, Miss (or Ms.) Susan Franklin, to Dr. Paul Smith, son of Mr. and Mrs. Simon Smith of Birmingham, Alabama. Miss (or Ms.) Franklin is the daughter of the late Mr. and Mrs. Robert Franklin.

— Announcing Second Marriages

Second marriages may be announced exactly like first marriages, by either the parents of the bride or the bride's mother, although it's not a necessity.

How Long an Engagement?

The length of an engagement may be governed by the time it takes to finalize the wedding plans. In order to reserve a club, hotel, restaurant, temple, or catering hall for your semi-formal or formal wedding, it may be necessary to reserve it at least one year ahead, even two years ahead in some highly populated areas in the United States.

A religious wedding may require premarital instruction. The Catholic Church is particularly strict, requiring "premarital preparation", that may take four to six months to complete. They also require previously married couples, whether Catholic or not, to obtain an annulment if they wish to marry within the Church — this may take months or even years.

Many bands, orchestras and disc jockeys reserve six months to a year ahead, and so do many photographers and florists. A wedding takes time to plan.

For those having a wedding at home, or anyplace that doesn't involve reserving a date so far in advance, a wedding engagement may last six months to one year, although it's important not to rush — the impending stress may not be worth it. Take your time and have a sweet, easy engagement. Don't let the stress of planning a wedding put a cloud over what should be the happiest time of your life.

The Broken Engagement

A broken engagement can be miserable to experience. It involves emotional suffering and financial loss. If the couple split by mutual consent, it's easier for everyone to accept. But they should do everything they can to reimburse their parents for their losses (if their parents were hosting the wedding). It's not fair for parents to shoulder the responsibility — especially if the bride and groom are employed.

If the bride breaks the engagement, it's up to her to return the ring to the groom. All losses must be sustained by her and her family.

If the groom breaks the engagement the bride is entitled to the ring. The groom also should offer to reimburse the bride and her family for any financial losses if they were hosting the wedding.

Whatever the reason for the break up, all gifts must be returned to friends and family. These include engagement gifts, shower gifts and wedding gifts. A handwritten note should accompany each gift. See Invitations chapter.

If the wedding invitations have been sent, they must be recalled. This is done by personal note, printed or engraved card, or telephone call. It's not necessary to give a reason. See Invitations.

In Summary

Now is *not* the time to think of broken engagements. You've got a lot of planning ahead!

The splendor and beauty of a church wedding.

The Ceremony

The ceremony is the most beautiful, significant part of the wedding celebration, and you should spare no effort in planning even its smallest detail. Whether in a church or synagogue, at home, in a park, or on the beach, the ceremony should be meaningful and memorable to you, your groom, families and guests.

Tradition, whether religious or cultural, plays a key factor in the wedding celebration and should be a foremost consideration. Often tradition is modified to keep up with our liberated lifestyles, but always remember that beauty lies within. Tradition provides a bridge to our history — the way our mothers, fathers and grandparents lived their lives and upheld what their parents taught them. The traditions that your family and your fiancé's family have passed down to you should be reflected in your marriage ceremony. It will make it meaningful for you and those who have shared your lives.

Talk with your fiancé about religious and cultural marriage traditions within your respective families. You may come from the same backgrounds, or you may be blending two cultures and religions into one wedding celebration. Discuss what you would like incorporated into your ceremony — traditions and customs that are meaningful to you both, your families, and your heritage.

Religious Instruction, Rules and Restrictions

Many religions require that couples take instruction before they marry. Some Christian churches also may require that one person be a member of the congregation. In Judaism, in most instances, the couple must be Jewish and one person must be a member of the temple. Give yourself enough time when planning your wedding to meet all religious requirements.

At your first meeting with clergy, ask for a brochure or pamphlet that details requirements, rules, and restrictions. Most churches and synagogues offer these guides for couples about to marry.

Fees

Many churches require fees for use of their facilities, as do some synagogues (independent of the gift you present to the officiant), and these sometimes can be exorbitant. You also will need to pay for any extras such as the organist, choir, harpist, vocalist and church attendant. Catholic couples also are expected to provide gifts for altar boys.

What If You're Living Together?

Most Christian religions regard cohabitation as a sinful state, therefore unacceptable. Many sects also refuse to marry couples living together. In Judaism, premarital sex — while frowned upon — most likely would not be grounds for refusal of the marriage ceremony. Either way, be aware of this before meeting with clergy.

Second or More Marriages and Religion

Religion can be a major stumbling block if you want to marry in a church or temple and were previously wed. Consult your minister, priest or rabbi about requirements and restrictions. Ask how long it will take to fulfill obligations necessary for remarriage. Then make your plans.

Second or More Marriages and Good Taste

It always amazes me when a "multiple bride" (my term for a bride who weds more than once) remarries in the precise manner she did the first time. Or, if previously married without the fanfare of a traditional wedding, she'll pull out all the stops the second (or third) time around. She wears a white wedding dress with veil and has a zillion bridesmaids. Then she hosts a big reception, tosses the bouquet, and sails away into the sunset with her current Prince Charming.

Good taste aside, whatever happened to the independence, autonomy, free thought and free spirit of the American woman. To look at remarriage today, you might not know it exists.

My advice: "Be different this time!" Let your personality and maturity shine. You're not tied to mama's purse strings anymore, or her tastes. This time do it your way. Be imaginative. Have the ceremony in a small romantic chapel or country inn. Use a friend's mountain retreat or beach house, or be married at your club with a fabulous cocktail party following. Don't have your father give you away. You've probably been on your own for some time, so walk yourself up the aisle. Show your independence. Have one attendant for yourself and one for your fiancé. Wear something dazzling with a comparable headpiece, and choose something equally chic for your honor attendant. If 50 or more guests are attending, ask friends to usher. Include your children if you have them and they are willing. Make this wedding your own — not a "not-so-instant replay" of the last one. Let your personality and that of your fiancé shine. Write your own vows and make your own rules.

Interfaith Marriages

Interfaith marriages often pose problems, but these can be overcome with patience and understanding. It is essential that couples openly discuss the differences in their religions, and that they become familiar with each other's faiths. This can be accomplished by meeting with clergy. At the first meeting, your parents should be included so they will understand and appreciate your concern for their feelings. All misgivings and questions should be discussed openly.

Many churches and synagogues offer counseling and seminars for those contemplating interfaith marriage. It is advisable that you participate in them *before* setting the date for your wedding.

The divorce rate for couples of different faiths is twice the average, so it's advisable to participate in counseling programs before you marry. They've proven very beneficial to interfaith couples. Counseling will make you aware of potential problems and enable you to go beyond the romantic notion of "the wedding" to the realities of married life. Ask your clergy about counseling.

An Orthodox or Conservative Jewish-Christian marriage may be difficult, because Orthodox and Conservative rabbis will not perform marriages between a Jew and non-Jew. Many Reform rabbis will, but most will not perform them in conjunction with Christian clergy. If it's been your dream to have a rabbi and minister or priest officiate at your wedding, it's best to begin looking now.

Before the ceremony — an elegant chuppa is draped from the ceiling for a Jewish wedding.

A traditional Greek Orthodox ceremony. The bride and groom wear crowns to signify that they are king and queen of their realm.

Start by asking recently married friends and relatives if they know of any rabbis and Christian clergy who would officiate together. Or you may call the Rabbinic Center for Research and Counseling, who will be able to provide you with a list of rabbis in your area who will officiate at interfaith weddings. If you have any concerns or questions regarding interfaith marriage, the Director of the Center will be glad to discuss them with you. Consult the Appendix for more information.

Once you choose the officiant, discuss the ceremony. If you are both Christians, your minister or priest can advise you on how best to conduct the ceremony. In most cases, in deference to the bride, the couple is married in her church (although the groom's pastor may offer a prayer or blessing, if the bride's pastor is in agreement).

Sometimes, to avoid hard feelings, it's best to have an interfaith wedding on neutral turf — a hotel, club, or restaurant. Your clergy may marry you there, or you may decide on a civil ceremony conducted by a secular officiant such as a justice of the peace. Having the latter does not mean your wedding must be less meaningful or beautiful. It means that you and your fiancé can take charge and write your own ceremony, incorporating different facets from both your religions and cultures. Most secular officiants offer beautiful wedding ceremonies for interfaith couples. Having an interfaith wedding also can be expensive. Ministers, priests, rabbis, or lay persons who officiate at these weddings can charge exorbitant fees. Ask what they are before you hire them.

For more information, read Rabbi Abraham Klausner's book, *WEDDINGS A Complete Guide to All Religious & Interfaith Marriage Services*. It's a must read!

Atypical Ceremony Sites

If you're planning on being married on a beach, in a park or at a museum, call city hall or the institution itself to inquire about availability and fees. To reserve the date, you'll need to leave a deposit. Be sure to ask when the balance is due, what restrictions apply, what the clean-up policy is, and if a permit is required.

Scheduling the Ceremony to the Reception

Schedule your ceremony so that it immediately precedes your reception, and be sure that it properly reflects your wedding, whether formal, semi-formal or informal. (See Part I of *For the Bride*.)

Don't Forget the Marriage License

I once did a wedding at the Boca Raton Resort and Club in which the bride and groom forgot to obtain a marriage license. The officiant refused to marry them on the grounds that he would be violating the law. After much wrangling, he consented, although the wedding date was later fudged when the bride and groom went to get the license the next day.

If you are having two wedding services, one in one state and one in another, you need to take a copy of your first license to the second service. If both ceremonies are to take place within the same state, or a civil and religious service are performed within the same state, the same rule applies.

Always take the precaution of calling the courthouse in the town where the ceremony is to take place to find out the state's requirements before you apply. Each state varies. Ask what form of payment is required, and remember, both of you must apply for a license. You also may need your birth certificates, a driver's license or other means of identification. You may need to prove your age if you're under 23. If you were previously married, you may need to show proof of a divorce or annulment. You also may need blood tests. Some states require tests for syphilis, others require AIDS tests, which may take as long as three weeks to process.

The Out-of-State Clergy or Officiant

Some states prohibit marriage by officiants who do not reside within the state. If you plan on being married by a dear friend or relative who lives out of state, check with local state authorities to find out requirements.

Premarital Physical and Genetic Examinations

Before you marry, get tested for *all* sexually transmitted diseases, even though it may not be required. I also feel it essential for couples to have complete physical examinations before marriage, and to be tested for genetic disorders that they may pass on to their children (hemophilia, for example, or sickle cell anemia). These tests would be at the discretion of doctors, based upon the couple's medical history.

If there has been a history of a mental disorder, each partner should be made aware of the other's background in detail. A meeting with the attending psychiatrist or psychologist should be scheduled.

If you are Jewish and are marrying a Jew, it is important to be tested to see if you are a carrier of Tay-Sachs disease, an illness fatal to children. Descendants of Jews of Central and Eastern Europe (called Ashkenazic) carry the disease, and 90 percent of the American Jewish population is of Ashkenazic descent. About one out of 25 carry the gene for Tay-Sachs. If both of you are carriers, it would be advisable to seek genetic counseling if you plan on starting a family.

Meeting With the Officiant

The first step in planning your wedding should be meeting with the officiant. At this meeting the date, place and time of the ceremony should be reserved, and the particulars of the wedding discussed.

At this time, clergy also will discuss religious obligations that must be fulfilled before the wedding.

Music and Its Restrictions

Many religions place restrictions on music that can be played during the ceremony. Some prohibit or restrict secular music. Others restrict certain religious music at certain times of the year, Lent

and Christmas, for example. Be sure to ask your clergy.

The church or temple organist will typically work with you to select and coordinate your wedding music. Make an appointment and review selections with them to ensure they're acceptable. Some churches and temples, for example, will not allow either Wagner's *The Bridal Chorus* ("Here Comes the Bride") or *The Wedding March* by Mendelssohn. Many churches feel the "Chorus" to be too tragic, while the "March" was written for a pagan wedding. Some rabbis, on the other hand, frown on the use of these selections because Wagner who composed *The Bridal Chorus* was an anti-Semite who tried to destroy Jewish participation in the artists' guilds of Europe. Mendelssohn, on the other hand, was a Jew who converted to Christianity.

Selecting Wedding Music

Because music adds so much to a wedding ceremony, it is crucial to spend the time to find the right selections. When thinking of possibilities, ask yourself if the music is meaningful to both you and your fiancé? Does it reflect the joining of your personalities? Is it significant to you both and the occasion of your marriage? Does it meet religious requirements?

I attend weddings every weekend, and it seems that most have a vocalist who sings Peter, Paul and Mary's *The Wedding Song*, or *Sunrise, Sunset* from *Fiddler on the Roof*. Wonderful contemporary and classical music abound — take your time to find the music that's right for you.

Your temple or church organist also will be more than glad to advise you on music that relates to your wedding. A formal wedding, for example, would lend itself to heavy, classical,

A traditional, formal church wedding.

religious music. On the other hand, music for an informal wedding might feature ballads, folk songs, or soft rock and roll. Music for a semi-formal wedding might be a mixture of light classical and romantic show tunes.

Whatever you choose, always hear the music in the place you'll marry. One guitar might get lost within the confines of a huge church, synagogue, or hotel ballroom. Two might be required. Whether you employ harpists, cellists, or vocalists, or have the church choir sing at intervals throughout the service, always hear the music in the ceremony place to determine if it's suitable to the surroundings.

Strive for variety in the music you choose and have changes in modulation. When guests are being seated, bold and happy "prelude" music should be played. If secular music is permitted, the prelude music may be contemporary and romantic. Always have music as guests enter, either by musicians or vocalists, or both. It sets the tone for your wedding. During the ceremony itself, you might have soft music played when the officiant, honored guests, or relatives read scripture or poetry.

Processional music, played when you walk up the aisle, should be solemn, but dramatic, with a definitive beat, one that's easy to walk to. (Don't forget the processional in *The Sound of Music*. It's wonderful, and one I rarely hear.) Once you have decided on your processional music, practice walking to it with the person who will give you away. At the end of the ceremony, play lively,

happy music for the *recessional*, something that mirrors your joy and happiness.

If your ceremony is at a club, restaurant, or hotel, the same rules apply, except the music will not be restricted. Meet with your band leader or disc jockey who can advise you on selecting music for your ceremony, and who may also provide you with the necessary musicians and vocalists. Hear the music played at the ceremony place before making a final decision. Many companies offer tapes, records, and CDs that feature

The groom kisses the bride's hand in a romantic pose after the wedding.

countless musical selections for ceremonies. For more information, consult the Appendix.

Music and Fees

The organist and other musicians or vocalists performing at your ceremony will charge for their services. Inquire about fees.

Wedding Programs for Ceremonies

Today many brides create decorative wedding programs that describe the sequential events of their ceremonies and list participants. They are handed to guests before the ceremony.

At one wedding I attended, an Orthodox Jewish couple made programs explaining all the intricacies of their service. They even designed an "artsy" cover of palm trees that contained their Hebrew and English names. These unique programs were a wonderful, informative guide to their wedding.

For those not so artsy, most invitation catalogues carry lovely, decorative programs.

The Guest Book at Ceremonies

The guest book, with plumed pen, is usually placed on a table at the ceremony for guests to sign as they enter. A relative or special friend, who is not a member of your wedding party, may be assigned to supervise, and should be presented with a corsage or boutonniere for assisting. After the wedding, the guest book becomes a cherished memento.

Guest books and plumed pens usually can be found at stationery stores. Also check the back of invitation catalogues. They make nice gifts and may be personalized with the names of the bride and groom and the wedding date.

What the Attendants Pay For

Weddings can be a financial burden for attendants, so the savvy bride and groom will use good judgment when selecting the bridal party. Female attendants are expected to pay for bridesmaids' attire that may include dresses, undergarments, shoes and jewelry. Male attendants pay for the rental of their apparel. All pay for transportation to and from the wedding and lodgings. The bride and groom or their families may pick up any or all of these expenses if they choose, or if an attendant can't afford the expense. Attendants also are expected to pay for a wedding gift for the bride and groom.

If you have an attendant who cannot afford to be in your wedding (and you're not in a position to help out), ask them instead to read scripture or poetry at your ceremony and get them a boutonniere or corsage. Hard feelings should be avoided at all costs.

A radiant bride escorted by her father.

Attendants - Their Selection, Number and Duties

The maid of honor (or matron if she is married) and best man should be the bride or groom's dearest friend or relative. The maid or matron of honor (you may have both, or two maids of honor or two matrons of honor) should assist you throughout the planning of your wedding. She should be a friend and confidant, and be willing to pitch in and help whenever you need her, both emotionally and physically. In the same way, the best man should be there to assist the groom. (There may be two best men.) These positions are ones of honor and responsibility, so make your selections carefully.

It's also up to the maid of honor to give a shower for the bride, which may be done in conjunction with the bridesmaids. It's considered in poor taste, however, for the immediate family of the bride to be obligated to give a shower if they are hosting the wedding. If you and the groom are paying for your own wedding, it's appropriate for either of your families to "shower" you (for more information, see Part III).

The best man should be responsible for the bachelor party. This he may give in conjunction with the groomsmen. Always make sure that the bachelor party is held at least one week prior to the wedding. I've attended many weddings, where the hard-partying groom wasn't in any shape to attend a wedding the next day — least of all his own.

Ushers and bridesmaids are chosen at your discretion, and are usually made up of close friends and family. For a formal wedding, you may have four or more bridesmaids, flower girls and a ring-bearer. A semi-formal wedding requires three or fewer bridesmaids, and may include a flower girl and a ring bearer. An informal wedding requires only a best man and a maid of honor.

Ushers should be determined by the number of guests at the wedding — one usher for every 50 guests. For this reason, the number of ushers need not match the number of bridesmaids. You also may have more ushers than required so that all close family members and friends are included.

Wedding Day Duties

The maid or matron of honor, and best man do not leave the bride and groom on the day of the wedding. They help them dress, and if necessary, organize and pack for the honeymoon. The best man makes sure he has the marriage license and the ring for the bride. If the officiant is to receive a donation, he presents it for the groom. He signs all pertinent documents as a witness. He makes sure the groom makes it to the ceremony in time and stays with the groom before and during the ceremony. He helps organize the groom's honeymoon preparations, ensuring that he has all documents, airline tickets, reservations, passports, etc., that the couple will need. If the groom's clothes are rented, he sees that they're returned.

The maid of honor keeps the groom's ring for the bride. She also signs all pertinent marriage documents as a witness. Before and during the ceremony, she arranges the bride's dress, veil and train. At the ceremony, she holds the bride's bouquet. After the ceremony, she stands in the receiving line. She also makes sure the bride has all the documents for her trip, and helps her get organized for the honeymoon.

The Essentials Kit

I also feel it's the maid of honor's duty to bring an "essentials kit" to the ceremony for emergencies.

This should contain a brush, comb, hair-spray, makeup, deodorant, tampons, bobby-pins, safety pins and a small sewing kit. *This is a must.* Every week I attend weddings where a small emergency occurs that no one's prepared for — the bride's veil or the flower girl's halo won't stay secured, or a hem falls down. An essentials kit will enable you to handle all contingencies.

How an Usher Ushers

Ushers are expected at the ceremony 45 minutes before the guests start arriving. The usher escorts a couple up the aisle by offering his right arm to the woman, whom he escorts to her seat while her husband (or date) follows behind. Or, he may precede a couple to their seats so that a woman may walk up the aisle with her escort. He escorts a group up the aisle by preceding them. Ushers should be there to help anyone who needs special assistance

If there are many more family and guests for one side than the other, have the ushers seat

The bride and groom after the ceremony.

guests proportionately so that the room doesn't look lopsided.

Seating of Guests and Family at Weddings

Guests are seated at ceremonies based on their affiliation with the bride or groom. In gentile weddings the groom's family and guests sit on the right, the bride's on the left. This is because the bride is on the left hand side of the groom. In Jewish weddings, however, the opposite is true, and it's done for a reason. In the Bible, Psalms, 45:9, it states, "...upon thy right hand did stand the queen..." In Judaism, every bride is a queen on her wedding day.

Close family members are seated as close to the front as possible on the appropriate side. The first rows of church pews are designated for the immediate family and are sometimes marked with ribbons or flowers. The bride may even include a "Within The Ribbon" card in the invitations of these family members (see the chapter on Invitations).

After all guests are seated, the grandparents are seated (the groom's first, the bride's last), and then the parents of the groom. The mother of the bride is the last person seated before the processional. She should be escorted by an usher who is a close family member if possible. In Jewish weddings, grandparents are part of the processional unless they are physically not able. In this case, they would be seated in the front row before the processional begins. As in Christian weddings, the first rows at the front are reserved for close family members and may be marked with ribbons, bows or flowers.

Children at Weddings - Participants and Guests

Children participate in weddings as flower girls, ringbearers, junior bridesmaids or junior groomsmen.

Girls age four to eight qualify to be flower girls and there may be more than one. A flower girl may be dressed in white, ivory, candlelight or blush in a gown similar to the bride, or she may be dressed in the color and style of the bridesmaids, or in a simple white or ivory smock. Whatever you decide to do, use common sense. Flower girls dressed like adults with heavy make-up look foolish. The flower girl may carry a small basket of flowers or a small nosegay. She may even carry a fire-side basket (without sides) containing short-stemmed roses tied with ribbons, that she hands to guests as she walks up the aisle. At no time should she throw petals, because people may slip on them.

There is only one ringbearer at a wedding. Boys age four to eight qualify. The ringbearer should dress like the groomsmen if the wedding is formal or semi-formal. His attire may be rented from the same shop as the groomsmen's. If the groomsmen are wearing suits, the ringbearer should also.

The ringbearer walks up the aisle carrying a pillow containing two plastic rings. (Don't place your real rings on this pillow, because they might not make it to the altar. The maid of honor and best man should hold the real thing).

Junior bridesmaids and junior groomsmen are young people from ages nine to 17. Junior bridesmaids should look like young women and should not be dressed in ultra-sophisticated bridesmaids attire, nor should they wear heavy makeup. Choose a style that befits a young woman in the same color, or color family and material as the bridesmaids dresses. Junior groomsmen, on the other hand, should match the male members of the bridal party.

Be forewarned that you take your chances when you have younger children participate in your wedding. They tend to be nervous, fidgety and many times throw tantrums. At one garden wedding I coordinated, the bride insisted on her three-year-old nephew as ringbearer. He refused to walk up the aisle and ran in circles around the trees during the ceremony.

Younger children also may steal the show. At another wedding I handled, the flower girl and ringbearer sat on the steps below the altar and had a lively conversation throughout the entire ceremony. The congregation was in stitches.

I often suggest having the flower girl and ringbearer walk up the aisle holding hands so that they won't be frightened. I also suggest having their parents seated in the front row. Once the children walk up the aisle, they can take their place with their parents. If your ringbearer and flower girl are mature, they may stand behind the best man and maid of honor during the ceremony.

Younger children as guests are easily bored with ceremonies and receptions and tend to be very restless and impatient. This also places a burden on their parents, who must watch their every move instead of having fun and enjoying your wedding. It should be noted, however, that children may be invited to informal family weddings at your home or that of friends or family.

Second Marriages and Children as Participants

If children from previous marriages are comfortable with your impending wedding, include them in your ceremony. Boys may be ringbearers, junior groomsmen, or groomsmen; girls may be flower girls, junior bridesmaids or bridesmaids, or they may read scripture or poetry at the ceremony. At a Jewish ceremony they may hold the chuppa

poles. If, on the other hand, they're having problems adjusting, don't force them to participate. If younger children don't want to be included, make plans for them to stay with your former spouse, relatives, or their friends during the wedding and while you're away on your honeymoon.

Transportation

Limousines can be expensive, but most brides and grooms reserve them to transport them and the bridal party to and from the ceremony. Some "stretches" are roomy enough to carry the bride, her parents and bridesmaids. If you can only afford one, it should take you and your parents to the ceremony place, and you and the groom to the reception after the ceremony is over.

If you can afford a fleet of limousines, the schedule is as follows: the first limo picks up the groomsmen (except for the best man) and gets them to the ceremony about 45 minutes beforehand. The next limousine picks up the groom and best man, who arrive about 30 minutes before the ceremony. The third limo brings the groom's parents, followed by the bride's mother and female attendants in another limousine. The last limo transports the bride with her father. Attendants and parents should make arrangements to have their cars taken to the reception so they have transportation home.

There are fun alternatives to the limousine when considering rented transportation. One is the horse and buggy, another is the trolley car that is large enough to transport the bride, her family and attendants to the wedding and reception.

Where Should the Bride Dress?

If a dressing room is provided by your ceremony place, my advice is to use it. A wedding gown should look its best and so should bridesmaids dresses. After a crushing ride in a car or limo, this may not be the case.

Everyone will look fresh and gowns will be wrinkle-free if you dress directly before the ceremony.

A Tip for the Bride

No matter what time your ceremony, always eat something beforehand. Nerves can wreak havoc on your wedding day, and many brides who forget to eat, chance fainting at the altar. I've seen it happen. If you are prone to fainting, make sure your maid of honor carries smelling salts such as "Revivo." If you're Jewish, however, consult with your rabbi about fasting before the ceremony.

The "Starter"

Many churches and temples have members who act as coordinators for weddings. I like to refer to them as "starters," and although you may pay a minimal fee for their services, they may be less expensive and more familiar with your ceremony location than a wedding consultant.

The starter arrives approximately one hour or more before the ceremony to help the florist set up, and to put the bridal party flowers in the appropriate room for the bride and her attendants. The starter also will pin boutonnieres on the gentlemen and corsages on the ladies. The starter knows the ins and outs of the ceremony place, and can advise where to set up photo equipment, where electrical outlets are, and how to secure the aisle runner.

Before the ceremony begins, the starter ensures that the ushers are doing their job, sees that the best man and groom are where they should be, and assists the bride and her attendants when they arrive at the ceremony.

Once guests are seated, the starter tells the musicians when to change from prelude to processional music. He/she gets the attendants in line and paces them as they walk up the aisle. The starter makes sure that the bride looks her best, adjusting her dress, train and veil.

If you are being married in a club, restaurant or hotel, your catering director may handle these details. If you have a wedding coordinator, be sure she meets with clergy at your church or synagogue to go over details well in advance of your ceremony. Similarly, she should meet with your catering director.

If your church or synagogue does not offer a starter and you can't afford a wedding consultant, give the job to a close relative or friend, someone who will be honored and glad to assist.

The Aisle Runner

Many churches restrict the use of aisle runners because people often trip over them. Traditionally, they were used so that the bride's feet would not touch the ground where evil spirits lurked. Today, many brides insist on them although they're merely symbolic. The cloth ones are expensive and are provided by florists, as are the soft paper variety that are cheaper and disposable. Aisle runners are anchored to the floor by the florist with either tape, pins, or both. The aisle runner is pulled to the end of the aisle by an usher (although it may be anyone of the bride's choosing) before the processional begins.

Most temples allow the use of aisle runners. In many Jewish ceremonies, the runner is pulled down the aisle by the florist, and cut and tacked before the ceremony begins. The last row of chairs is roped off on the center aisle with tulle or satin ribbons, and guests are seated from the sides. The rope is removed before the grandparents walk up the aisle.

The Receiving Line

A receiving line provides the bride and groom with the opportunity to individually thank their guests for attending their wedding. It was designed to take place after the ceremony, or at the reception site before it begins. If you decide to have one, I recommend a "short-order" receiving line to move guests along. Try to keep the conversation short because no one likes to stand in line.

In a short-order receiving line, the mother of the bride is first followed by the mother of the groom. The bride and groom take their place beside her and finally the maid of honor. (This solves the problem of "who to put where" if the parents of the bride or groom are divorced.)

The fathers and best man are not included (although they may be if the bride and groom so choose). The idea is to get them mingling with the guests departing from the receiving line to ensure everyone feels comfortable. If your divorced father is hosting your wedding and insists on being in the line, place him on the other side of the groom. (If he is remarried, place his wife beside him.) If your mother is deceased or not in attendance, your father may take her place in the receiving line if he is hosting the wedding. A close female relative of yours may stand beside him, or if you like, and if your father has remarried, his wife.

The person(s) who are hosting the wedding, however, come first in the receiving line. In other words, if you and your fiancé are hosting your wedding, you would be the first two in line, with the mother of the bride and the mother of the groom following, and your maid of honor last.

Today, many couples skip the receiving line. Often churches, on a tight schedule, don't have time for them and neither do reception places. "Receiving" 100 or more guests can take well over an hour. Most couples who have pictures taken after the ceremony also find it impossible to host a receiving line. Orthodox and Conservative Jewish couples who practice "Yichud" (seclusion) after their ceremonies don't have receiving lines either.

If you don't have a receiving line, be sure to greet each of your guests at the reception by visiting each guest table. It's important for your guests to know how much you appreciate them being there. (For an interesting twist on the receiving line, see Entertainment chapter.)

The Rehearsal and the Rehearsal Dinner

It is always advisable to have a rehearsal if you're having a semi-formal or formal wedding. It gives everyone an idea of what they *should* be doing. All should be present, including the officiant, bride and groom, musicians, parents and grandparents and the attendants. This also includes the ringbearer and flower girl's parents, who are invited to keep a watchful eye on them. The officiant takes charge of the rehearsal, directing and instructing everyone through the various steps of the ceremony. A rehearsal should last no longer than 45 minutes, for it can be stressful. It's my advice, if possible, to have it two nights before the wedding, not the night before. Then everyone can relax and enjoy the rehearsal dinner, without worrying about the wedding the next day.

After the rehearsal, there's usually a dinner for *all* participants (including the ringbearer and flower girl's parents), typically given by the groom's parents. If both families are sharing the expense of the wedding, both may host the rehearsal dinner. Or, the bride and groom may give the rehearsal dinner as their contribution. On the other hand, if they're hosting their own wedding, it would be appropriate for both sets of parents to give them the rehearsal dinner. Many families also like to include close family members and friends who've arrived from out of town.

At the rehearsal dinner, it's customary for the bride and groom to give gifts to their attendants and to each other. It is also proper to extend gifts to their parents if they're hosting the wedding.

It should be noted that many rabbis will not conduct rehearsals, because traditionally the bride and groom should not see each other before the wedding. The rabbi and or catering director normally instruct everyone, except the bride, before the start of the ceremony.

Divorced Parents and Your Attitude

Divorced parents sometimes create dilemmas that must be faced head on, especially when planning a wedding. Who's going to pay? Where are they going to sit? Who will walk me up the aisle? What about step-parents? If the divorce was amicable, these problems will be minimal. If not, you and your fiancé will be key factors in keeping your divorced parents happy on your wedding day.

Don't expect estranged parents to come together on your day just to make you happy. You might ask them to try, but respect their wishes and work around their problems. Don't expect them to sit together, or together walk you up the aisle. If one parent is remarried and bringing a spouse to the wedding, make sure the other has an escort.

Provide step-parents with corsages and boutonnieres.

If you would like photographs of your divorced parents together, ask in advance. If they say "No," so be it. Have a list prepared for the photographer so that he knows whom to group together for photographs. Include all step-parents.

If one parent is funding the festivities and one refuses to contribute (even if they're able), it's up to the bride or groom to decide if they should be relegated to "honored guest" status, meaning they have no role in the wedding planning.

The key is to try to work together, if possible. If not, work around the problems of divorced parents and keep your expectations low. In that way you won't be disappointed.

THE CHRISTIAN WEDDING
Prayers, Biblical Verses, Love Poetry and Secular Readings for Christian Weddings

Protestant churches allow secular readings, besides Biblical verses and prayers during ceremonies. Within the Catholic Church, however, only Biblical verses and prayers are permitted, and many are included in a booklet provided for engaged couples called "Together for Life." It seems, however, that all I hear at weddings is from the Bible, 1 Corinthians 13: 4-13: "Love is always patient and kind; it is never jealous; love is never boastful or conceited..."

Through the ages many beautiful love poems and verses have been written that may be included in Protestant marriage ceremonies. Just like wedding music, the verses, prayers, poetry and secular readings that you choose for your ceremony should take much thought and effort to ensure they are uniquely yours.

Bridal Attire

Good taste is the only rule governing dress at the ceremony. If marrying in church, it might be more appropriate to wear a traditional gown than a slinky sheath that would be fine, for example, if marrying in a hotel (see Wedding Gowns and Bridesmaids Dresses chapter).

Who Escorts the Bride Up the Aisle?

Traditionally, the father of the bride escorts her up the aisle. If there is a step-father involved, the birth father takes precedence. However, the decision should be the bride's based upon her comfort level. In more amicable situations, I have witnessed both men escort the bride up the aisle. If your father is deceased, you may have a close relative escort you up the aisle or you may decide to walk alone.

Seating of Divorced Parents

The divorced mother of the bride will sit in the first pew with her husband or an escort. The father of the bride would then take his place, with an escort or wife, in the third or fourth pews. If neither are remarried, are amicable and don't have escorts, they may sit together. The same holds true for the seating of the groom's parents.

Churches and No Rice

Traditionally, rice — symbol of fertility and good luck — was thrown at the bridal couple when they left the church. Today, however, most churches will not permit it, because it can be harmful if you slip on it and hazardous to birds who can't digest it. Most will ask that you throw bird seed instead. It may be purchased in decorative little pouches through invitation companies. Regency Thermographers call them "Seeds of Love." Be sure to ask your clergy if bird seed is permissible.

Churches and Floral Decorations

Many churches restrict the use of flowers at wedding ceremonies, but if you're having a grand affair (and you ask nicely), they may grant you permission to be more "flowery."

Most times, Protestant churches allow a bouquet on the altar or on either side of the altar (called altar bouquets or arrangements) that may be taken to the reception after the ceremony. In Catholic churches, flowers are not permitted on the altar but may be placed on either side. Sometimes altar bouquets may be moved from the church, depending on your clergy. As one priest told my husband when he went to move the bouquets, "Don't touch those flowers. They belong to God!" He put them back.

Flowers, bows, or a combination of the two are permitted on the pews, as long as they are not attached with tape. Your florist will attach them with "pew-clips." (If you are making your own bows, ask your florist to lend you pew-clips and please return them.)

Decorations, Flowers and Set-Up Time

Many churches schedule weddings within two- to two-and-a-half hours of each other. This allows little time for decorating beforehand, little time for pictures afterward, and not much time to remove flowers and decorations before the next ceremony begins. Be sure to discuss this with your minister or priest, and have everyone prepared if there is limited time between ceremonies for set up or rip down of flowers or decorations.

The Unity Candle

The unity candle has become a part of many Christian weddings, symbolizing the joining of two families. It is composed of three candles, one in the middle flanked by two smaller ones on either side. It is usually placed to the side of the altar.

After the mother of the groom is escorted up the aisle, she walks up to the unity candle and lights one of the small candles. The mother of the bride lights the other. Sometime during the ceremony (at the discretion of clergy), the bride and groom will step up to the unity candle, and from each of the two smaller candles, light the large one in the center.

Many churches or florists provide unity candles for ceremonies. If not, invitation companies sell them in their catalogues.

The Christian Processional

The processional may be done in several ways. If the ushers are not walking up the aisle, they may enter from a side door at the rear of the church and walk with the groom, best man and clergy to the altar. All turn and face the aisle to await the procession.

If the ushers walk up the aisle, they start the processional. They may walk alone, in pairs, or one bridesmaid and one usher may walk together. The shorter ones should go first. If the brides-maids don't walk with the ushers, they come next, singly or in pairs, followed by the maid of honor, then the ringbearer, followed by the flower girl. They may walk up the aisle together. Then comes the bride, who is on her father's *left* arm.

The processional should be paced and all members should walk slowly, leading with the left foot. When the first attendants reach the fifth pew, the next attendant may begin. It is advisable for the bride to wait until the flower girl reaches the

The Christian Processional.

114

altar before she starts. A change in music will be her signal to begin.

At the Altar

In the Protestant wedding, the couple takes their place in front of the altar with the maid of honor beside the bride, and the best man beside the groom. All other attendants stand beside them on the appropriate side.

Once the bride and her father reach the altar, the minister will ask, "Who gives this woman to this man?" Her father may answer, "I do." or "Her mother and I do." He may then lift his daughter's veil, kiss her and wait for the groom to approach. Or, he may lift the veil, kiss her and lower it, leaving the groom to lift the veil at the end of the ceremony. He'll then offer his daughter's hand to the groom and sit down in the first pew on the left. The bride and groom will then approach the altar, where she will hand her bouquet to her maid of honor.

In the Catholic ceremony, the father of the bride does not give his daughter away. He walks her to the altar, lifts her veil to kiss her and is seated. (It is better that the veil remain lifted, because Communion is a part of most Catholic weddings.)

Attendants at a Catholic wedding are usually seated in the front pews of the church. The maid of honor and best man are the only two who accompany the bride and groom to the altar, who are usually seated in chairs facing it. However, if there is room behind the rail, all attendants may remain standing during the ceremony.

Long-Stemmed Roses for Mothers

At the end of many Christian services (before the recessional begins), the bride gives a long-stemmed rose to each mother. These roses, decorated with ribbons and tulle, are usually left on or near the altar by the florist. It's a sweet, thoughtful way to end the ceremony.

The Recessional

At the end of the ceremony, the maid of honor will hand the bouquet to the bride (don't forget!), who will then take the groom's arm and walk down the aisle. This starts the "recessional." Even if you're happy and relieved that the whole thing is over, don't walk fast. Take pride in your marriage, and remember that all those who came to your wedding want to see you.

The bride and groom should be followed by the maid of honor and best man, who may be paired or walk singly. Then come the bridesmaids (paired with the ushers or paired together), then the ushers (paired), and the flower girl and ring-bearer, walking together (or they may wait and exit with their parents). Next to leave is the mother and father of the bride, then the mother and father of the groom. The grandparents and other family members are next, followed by the guests.

Rings and the Ceremony

A ring is not essential to be married, but it is a centuries-old custom and tradition. In the single-ring ceremony, the groom gives a ring to the bride. In a double-ring ceremony, they give a ring to each other.

THE PROTESTANT WEDDING

The Protestant wedding can be a unique, wonderful experience, especially if the bride and groom plan it with all the tender loving care it demands This service can be a part of them — an extension of their personalities and love for one another. They may choose religious or secular readings (or both), besides the poetry and music that will make *their* ceremony uniquely their own.

I have witnessed many beautiful, meaningful Protestant weddings, but I also have suffered through many featuring 15-minute "canned" services, designed to get everybody into the church and out to the party as fast as humanly possible. The wedding ceremony should be meaningful — one that everyone will remember. Put your heart and soul into planning yours.

Everyone may participate at a Protestant service. The congregation may join in the celebration through the reading of verse or singing of hymns, or with prayer, readings and song.

Think of the ceremony that you and your fiancé can plan. Your favorite scripture may be read at the service, your favorite hymns sung, your favorite poetry or verse read by your dearest relatives and friends. You can spend many happy hours together making this ceremony as meaningful, significant and memorable as you like.

Below I offer the basic structure of a Protestant service. Add your favorite music and verse and include your dearest relatives and friends. Take advantage of this wonderful opportunity to make your ceremony one everyone will remember.

The Basic Structure

After the bride walks up the aisle to meet her groom, the minister may welcome all to the church and to the wedding. The greeting may be formal, "Dearly beloved: We are gathered together here in the sight of God and in the face of this company, to join together this man and this woman in holy matrimony..." or informal, "I wish to welcome all here on this beautiful, glorious day to witness the uniting of Mary and Andrew in holy marriage." On the other hand, the welcome may be a reading of verse, poetry or scripture by your dearest friends or family.

The minister may then deliver a sermon if you or your groom so choose. If he has known you, he might provide the congregation with anecdotes about you, the joy you've known, the sorrows you've shared, the strength, courage and happiness you've given to one another. If he doesn't know you well, the sermon should reflect the goodness of marriage and its responsibilities.

The second part of the service involves the declaration of intent, in which the minister asks for a commitment from the couple to each other. The most traditional one, asked first of the groom: "Will you have this woman to be your wedded wife, to live together in holy matrimony? Will you love her, honor and keep her in sickness and health, in sorrow and in joy, and, forsaking all others, be faithful to her as long as you both shall live?" (Many couples prefer to change this to "as long as you both shall love." I don't advise this since marriage should be regarded as a lifelong proposition. All couples go through times when their love is tested.) The questions are then asked to the bride. The minister may then ask the congregation to bless you and ask them to offer you support in your marriage. He will then ask who gives the bride in marriage. (At many Protestant ceremonies, this question is asked directly after the processional.)

The Vows

Those solemn words of love and commitment that you speak only to one another are called the vows. The most traditional is the one following, the very words that Prince Charles and the Lady Diana Spencer spoke to one another. For the recitation of the vows, the bride and groom join right hands. The groom speaks first: "I, (groom's name), take thee, (bride's name), to be my wedded wife. To have and to hold, from this day forward, for better, for worse, for richer, for poorer, in sickness and in health, to love and to cherish, till death us do part. According to God's holy law; And thereto I give thee my troth."

Vows may be traditional as the one above, or you may write your own, or may read a poem to each other, or you may memorize a statement. If you tend to be nervous in these types of situations, I don't advise it. You may get together with clergy, and with their help write vows that are personally meaningful. The clergy member may recite them to you during the ceremony (so you don't forget what you're supposed to say), and then you may repeat them to one another.

The Rings

In this ceremony, rings may be given by the bride and groom to each other, or just by the groom to the bride. When the groom places the ring on her finger, he is affirming his love and his marriage with a symbol. As he does, he may say:
— With this ring, I thee wed, in the Name of God. AMEN.*
— With this ring I wed you, and pledge my faithful love. *
— I give you this ring as a sign of my vow, and with all that I am, and all that I have, I honor you.*
— This ring I give you in token and pledge of our constant faith and abiding love. *
— With this ring I thee wed; in the Name of the Father, and of the Son, and of the Holy Ghost. AMEN.

If the bride gives a ring to the groom, she does it

at this time, repeating the same words. Then the service ends, with: "For as much as _____ and _____ have consented together in wedlock, and have witnessed the same before God and this company, and thereto have engaged and pledged their troth, each to the other, and have declared the same by giving and receiving a ring and by joining hands, I pronounce that they are "man and wife" or "husband and wife." The last statement that the minister says may be, "What God has joined together let no man put asunder."

THE ROMAN CATHOLIC WEDDING

For Catholics the wedding ceremony is a *sacrament,* meaning God is with the couple when they marry. Newlyweds need God's grace to help and support them, to give them strength and encouragement and to grow deeper in love. The sacrament of marriage helps a couple achieve these goals.

The Catholic ceremony usually takes place within the mass and may include communion. Ceremonies are usually held during the day and aren't performed during the holiest days of the year — Good Friday, for example. If you'd like an evening wedding, many Catholic churches consent to those held Friday night. Sometimes a ceremony may be held outside of the sanctuary at the discretion of the priest, who must get a "dispensation from place" from the bishop.

Catholics also may be married in church without benefit of a mass. In our area, one of the deacons performs a shorter, simpler ceremony. Many Catholics, who don't want to burden their non-Catholic guests with a heavy religious service, prefer this. This ceremony is also appropriate for an interfaith wedding by Christian participants, a Protestant and a Catholic for example.

* Footnotes, see page 356.

Requirements

The Catholic Church can be explicit in its marriage requirements, that may be time-consuming and difficult to fulfill. If you're planning a Catholic wedding, be sure to meet first with clergy before setting a date.

Each of you must have a certificate of baptism, and although confirmation is not necessary, it's felt that it strengthens the faith. If you have been married, proof of an annulment must be provided, even if you're not Catholic. The posting of banns is no longer required.

You and your fiancé must also go through a premarital investigation with a priest. He may ask you all sorts of questions about your intentions, your prospects for children, if you're free to marry or if there are any impediments. The idea is to get you talking about key issues before you're married.

All couples must go through the marriage preparation process involving classes, interviews and seminars which may take four to six months to complete. Think about this when considering a date for the wedding. It's up to the priest to determine how much, or how little, preparation you'll need.

The Structure of the Catholic Service

Since most Catholic ceremonies are held within the mass and rigidly structured, I won't take the time to go into it here. Biblical readings and music can be added at the discretion of the priest, however, and chosen by you and your fiancé in accordance with clergy. Just like the Protestant ceremony, you may choose your own vows and rings may be exchanged.

When two Catholics of mixed rites marry, the couple usually marry in the church of the person who's more religiously active. A "dispensation from place" and a "dispensation from form", however, must be granted if the marriage is to be moved from the Roman Catholic Church.

A Bouquet for the Virgin Mary

At some Catholic weddings, the bride offers a small bouquet to Virgin Mary. This is done during the ceremony, when she leaves the altar to drop a small bouquet at the shrine of the Virgin.

THE CHRISTIAN ORTHODOX WEDDING

Christian Orthodox weddings, including Greek, Russian, Antiochian and Serbian are ceremonies beautiful to behold, steeped in tradition, quite different from all other Christian marriage rituals.

Within the Orthodox religion you may marry outside the faith, provided the person is a Christian baptized in the name of the Trinity — a "trinitarian." Marriage between an Orthodox and an unbaptized person is not permitted. It is also possible to marry three times within the church, provided you meet religious requirements and have a civil and ecclesiastical divorce.

There are certain times of the year when marriages are not performed, including periods of fasting, after Easter and Christmas and the day preceding a holy day. Confer with your priest before setting a wedding date.

The couple must first meet with the priest to discuss their forthcoming marriage, bringing certificates of baptism and or confirmation and proof of civil divorce if previously married. Depending on clergy, premarital counseling may be required. It is also necessary to fill out affidavits swearing to your religious and marital history. Before the Greek ceremony takes place, the *koumbaros* (best man) must also swear in an affidavit that he is Orthodox and active in the faith. These are submitted to the bishop for approval.

The koumbaros holds a special place in the Greek Orthodox ceremony, representing the Greek Orthodox community, who symbolically support the pair as they take their first steps as a married couple.

Just like the Catholic ceremony, the Orthodox ceremony is considered a sacrament, meaning God is in attendance, giving the couple his strength and love. But that's where the similarities end. Vows are *not* exchanged at an Orthodox wedding, because marriage is not considered to be a contractual agreement between two people. Marriage is the *union* of two people in love that is witnessed and blessed by God.

Organs may be the only instruments allowed to be played *during* the ceremony. Some clergy, with the bishop's approval, may be flexible and allow other instruments to be played only for the processional or recessional. Be sure to confer with your clergy.

Like the Orthodox and Conservative Jewish ceremonies, the Orthodox Christian service contains a separate betrothal ceremony. Before the wedding begins, either outside the church doors or in the vestibule, the priest meets the couple to ask their intentions. At this time, gold rings held by the best man are blessed by the priest, and exchanged by the best man on the hands of the couple three times. Then the groom places the ring on the fourth finger of the *right* hand of the bride, and she places one on the fourth finger of his right hand.

The marriage ceremony begins when the priest, who holds an icon, leads the procession to the altar followed by the couple and their attendants.

At the altar, a white carpet or cloth is placed for the bride and groom to stand on and they are given lighted candles to hold throughout the service. Then the *crowning* or marriage ceremony begins. Two crowns, made either of flowers or metal joined by a ribbon, are placed on the heads of the bride and groom, symbolizing that they are now king and queen of their realm. Then the service continues with readings of scripture and the drinking of wine. After this, the priest leads the bride and groom around the altar three times, followed by the best man who holds the ribbon that joins the crowns, signifying that the bride and groom are not alone as they take their first steps as a married couple — the community walks with them.

In the Orthodox service, walking around the altar three times signifies the eternity of marriage — having no beginning or end — and the holy trinity — Father, Son and Holy Ghost. The priest then speaks to the bride and groom about the responsibilities of marriage. The ceremony ends and the recessional begins.

THE JEWISH WEDDING

Within Judaism fall three different points of view expressed by the Orthodox, Conservative and Reform movements. They are alike, but there are differences between the communities in their interpretation of Talmudic law. It can be correlated to the difference between being a Methodist, Presbyterian or Baptist within the Protestant faith, or a Russian, Greek Orthodox or Roman Catholic within the Catholic faith.

For that reason, I'm going to address Jewish weddings in general terms, noting particular differences, while also recognizing that there are differences of interpretation within each community.

In General

For all Jews a wedding is a *mitzvah* — a commandment — and the wedding service is sacred and sanctified. Jewish lore says that when Adam and Eve were married in the Garden of Eden, God braided Eve's hair, and stood as Adam's witness. He even created 10 chuppot (marriage canopies) for the couple's wedding. When the ceremony ended, the angels in their happiness shouted ``Mazel tov'' (good luck).*

In the days of the Talmud, Jewish law said that a couple had to perform three basic acts before they were legally married. One was the giving by the groom and the acceptance by the bride of a gift of value (usually a ring), as he recited the legal formula of acquisition and consecration, "Be thou consecrated to me with this ring in accordance with the laws of Moses and Israel." The ketubah (marriage contract) had to be signed and given to the woman. These acts had to be witnessed by at least two people, except for the final act — sexual intercourse.

The customs that have become so much a part of Jewish weddings — the chuppa, for example, or the breaking of the glass at the end of the ceremony — are just traditions. In the Reform ceremony, a ketubah is not required, although I've never attended a Reform ceremony that didn't have one. At this ceremony, however, the rabbi may give the couple a Certificate of Marriage that he signs and two people witness.

In Judaism, marriage customs passed from generation to generation have become an integral part of their ceremonies. As Rabbi Ezring from Temple B'Nai Torah in Boca Raton, Florida states, "Customs which become so dear to the Jewish people have the force of law."

Weddings, the Jewish Calendar and Mourning

Weddings are forbidden on the Sabbath and during certain major holidays and festivals. These include Rosh Hashanah, Yom Kippur, Sukkot, Passover and Shavuot. There are other restricted times if you are Conservative or Orthodox and even if you are Reform, be sure to confer with your rabbi before setting your wedding date.

If a member of your immediate families dies after the *wedding date is set,* the wedding will most often take place although not with the usual fanfare. The best thing to do is confer with your rabbi.

The Traditional Ketubah

The traditional ketubah is a marriage contract that is binding for Orthodox and Conservative Jews. Centuries ago, ketubot were written in Aramaic, the legal language of the Judean state and focused on the groom and his responsibilities to his wife — that he acquired her in the appropriate manner and that he would support her. It was witnessed and given to the bride as her possession. It is still read today during the Orthodox and Conservative wedding ceremonies.

This had to be the first Emancipation Proclamation for women. In the first century, it gave women rights and legal status within a marriage. It focused on material belongings shared between husband and wife and gave the wife her fair share. This made divorce a costly proceeding for the husband, who in those days could cast off a wife at will. Over time, the ketubah was seen as the document that cut the divorce rate and strengthened the Jewish family.* In the Orthodox and Conservative ceremonies, the traditional ketubah is still read and given to the bride. The modern ketubah used by Reform rabbis is an

* Footnotes, see pages 356.

A ketubah by artist Claire Mendelson.

updated version that reflects the changing needs of today's society.

The Wording of the Traditional Ketubah

In the traditional ketubah, divorce and its implications are clearly spelled out. For a divorce to be granted if you are Orthodox or Conservative, a *get* (a religious sanction for divorce) must be given from the husband to the wife. If a husband wanted to deny his wife a get, she would not be able to remarry within Judaism. Orthodox and Conservative rabbis will not perform second marriages without a get, and Orthodox and Conservative Jewish women are bound by the ketubah.

121

A festive ketubah by Claire Mendelson.

A Conservative Approach

Conservative Judaism follows many of the same tenets as the Orthodox when it comes to marriage and divorce. However, Conservative Judaism is more tolerant of a woman's rights within the faith, and does offer solutions to the problem.

An Essential Premarital Agreement for All Conservative Jewish Couples - And an Essential Addendum to the Ketubah

Many Conservative rabbis ask that a premarital agreement between husband and wife be signed at the time of their marriage, in which they agree to a Jewish divorce if a civil divorce occurs. This protects the rights of the woman, who is no longer at the mercy of her husband to grant her a divorce.

For this reason, also, the following addendum has been added to the traditional ketubah in case the marriage ends in civil divorce: "husband and wife will invoke the authority of the "Beth Din" (Canonical Court) of the Rabbinical Assembly and the Jewish Theological Seminary or its duly authorized representatives, to decide what action by either spouse is then appropriate under Jewish matrimonial law; and if either spouse shall fail to honor the demand of the other or to carry out the decision of the "Beth Din" or its representatives, then the other spouse may invoke any and all remedies available in civil law and equity to enforce compliance with the "Beth Din's" decision and this solemn obligation." *

If you are a Conservative Jewish woman, I think it in your best interest that you and your fiancé sign a ketubah that contains the above addendum. It should be noted that many Conservative rabbis will not accept it, but there is a ketubah containing a clause called the Liebermann Condition that in effect says the same thing. It might also be in your best interest to sign a premarital divorce agreement like the one below, that may be issued by your rabbi.

An Example of a Premarital Divorce Agreement for Conservative Couples

"In the event that the covenant of marriage entered into this _____ day of _____ 19_____, by (husband)_____ and (wife)_____ shall be terminated or if they shall not have dwelled together for six

A Jewish wedding under the chuppa.

consecutive months, the (husband)_____ and (wife) _____shall voluntarily and promptly upon demand by either of the parties present themselves at a mutually convenient time and place to terminate the marriage and release each other from the covenant of marriage in accordance with Jewish law and custom."

"This agreement is recognized as a material inducement to this marriage by the parties hereto. Failure of either of the parties to voluntarily perform his or her obligations hereunder if requested to do so by the other party shall render him or her liable for all costs, including attorneys' fees, reasonably incurred by the requesting party to secure his or her performance."

"Entered into this _____ day of _____ 19 _____." *

This document is signed by the bride and groom and two witnesses.

The Ketubah and Reform Judaism

The ketubah means little to Reform Jews, who

* Footnotes, see page 356.

A formal Jewish wedding under a remarkable chuppa..

recognize the legality and finality of the state's dissolution of marriage. It does, however, have symbolic meaning, and is usually signed by both parties at the time of their marriage.

The Beauty of the Ketubah

In this chapter, I am featuring some examples of unique, beautiful ketubot by artist Claire Mendelson. If you wish to have an artist design your ketubah, please note that it can take at least three months to complete and can be expensive. For information on how to contact Ms. Claire Mendelson, see the Appendix.

The Marriage Ceremony

While ritual and celebrations before and after the ceremony differ from community to community, there are common factors.

The Bridal Veil

The veil goes back into Biblical history when Laban, Jacob's uncle pulled a nasty trick. Jacob was in love with Rachel, Laban's daughter. But before he could win her hand, Laban required Jacob to work for him for many years. Jacob fulfilled his part of the bargain, but when it came time to marry Rachel, Laban hid his other daughter, Leah, under a heavy bridal veil (today known as the blusher) and married her to Jacob instead.

Today, in Orthodox ceremonies, to ensure that the correct bride is veiled, custom dictates that the groom and witnesses see the bride before the ceremony, and they place the veil over her head. In this way, the groom symbolically knows he is marrying the right woman.

In Reform ceremonies, the veil is merely a part of the bride's attire, although the blusher is still commonly used. During the ceremony it may be raised by her mother, maid of honor, or groom when she drinks the wine. In any event, it is lowered over her face again after she drinks. In most ceremonies, this veil will not be lifted again until the ceremony is over and she is married.

Yarmulkes

In Conservative and Orthodox and in many Reform weddings, yarmulkes (skull caps) are required of all male guests. It is up to the bride and groom to make them available.

Yarmulkes come in many colors and fabrics and can be ordered with the bride and groom's names and date of the wedding. They are offered to male guests as they enter the ceremony and are a nice memento of the occasion. Most temple gift stores carry yarmulkes and can order them for you in the color and fabric you prefer.

Flowers and Decorations

Unlike churches, temples welcome flowers and decorations. They're symbolic of the first wedding in the Garden of Eden.

If you are having your wedding in a hotel or club, be sure to ask about restrictions on ceremony or reception flowers and decorations. Some restrict the use of candles in centerpieces, for example. Also be sure there is enough set-up time before your ceremony for decorations and flowers and enough rip-down time once it's over. Elaborate Jewish weddings take time to create.

Who Escorts the Bride and Groom?

In the Jewish ceremony, both parents give a child in marriage, ergo, both parents walk the bride and groom up the aisle. If one of the parents is deceased, the other may walk alone with the bride or groom. There really are no set rules to follow.

The Processional

There are no rules about how the processional should be conducted but there is custom to consider. The cantor may be the first up the aisle or the rabbi. Then the groom's grandparents, and the bride's grandparents with the ushers following, or in Conservative and Reform Judaism, an usher with a bridesmaid. The last to appear is the best man, before the groom is escorted with his parents up the aisle (mother on the right, father on the left).

After the groom is escorted up the aisle, the bridesmaids may walk up the aisle, or a bridesmaid with an usher if the wedding is Reform or Conservative. If a flower girl or ringbearer is a part of the ceremony, they immediately precede the bride, who is then escorted up the aisle by both her parents, once again the mother is on the right, the father on the left.

The Processional and Divorced Parents

If the parents of the bride or groom are divorced and friendly, they should walk their children up the aisle. If they're not on good terms, the mother may be escorted up the aisle by a close family member and take her place at the chuppa with her

A Jewish Processional.

husband following. The bride or groom may then walk, unescorted, up the aisle.

The Chuppa

When the rabbi reaches the chuppa he will stand behind a small table facing the assembled guests. A floral arrangement may be placed on the table and candles may also be used. The kiddush (marriage) cup(s) also will be on the table, along with the glass that is wrapped in a linen napkin that will be broken at the end of the ceremony.

The ushers will then walk up the aisle, together or singly, and take their place to the left of the chuppa. If ushers and bridesmaids walk together, the ushers will go to the left, the bridesmaids to the right. The best man then walks up the aisle and takes his place under the chuppa, to the left. All will turn to look down the aisle to wait for the groom with his parents. After they walk up the aisle, the groom's parents will enter the chuppa and stand to the left. The groom will stand directly in front of the rabbi, but face the aisle to watch the procession. The bridesmaids then proceed up the aisle, followed by the maid of honor, who will stand to the right under the chuppa. The flower girl and ringbearer are last and will take their respective places behind the ushers and bridesmaids. If younger children are involved, it's best that seating arrangements be made for them in the first row with their parents.

The bride will then walk up the aisle with her parents. Before they reach the chuppa, the procession will stop so that the parents of the bride may lift their daughter's veil to kiss her — lowering it once again before they enter the chuppa. They will stand to the right. The groom then walks outside the chuppa to escort his bride inside, symbolically escorting her into their new home (one of many, varied meanings of the chuppa). The ceremony then begins.

The chuppa has various symbolic meanings within Judaism, but its history should not be overlooked. In the Middle Ages, Jews married and then went into a wedding tent or *tent of consummation*. The bride left the tent with proof of her virginity. As customs changed, however, the wedding tent was dropped, but the chuppa remains. Symbolically, it is the last remnant of the tent of consummation.

Today, the chuppa has varied interpretations within Judaism — for some it is the symbol of a new home, under which the bride and groom stand to begin their new life together. For others, the four, open sides represent the tent of Abraham that had doors on all sides symbolic of his never-ending hospitality.

There are no laws about how a chuppa should be made or what it should look like. It's basically a fabric canopy supported by four poles. The poles may be held by family or dear friends during the ceremony or the chuppa may be self-supporting. Many synagogues offer their own. Florists also rent and decorate chuppot, or a bride and groom may create their own, that they may pass down to future generations.

The Seven Marriage Blessings

Within the Conservative and Orthodox Jewish wedding ceremony the Seven Marriage Blessings — Sheva B'rachot — are read in their entirety. They may be chanted by the rabbi or by a cantor in Hebrew and translated into English. They may be read by guests or family members. In some Reform ceremonies, they're read in their entirety, at others only some are read. It's up to the bride and groom.

The Seven Marriage Blessings are prayers to God which rejoice in Creation. These blessings culminate in the last two, which specifically address the bride and bridegroom.

The Rings

In all Jewish weddings, the groom places the ring on the bride's finger and says, "Be thou consecrated to me with this ring in accordance with the laws of Moses and Israel." This is the legal formula of acquisition and consecration.

In Orthodox weddings, the ring must be a smooth gold band without stones or adornment (an unending circle of love), and is *only* given by the groom to the bride. In Conservative and Reform ceremonies, the bride is permitted to give the groom a ring.

Wine and the Kiddush Cup

Wine is an integral part of Jewish life. Wine and the wine cup are symbolic of the sweetness of life. In the Conservative and Orthodox ceremonies, two kiddush cups are placed on the table under the chuppa: one for the betrothal and one for the marriage ceremony. In the Reform ceremony, one cup is usually used. Either way, both the bride and groom drink from the same cup. The cup(s) used may be a family heirloom. They may be decorative or plain. They may be new and, just like the chuppa, symbolize the beginning of your new life together. They may be painted or inscribed with your names and wedding date and may become a cherished memento of your wedding. There are no rules.

The End of the Service - A Shattered Glass

At the end of a Jewish wedding, the groom steps on a wine glass and shatters it — a custom that goes back centuries. Many meanings are attached to this custom. Some say that it breaks the solemn tension of the wedding service and marks the beginning of the celebration to follow. Others see its sexual connotation — the breaking of the hymen. Many see it as symbolizing the destruction of the temple in Jerusalem.

But what glass should be broken? Sometimes the betrothal cup is used if two cups are incorporated into the ceremony. If only one cup is used and the bride and groom wish to keep it as a memento, a separate glass may be used, wrapped in a linen napkin. Many clubs and hotels use light bulbs wrapped in a napkin. But I find this neither romantic nor traditional. Besides, who would want to keep a broken light bulb for a keepsake?

Many companies offer wine glasses sewn into decorative, fabric pouches embroidered with the bride and groom's name. When the groom steps on the pouch, the pieces of shattered glass stay within. This is a wonderful memento for any bride to cherish.

The Recessional

The bride and groom are the first to walk down the aisle. They are followed by their parents, the attendants, the rabbi and cantor and the grandparents.

Yichud

Traditionally, after the ceremony the bride and groom spent time alone together in seclusion, which is called "Yichud." In ancient times, the marriage was consummated during Yichud. Today, the Orthodox and Conservative require it — a time for bride and groom to be alone, to share their happiness together (they may even consummate the marriage).

Orthodox and Conservative Jews fast before their weddings. During Yichud, they may break the fast. There are no rules about what may be eaten, although it's traditional that the bride and groom feed one another.

In Conclusion

I have come to love Jewish weddings. They have so much meaning — their traditions and customs are some of the most beautiful I have ever witnessed. They can also be very elaborate with no expense spared. In her book, *The New Jewish Wedding* by Anita Diamant, published by Simon & Schuster (a must read for everyone having a Jewish Wedding), she relates a parable from the seventeenth century that I repeat here:

A group of people who have been to a wedding are on their way home. One says, "It was a beautiful wedding. I liked the food." Another says, "It was a great wedding. The music was marvelous." Still another one says, "It was the best wedding I ever went to. I saw all my good friends there and we had a terrific time." Reb Nachman, who has overheard them, says, "These people weren't really at a wedding."

Then another wedding guest joins this group and says, "Baruch HaShem! (Blessed be the Name!) Thank God those two got together!" At that Reb Nachman says, "Now, *that* person was at a wedding!"*

THE AT-HOME WEDDING

The "at-home" wedding requires intense planning and work and may be infinitely more stressful than weddings held at clubs, restaurants or hotels. If the wedding happens to be a small, informal affair, it should pose no problem, but a large, formal or semi-formal wedding held at

* Footnotes, see page 356.

one's home can be a mind-boggling experience. The responsibility for the entire wedding becomes YOURS, not the catering director's. Sometimes it's just not worth the stress or work that's involved (not to mention the cost).

Research all possibilities before planning a large wedding at home. If you decide to do it, get a wedding coordinator with lots of experience.

THE DOUBLE WEDDING

A double wedding normally occurs when two sisters plan on getting married at the same time, and will save effort and money because the planning and expense can be shared equally. As long as the participants agree with each other and work well together, this type of wedding can be enjoyable. Here are the basic rules to follow:
— The brides should be dressed similarly, depending on the formality of the wedding, with the same length train and veil.
— The men in both parties should be dressed identically.
— Each set of female attendants should have different dresses, but they should reflect the formality of the wedding. For example, if one set is long, the other should be also. Colors, while different, should not clash.
— The brides' bouquets should be different in design and the flowers may be different, but the colors must be compatible. The flowers the attendants carry should be different in type and design, but the colors should complement each other. The men's boutonnieres should be different flowers or colors, but must be compatible.

The Ceremony:
— The grooms enter with clergy and stand on either side of him with their best men behind them. The older bride's groom stands on the left, and the younger bride's groom stands on the right.
— The procession begins with the older bride's attendants, who take their place to the left of the altar. The younger bride's attendants take their place to the right. All turn to look down the aisle for the brides.
— The procession begins with the older bride escorted by her father. When she reaches the altar, she takes her place with her future husband and stands to his right. Her father stands behind them.
— The younger bride then follows to different processional music. She may be escorted by a close relative or her mother, or she may walk alone. When she reaches the altar she stands beside her future husband to his right. Her escort is seated.
— If clergy asks, "Who gives this woman to this man?" The father replies, and then moves behind his younger daughter until the question is asked of him again, and then he sits down.
— The vows are asked of the older bride first and then the younger. All other aspects of the ceremony may then be incorporated into one.
— The recessional begins with the older bride leaving first followed by her bridal party. The music should change when the younger bride begins her recessional.
— If there's a receiving line, the mother of the brides is first, followed by the mothers of the grooms, then the oldest bride with her groom and maid of honor. The younger bride follows with her groom and maid of honor. The fathers and best men should be mingling with guests as they leave the receiving line.

THE MILITARY WEDDING

Many brides choose to have a military wedding if they or their future husband is in the military. The two things that differentiate this wedding from a civilian one, are the dress of the bridal party and the "arch of swords" after the recessional.

Military men wear dress blues for semi-formal weddings held during the day in winter, whites in summer. For that formal, evening wedding, they wear their formal, evening dress uniforms. They are not permitted to wear boutonnieres, and only officers are permitted to wear swords.

The bride should dress accordingly. If the wedding is a formal, evening affair, for example, she should wear a formal wedding gown. The bridesmaids also should dress appropriately. If the bride is in the military, she may wear her dress uniform or a wedding gown. Either is correct. If the bridesmaids are in the military, they may wear either their dress uniforms or bridesmaids attire. This is up to the bride, although everyone should be dressed either in military or civilian garb. Don't mix the two.

Male attendants may be mixed, if the bride and groom have family or friends outside the military that they want to include. Male attendants not in uniform should dress according to the formality of the wedding and should have boutonnieres.

The dramatic ending to this wedding is the arch of swords. The military groomsmen walk up the aisle and weather permitting outside, form two lines, facing each other. They then draw their swords, forming an arch for the bride and groom to walk under as the final act of the recessional. This may be done inside if the weather is bad and your clergy or officiant doesn't object.

If you are being married at a military facility, it's best to speak with the chaplain or the officiant about requirements and specifications. Military standards may be more stringent than those you would encounter at a church, temple, club or hotel.

For example, guests may be asked to provide identification to gain entrance to a military base. This information should be included in your wedding invitation. Also, if being married on a military site, or at a military academy, it's best to start early and give yourself at least a year to plan it. Begin by contacting the chaplain's office.

YOU, YOUR PARENTS OR CLOSE FAMILY MEMBERS AS OFFICIANTS

If your father is going to officiate at your ceremony, you may be walked up the aisle by a close relative, an uncle, a brother, or even your mother. However, you may choose to walk up the aisle by yourself. If you are going to be "given" in marriage, it's your mother who should do so.

A close family member officiating at your ceremony should pose no problem. If they're coming in from out-of-state to officiate, it's best to check with local state authorities to find out what the requirements are. Give yourself plenty of planning time to complete these requirements.

If you are marrying a minister, priest or rabbi, you'll be married in their place of worship with a colleague or superior officiating. The same if you are the minister, priest or rabbi.

If the bride is a minister, priest or rabbi, she should wear wedding dress which coordinates to the formality of the wedding.

The happy couple is greeted by petal throwing well wishers.

A beautiful reception room awaits the entrance of the bride, groom, bridal party, family, and guests.

The Reception

A reception may be lavish and grand or small and simple, but whatever you plan, make it a happy, fun occasion. Don't stress yourself or your family by going over budget — don't put yourself, and them, under undue pressure. The reception is the greatest single expense of a wedding, and because it is, it can be the most stressful. If you and your fiancé are working, help as much as you can. If you're living together, it's best to pay for your own reception, but you may accept contributions in lieu of gifts.

In my old bridal books not much is said about receptions. In those not-so-long-ago days, you needed only three basic things to guarantee their success — your family and friends to wish you well, a wedding cake, and champagne or sparkling wine to toast the future. Receptions have come a long way since then.

Your reception will be your *first* party as husband and wife, and whether you choose to have a formal ball at a grand hotel, or a picnic on a beach, it should reflect your personalities and tastes — but don't go into debt. That's no way to start a marriage. Put aside what you can afford and stick to a budget. A wedding can end up like a hangover — after you've spent thousands of dollars on a four-or five-hour party, you might not feel so good when you wake up the next morning.

Because the average cost of a wedding in the nineties will easily exceed $20,000, I strongly feel that apart from tradition, both families should share the cost. I can't stress this enough. A man and a woman are getting married, therefore, the wedding becomes the responsibility of *both* families. The groom should emphasize this to his parents.

Once you know how much money you and your families can contribute, you can realistically begin to plan your reception.

RECEPTIONS - GENERAL INFORMATION

Accessibility - from Ceremony to Reception

Look for a reception location that is close to your ceremony site. It should take guests no longer than 30 minutes to get to your reception from the ceremony. This will be greatly appreciated by your out-of-town guests, who should not have to drive long, unfamiliar distances to attend your reception.

The Receiving Line - To Have or Have Not?

If you want a receiving line have it directly after the ceremony — not at the reception. If you have

100 guests and calculated it would take each one 30 seconds to get through the line, it would take almost an hour. An hour is too much time to waste at a four-or five-hour reception.

The receiving line was initiated so the bride and groom could thank each person attending. If you don't have a receiving line after your ceremony, visit each guest table at the reception to offer your thanks. For a fun alternative, see the Entertainment chapter.

Wine and Beer Receptions

Many brides choose to have a wine and beer reception either because it's less expensive, or they don't believe in serving hard liquor. However, at a semi-formal or formal wedding, guests should have the option of choosing their own liquor. Wine and beer receptions, on the other hand, are perfect for informal affairs.

Small Children and Receptions

Unless specifically invited, small children should not attend formal or semi-formal receptions. A reception is a boring function for them. Moreover, due to the length and/or time of day of the reception, children can become tired and cranky. It's not fair to their parents, who should be enjoying themselves.

If there is a ringbearer or flower girl, provisions should be made for a baby-sitter to be at their home or the home of family and friends. If your reception is at a hotel or club, baby sitting may be provided or arranged for a fee.

Seating the Bride, Groom, Bridal Party and Families

Seating options abound for the bride, groom and bridal party. Many couples choose to sit at a small table just for two — the *love dais*. Others like to sit at a long dais with members of their bridal party. Many couples like to sit with their maid of honor and best man and their dates or spouses. I've even been to receptions where the bride and groom sit with their parents and grandparents. The decision is yours to make, but seat your bridal attendants with their spouses or dates so that everyone feels comfortable. If you have a large party and want all members and escorts to sit at a dais, have your caterer construct a double-decker one. One dais (erected on a platform) seats the bride and groom, maid of honor, best man and escorts. The one below it seats the rest of the bridal party and escorts.

If your parents are not seated with you, position them close to you. Then seat other members of your families and next the guests. If your parents are divorced, they should have their own tables with families and friends. These should be situated on either side of the bride and groom's table. Divorced parents should not have tables side by side.

Place-Cards and Guest Seating

Place-cards are used to get people seated in an orderly fashion and are *a must* at formal and semi-formal weddings for either a buffet or sit-down dinner. They are usually placed in rows in alphabetical order on a table directly outside the dining room. There is one place-card per couple and one for each single guest.

They should be handwritten by someone with good, clear penmanship, or better yet, by a calligrapher. The place-card should designate a couple's name or the name of a single guest and their table number. For example, Mr. and Mrs. Gordon Smith — Table Four, or Mr. John Frank — Table

The bride and groom sit at a "love dais" surrounded by friends and family.

An elegant reception room for an afternoon buffet.

Six, or Mr. John Frank and Guest — Table Two. (Numerals may be used and it's a nice touch to take the time to find out the name of a single person's guest.)

Place-cards also may be placed directly on guest tables. An alphabetical list of the guests is given to the maître d' who stands at the door. As each guest enters, he advises them of their table number. (In this instance, there is one place-card for each guest). This is called *maître d' seating*. If you have 100 or more guests, this time-consuming process is not advisable.

Another alternative is a placard containing each guest's name and table number written in calligraphy. This is placed on an easel outside the dining room. The guests find their table number on the placard and when they reach their table, find a place-card designating their seat. Again, there is one place-card for each guest. The placard, with all the guests' names listed, makes a cherished memento of the wedding.

TIP: Seat couples together who know each other and, if possible, seat singles together to make them feel more comfortable.

The Wedding Cake - Some Charming Customs

A cake is to a wedding what apple pie is to America. It's traditional. You can't have a wedding without one. Its history can be traced to the Pilgrims, who brought the custom from England. In those days, the wedding cake was basic fruitcake. It wasn't until the 1800s that the white wedding cake became popular in the United States, due to the introduction of finely ground flour, baking powder and baking soda.

In many parts of the United States the tradition of the fruitcake continued but became known as the *groom's cake*. It was placed next to the wedding cake and later cut, boxed and presented to departing guests. Legend has it that any single guest who placed it under their pillow would dream of their intended, and for that reason groom's cake was also called "dreaming bread."

Wedding cakes by "Sweet Tiers", Hobe Sound, Florida.

The splendor of a Sylvia Weinstock cake.

Sylvia does it again!

Grooms' cakes today are not necessarily fruit-cakes. One of my clients had her chocolate groom's cake shaped like a huge football. Another, whose fiance was an avid fisherman, had his carrot cake made into the shape of a huge marlin — covered in blue-green frosting.

Traditionally, the bride first cuts the cake. The groom places his hand protectively over hers,

symbolically protecting her person throughout life. They should then take a piece of cake, inter-twine arms and *jointly* feed one another. This custom derives from the ancient Greeks and Romans who believed that taking cake simultane-ously created a mystic bonding between the cou-ple, guaranteeing a happy union.

Saving the top layer for the first anniversary derives from an old custom — if a cake can last a year, the marriage is bound to be a long one. To save the top layer, seal it in three freezer bags (one over the other), and place it in the freezer. A couple of days before your anniversary, move the triple-bagged cake to the refrigerator to thaw. Chances are, it'll be as good as new.

Shopping for Wedding Cakes

Shopping for wedding cakes can be fun and fattening! Try several bakers *who specialize in wed-ding cakes.* This is important. What makes a cake a culinary delight is the quality of the products that

The groom and friends strut their stuff.

The bride and groom cut the cake.

go into it. A bakery that specializes in wedding cakes will tend to use finer ingredients than a supermarket or commercial bakery, and you may find there's not much difference in the price.

Betty Baird, owner of Sweet Tiers in Hobe Sound, Florida, and baker of Burt Reynolds' and Loni Anderson's wedding cake says, *"The cake is the focal point of the reception.* It shouldn't be so large as to overpower a small room or so small that it isn't noticed."

Betty is a specialist in *fondant* cakes — those that look like they're covered with smooth glass instead of icing. A layer of butter-cream frosting or jam is put over the cake and then fondant (a smooth, sweet confection) is rolled out and molded over the cake. The cake is then decorated with handmade flowers or lace made of either butter-cream frosting, sugar or fondant. These cakes are elegant and expensive.

Not everyone, however, likes or can afford fondant cakes. The important thing is to get a good-looking, tasty cake. Betty suggests elegant butter-cream cakes that look sensational and taste great but aren't as expensive as fondants. The *look* and *taste* of your wedding cake should be your primary concerns.

If you want a wedding cake from a specialty baker it's best to order six to nine months ahead of the date — or sooner if possible. Shop around, compare cakes and prices and make sure you taste the cakes. A reputable baker will be delighted you asked. Next, look at their pictures to see how you want your cake decorated. Too many clients have told me, "My cake wasn't decorated the way I wanted. I was disappointed."

If you want a dazzling wedding cake from a specialty baker but think it's too expensive, ask the baker to make a smaller cake that can be put

A formal reception room awaits the bride and groom.

on risers to make it look bigger. Then have him make a large sheet cake (the same batter and frosting) to keep in the kitchen. This will be sliced and cut, and along with the wedding cake served to the guests. No one will be the wiser.

Tell the baker the number of guests you'll have and let him be the judge of how big your cake should be. Make sure the baker or one of his assistants will go to your reception to set up your cake — don't leave this task to your caterer. Ask about delivery and set-up fees and get everything in writing.

Time to let your hair down and have fun.

The Cake Top

Love that Lladro? Many brides buy or are given Lladro or other expensive pieces of crystal or porcelain to use as cake tops — but I advise caution. Too often a hurried waiter or guest bumps the cake-table and off falls the cake top (or the cake top is lost or stolen before the affair begins).

Buy a tasteful but inexpensive cake top and leave the beautiful china and crystal in the break-front to be treasured, not cried over.

Another alternative is to have the florist make a "cake crown," a small bouquet of fresh flowers for the top of the cake. It's pretty, can't be broken — and doesn't have much value. I've never seen anyone steal a cake crown.

If you're lucky enough to have Sylvia Weinstock, that incredible baker of custom cakes, bake yours, you won't need a cake top. Those unique, handmade, delicate sugar flowers that adorn her cakes speak for themselves.

Sylvia Speaks

Most caterers regard a wedding cake as an obligatory piece of tradition that has little culinary value. Not Sylvia Weinstock. Sylvia believes that a wedding cake "... is almost as important as the bride...it's an integral part of the celebration...it's the show piece." She says that when people walk into a reception, the cake is the first thing they see and for that reason it becomes the focal point. But to Sylvia, the taste is as important as "the look." A wedding cake must be delicious.

Most caterers advise serving dessert with dinner — but not the cake. They regard the cake as a mere formality to be cut and served long after dinner is over. I can't tell you the number of my clients who have said, "Who cares about the cake?

They always taste awful and no one eats them anyhow." This may be true more times than not, but why spend good, hard-earned money for an inedible cake? I think we have to start thinking like Sylvia.

Sylvia says that the cake *should* be served as dessert — but not with dinner. She suggests serving lighter fare when dinner's over, perhaps strawberries dipped in chocolate or a sorbet. But the pièce de résistance should be the cake. "The cake *is* dessert," says Sylvia, "and it should be so good that it sings to you when you put it in your mouth." I agree.

Here's some tips from Sylvia on how to choose your wedding cake:

— Before you go to a baker do your homework. Know what your centerpieces will look like and their colors. Know the color of the linens. Know the dimensions of the reception room, the height of the ceilings and the color of the room. Does the room have a formal ambiance, informal or somewhere in between? How many guests will be attending? All of these factors will influence the baker's design of your cake.

— Make sure the wedding cake reflects the formality of your wedding and captures its mood.

— The cake should relate to the room it's in. In a room with low ceilings, for example, you would not have a twelve-foot cake.

— The size of the bride and groom should also be taken into consideration. If they're both small, they shouldn't be dwarfed by a huge cake. If they're tall, they shouldn't have to lean over to cut a small cake.

— In terms of design, the cake should fit comfortably in its surroundings and blend with it. Will it be placed in a ballroom with crystal chandeliers, for example, or will it be outside in a garden?

— The cake should not be grandiose if this is your second (or more) marriage. Make the cake simple but elegant.

— Take the time of the reception into consideration. If it's a late evening affair and you're serving cake at two in the morning, make it light — a lemon cake, for example. If the reception is in the early afternoon you may serve heavier fare — a chocolate or carrot cake.

— The cake should reflect the colors of the reception room — not necessarily the bridal party colors. For example, if the table cloths are peach and the centerpieces are composed of peach and lilac flowers then the cake should reflect those colors.

The best man makes a toast. Love, happiness, and health to the bride and groom.

If, however, you were to use purple and hot-pink flowers and hot-pink table cloths, it might be better to go with an all-white cake. A hot-pink and purple cake will be too flamboyant. When in doubt — go white.

— The cake should taste as heavenly as it looks.

Sylvia's cakes are show-stoppers and not just for their look (covered in hand-made sugar flowers, they're dazzling), but their taste. These cakes are made from the finest imported ingredients. There's no Crisco or oil in this butter-cream frosting. It's the real thing — which is one reason Sylvia's cakes are superior.

Not everyone can afford a Sylvia Weinstock cake, but it might not be a bad idea to call her for an estimate before purchasing yours. It may not be as expensive as you think.

Sylvia's cakes are packed and flown all over the world, and they're fresh, never frozen. Once they're retrieved from the airport, they're put together just like any wedding cake. Sylvia says they've never had a problem.

The Toast

The toast, a traditional way to wish the bride and groom well, is a centuries-old tradition that began in France and remains with us today. In the early 1500s, toast was put in the bottom of glasses to absorb impurities in wine. At weddings, newlyweds were expected to drink from a single cup of wine. In deference to their families, the cup was passed to them and each person drank from it. The last person to drain the goblet got to eat the toast, which was an honor, and was applauded. The custom, although much modified, remains with us today.

Ever wonder why people clink their glasses or break them after toasting? The devil made them

do it! The ancients believed that the clinking of wine glasses produced a chiming sound like bells. Bells supposedly repelled Satan, while the breaking of glass drove off evil spirits.

The first toast at the wedding is given by the best man, then by the maid of honor if she chooses, followed by parents and other members of the immediate family. The most beautiful, meaningful, tearful toasts I've heard, however, are when the groom toasts the bride and she him.

Here are some tips for good toasting:

— *It should last no longer than five minutes.*
— *It should never embarrass anyone.*
— *The person giving it should be prepared.*
— *For good luck, toast only with wine or champagne.*

Toasts don't have to be funny or poetic. The best man may stand and say, "Here's to Barbara and Tom, may they always be as happy as they are today." The woman's name always comes first. Everyone then rises and drinks to the bride and groom who remain seated. The bride and groom should be seated or standing close to the best man when he gives the toast — this makes for meaningful pictures. After all the toasts are completed, the best man might read congratulatory telegrams, or a special letter written by a relative who was unable to attend.

Linens and More for Your Receptions

Linen colors should be coordinated to the color of the reception room (see Flowers chapter). Many reception places offer a variety of linens, but if they don't have the color you need or the desired length, you can rent them from a party rental store. Consult your caterer for a reputable store in your area.

At a *formal* wedding, all tablecloths — including those on the cake and place-card tables — should touch the floor. There's nothing worse than exposed table legs.

If you really want to be extravagant you might rent overlays. These are short tablecloths in different designs and colors that are placed over floor-length, solid-colored tablecloths. Your tables may be covered with long, white cloths, for example, topped with shorter, pink lace overlays. As an elegant extra you might rent pink lace napkins.

Party rental stores also can provide chair covers if the chairs in the reception room are old, or upholstered in ugly fabric, or do not match the color of your linens.

Party rental stores will deliver tablecloths, napkins and chair covers, but many won't put them on. Your caterer will have to do it (although some may refuse to do so) and most will charge you for it. Make sure the cost is included in your contract, and that the caterer will store your rentals in a safe place until they are picked up. (Many caterers request that they be picked up immediately after the affair.)

Call your party rental store the day before the wedding. Have it verify your order — the wedding date, time, color and number (of linens, etc.) that are to be delivered. (Get a receipt with all details in writing.)

Entertainment

In my opinion, good entertainment is *the* key that makes parties swing! (See Entertainment chapter.) Before visiting reception possibilities, ask your band or orchestra leader or D.J. how much space they require and if they have special electrical needs.

When you look at a possible reception room,

position the guest tables (in your mind) where you want them. Then mark off the space required by the entertainment. Next, mark off the dance floor — it should be 20 feet by 20 feet for 100 guests. Ask the caterer for a floor plan drawn to scale.

It's critical that you make sure there's enough room for dancing and entertainment when inspecting reception possibilities. (Make sure the room also has adequate outlets and power to accommodate the entertainment.) A cramped room and a too small dance floor can put a crimp in the party.

Flowers and Decorations

The formal or semi-formal reception requires centerpieces on the tables. These may be elaborate arrangements or simple pots of blooms (see Flowers chapter). At a *theme* reception, flowers and decorations should reflect the mood of the party. What's the point of a luau reception if nothing else looks like a luau but the food? Centerpieces might be large shells filled with exotic, *island* flowers — birds of paradise, for example, or a queen protea. How about renting some palm trees to go around the room? Your choices are endless.

Favors and All Those Little Extras

Most times at formal, semi-formal, even informal weddings, brides offer favors to guests. Each couple may receive a favor placed at the woman's plate and at the plate of each single guest. A favor may be elaborate or simple; it's up to the bride's taste and budget.

The most simple and traditional, especially among Italians, is the jordan almond, a confection that symbolizes both the sweetness and bitterness

The beauty of an elegant traditional reception.

The priest offers a blessing.

of married life. These are normally wrapped in net and tied with a ribbon that's imprinted with the bride and groom's name and the wedding date.

Many couples buy splits of champagne that may be fine quality or inexpensive. Others may choose match books inscribed with their names and wedding date. The choice is yours.

You also may have napkins printed with your names and wedding date in any design you wish — love birds, for example. These should be placed on the bar and or passed with the wedding cake. Many couples also have menus printed that are placed at each guest's plate. All of these little extras can be found in the back of invitation catalogues.

RECEPTION TYPES

The Informal Wedding

A reception for an informal wedding may be a picnic in a park, a beach party, a cocktail party at your home or at your club. If your reception is at home, you, your family and friends may decide to do the cooking, or you may have it catered, or you may simply decide to serve champagne and cake. If you want to dance, hire a disc jockey, a band, or play music on a compact disc or tape player. Your choices are limitless. The only rule — *keep it informal.*

If you plan on hosting the reception, consult a bartending book so you'll know how much liquor to buy, and a party cookbook providing you with recipes and advice on how much food you'll need.

If you're having the reception catered be sure to ask friends, relatives, or business associates for references. Hire a caterer who supplies linen, silver, serving dishes, etc. You don't want to bother with those details on your wedding day. And be sure to sample the *cates* — the food the caterer will be serving.

The caterer also may provide the liquor — but you'll pay more. To save, buy your own. Be sure to ask the caterer's advice about what you'll need. Most liquor stores allow you to return unopened bottles. Be sure to keep the receipt.

The Formal and Semi-Formal Wedding At Home

A semi-formal or formal wedding at home, the type you saw in *Father of the Bride,* is no easy task. It requires an expert's assistance. If your family's home is large and beautiful with sumptuous gardens or a memorable view of a lake or ocean, it only makes sense that it should be *the* place to have your reception. Just don't attempt it alone. Can you see yourself on the morning of the wedding in a robe and hair in rollers, directing the guys on where and how they should put up the tent?

After you check their references, hire an experienced wedding consultant who specializes in this type of wedding. Once she's employed, let her do the work, but meet on a regular basis and confer with all vendors she's considering. Go see the florist and samples of his or her work. If you're thinking of a tent, see one set up. Sample in advance all the foods the caterer will be serving. See the linens, china and serving dishes. Go hear the band, etc. If you don't like something or someone the wedding consultant has employed, tell her to find an alternative. Always sign a contract with a wedding consultant specifying her duties in detail. Include all vendors that will be used but negotiate their contracts yourself.

THE CATERED WEDDING

The catered wedding refers to any wedding in which food and liquor is provided by an outside source. In fact, the word *cater* means "To provide ...things desired." Today, most catered weddings take place at country clubs, catering halls, hotels, temples and restaurants. If you decide on a catered reception, be aware that many of these places reserve a year or more in advance.

Many private clubs and country clubs open their doors to non-members for weddings and private parties. Others will allow non-members provided a member of the club will act as a sponsor. If you're thinking of a private club or country club for your wedding, be sure to check on restrictions. Many temples provide facilities but

The first dance.

there may be restrictions. Many of them require a kosher caterer and food. Others may insist on the use of certain bands or florists. Be sure to ask about restrictions when you meet with the person in charge, and follow the guidelines specified in this chapter for the formal or semi-formal wedding.

The First Step - Referrals

Once again, *referral* is the key to finding just the right spot for your reception. Ask recently married friends, business associates or relatives where they had their receptions and if they were happy. Ask what they would change if they had it to do again. This will give you good insight into the problems (if any) they encountered.

Reputation and *word of mouth* are "key" factors in finding a good place for your reception. It takes a catering business years to build a solid reputation. They must be consistent, providing each bride and groom, their families and guests with good food, good service and a pleasing ambiance. The place, whether a country club, restaurant, hotel or catering hall, must be kept in good repair and be exceptionally clean. Scheduling must be flexible — receptions should not be booked one on top of another. Pricing should be competitive.

If you want an honest opinion about a place ask a former bridesmaid — they're a great source of information. Unlike the bride, who gets wrapped up in the euphoria of the occasion, bridesmaids tend to be more realistic. The bride will tell you, for example, "Everything was perfect. It was heavenly. I wouldn't change a thing." The bridesmaid, once the bride leaves the room, will say, "It was all right. But everyone was starving — it took over an hour for them to serve the main course after the salad."

Comparative Shopping a Must

Once you have a list of options, it's time to call to see if they have your date and time available. If so, make an appointment with the person in charge of catering, who's normally titled the catering director or manager. At this meeting discuss the type of reception you would like — whether cocktail hors d'oeuvre, lunch, brunch, buffet or sit-down dinner. Also, have a figure in mind of how many people will be attending. Many brides choose the place first and then make up their guest list — having to cut it if the place is too small.

Next, check the facilities. Go to the room where the cocktail hour will be held. See the room where the dinner will be served. Is there enough room for your guests and the band, orchestra or disc jockey if there's dancing?

If your ceremony will be in the same place as the reception, make sure the room is adequate. Mark off the aisle to ensure it will be wide enough. Make sure there's sufficient room for your guests. If you plan on a harpist or organist, be sure there's enough room for their instruments. If you plan on an arch, chuppa, rental trees or candelabra, be sure the room can handle them. Ask if there will be enough time to decorate before the ceremony and enough time to rip it down if there's another wedding after yours.

Make sure the place is clean. You should not see dirty carpets or walls. See that it's well maintained. You should not see holes or cigarette burns in the carpet, or rips in the upholstered chairs, or peeling paint or wallpaper. Check rest rooms to see if they're dirty or need paint.

Make notes about what you like and don't like about the places you've seen. Jot down any extras the catering director will throw into the *package*. Take your brochures home to study them.

The "Package" Deal

Most catering businesses sell their receptions in *packages* containing everything the bride will need for her reception, from appetizers, to desserts, to liquor. Packages are based on the amount of food served, how it's served and the types of food. Beef, for example, costs more than chicken. Some packages also may include the wedding cake and a champagne toast. There also are packages for buffets, sit-down dinners, cocktail hors d'oeuvre receptions, lunches and brunches. All packages and rates should be detailed in their brochures.

Compare and study your brochures to see what type of reception is best for you and your budget.

The Catering Director and Maître d'

The catering director at a hotel, club or restaurant is the person that helps you plan and structure your reception within your budget. This will take time and effort on both parts, so it's essential you develop a good rapport. When the big day finally comes, the catering director who helped plan it should be there to supervise it, not someone you've never met before.

At this point, it's best to mention the distinction between the catering director and the maître d' or captain, who will be in charge of *serving* the reception. While the catering director or manager structures the affair, it's the captain or maître d' who will oversee it. He's in charge of the reception — start to finish. While the catering director darts in and out to make sure things are progressing well, it's the maître d' or captain who stays throughout to see that everything is as close to perfection as he can make it.

A Word of Advice

The people in charge of catering at hotels, clubs or restaurants are sources of invaluable information because they handle hundreds of weddings. They are experts in their field. But you should recognize that they also are *sales people* whose job it is to sell you their establishment. Most catering directors are paid a salary plus commission — the more they sell to you, the more money they make (and so does the club, hotel or restaurant).

Many brides ask catering directors for recommendations for bands, flowers, even gowns. But be aware that many catering directors are paid "referral fees" by the businesses they refer. If a bride and her family don't bother to survey the market and rely solely on the advice of the catering director, it denies them the opportunity of seeing goods and services that might be better suited to their needs, tastes and budget. Keep yourself open to the suggestions of the catering director but do your own research before making any decisions.

Interviewing Catering Directors

Interview catering directors to determine if they're responsive to your needs. Note whether they appear burned-out, excessively tired or irritable. Also make note of their interest level. Do they appear interested in you and your wedding, no matter how small it may be?

Take notes. This will enable you to keep a record of what each catering director and establishment has to offer, so there won't be any misunderstandings or confusion later.

Make sure the catering director acquiesces to your needs, not his.

Make suggestions — "Could the dance floor be moved to the middle of the room?" — and see if they're receptive to your ideas. The last thing you want to hear is, "Well, we normally don't do

The bride, groom, bridal party and families before the reception.

Let's party!

that…" or "If you insist…" This is your wedding and you have the right to do it your way. You're paying for it.

Ask the catering director for names and phone numbers of the newlyweds at the last five weddings they've catered. Call to ask these "referrals" if they were happy with the catering director and their hotel, club or restaurant. Ask if they had any complaints. Some are easily rectified — "They forgot the champagne glasses for the toast!" Some are not — "They're under new management and just can't seem to get it together."

Call the catering director, leave messages and see if your calls are promptly returned. If not, and you still want to reserve them, ask for another catering director. Or at a small establishment, ask to work with the manager, even the owner. If they want your business, they'll be glad to accommodate you.

Things to Ask

—- If the place is small, ask the catering director how many weddings will take place at the same time as yours. You don't want the band from your wedding competing with the one in the next room. It's also embarrassing to walk into the ladies' room and find three other brides freshening up. If your reception place is large this shouldn't matter.

— If your reception is at a hotel or club with guest rooms and you plan on having family and friends stay there, be sure to ask your catering director for discounted rates. A free room should also be offered for the bride and groom's wedding night. The number of rooms reserved for family and guests, their rate, and the room for the bride and groom should be in your contract.

— If you are considering a sit-down dinner ask the catering director for a *tasting*. The chef will prepare small quantities of *reception* food for the bride and groom (or host and hostess) to sample before the wedding. Anything you don't like should be changed at this time. If you're having a large wedding, you shouldn't pay for a tasting.

— If you're having a large reception make sure the caterer stations attendants in the rest rooms to keep them tidy. Ask for them even if there's an additional charge. This is also advisable if the place has more than one reception or party going on at once using the same rest room facilities.

— Many catering halls offer arches, chuppot, pedestals, mirrors, votive candles and potted trees free of charge. This can save a fortune so be sure to ask about them. Most hotels, clubs and restaurants, however, don't offer these extras. They must be obtained through your florist.

— Ask how many valet parkers will be available. There should be one valet for each 50 guests. If there are less, your guests will be sitting in line in their cars instead of having fun at your reception.

— Ask what size the dance floor is. The dance floor should be 20 x 20 if you have 100 guests and scaled upward or downward proportionately.

— If you are employing a large band or orchestra, or stage entertainers for your reception, or high-tech videographers whose electrical and lighting requirements far outweigh what the hotel, club or restaurant has to offer, have the band leader, entertainment director, or videographer discuss in detail what's needed with the catering director. Have it written into your contracts (entertainment, video and reception), whose responsibility it is to provide the extra equipment and what the charge is.

Negotiations - Be Prepared

Know what each restaurant, hotel or club in your area has to offer, what kind of packages they have (whether for buffet, cocktail-hors d'oeuvre receptions or sit-down dinners) and the price. Most packages are based on the type of food served. A sit-down chicken dinner, for example, will be the least expensive followed by beef and lobster. In the same way, lobster canapes at a cocktail-hors d'oeuvre reception will cost more than chicken fingers, or cocktail hot dogs wrapped in pastry.

If you're having a large, expensive wedding there's no reason to pay for all those little extras — "white glove service" (waiters wear white gloves when serving), cake cutting, an exorbitant fee for valet parking, or a room at the hotel for the bride and groom. With the cost of a wedding reception today, these should be included in the package. Receptions are negotiable. When you meet with the catering director don't forget that you're there to get the best deal you can.

Let me give you examples. One of my clients, a very bright girl, interviewed the catering director at a local hotel where she wanted to have her reception and got an estimated price. She then went to a catering director at another hotel and was quoted a price that was considerably less. She went back to the first catering director, gave her the estimate from the second and said, "If you want my business, beat this." The catering director did, and added a few extras like white glove service.

Recently, two of my clients were discussing their receptions. One was a bride paying for her own reception, the other a prosperous-looking mother of the bride. Both were having their receptions at the same club. What came out in the conversation was that the mother-of-the-bride was paying for white glove service, passed (called "butlered") hors d'oeuvres and cake cutting. The bride was not. She was also paying less for valet parking than the mother of the bride. The irony was they both had the same catering director. The young bride said it best, "I think he felt sorry for us, having to pay for our own wedding, but my fiance did bargain a lot."

How, you ask, could this happen? The reasons are simple:

—— *Numbers.* Catering businesses make more on a larger wedding than a smaller one. The catering director can afford to throw in an ice sculpture, or free butlering of hors d'oeuvres, or free valet parking to the bride having the larger wedding. Although this is not likely to happen at large convention hotels where prices rarely vary.

— *The date.* A June 5th reception (in the middle of wedding season) puts the catering director in the driver's seat. They can pick and choose clients waiting for the June 5th date, so it's doubtful they'll be open to negotiation or throw in many extras.

November 10th, on the other hand, may be difficult to book. The catering director might upgrade the entree, throw in an ice sculpture and cake, free valet parking and butlering of hors d'oeuvres. An *off-season* wedding offers many advantages.

— *Negotiating skills.* Just like the young couple paying for their own wedding (who got the better deal than the prosperous-looking mother of the bride), it's important to be a good negotiator and to have knowledge of what comparable clubs, restaurants and hotels in your area have to offer. No matter what the date or the numbers, you should not pay significantly higher prices, or get less than what you could have at a comparable place elsewhere.

GENERAL INFORMATION

The Evening Reception and Your Budget

Saturday night is the most desirable night for formal and semi-formal receptions, followed by Friday and Sunday nights. If you want an evening affair, don't rule out Friday or Sunday if your restaurant, hotel or club has your Saturday night booked. Another advantage is it's often cheaper. It's more difficult for catering directors to book Friday and Sunday nights and this is usually reflected in the price.

The Cocktail Hour

A cocktail hour always precedes a sit-down lunch, brunch or dinner. This allows guests to go to the reception, mingle with friends and have refreshments while waiting for the bride and groom, who usually have photos taken after the ceremony.

It's essential that guests be offered food and drink the minute they get to the reception (if alcohol is served food must be provided). This is particularly important for those odd-hour weddings in between meals. If the wedding is at noon, for example, guests will have had breakfast but not lunch and won't arrive at the reception before 1 p.m. or later (depending on the length of the ceremony and travel time to the reception). That's a long time without food. Jewish weddings on Saturday night in summer also pose problems. Many times sundown isn't until after 8 p.m. By the time guests get to the reception it's after 9 p.m. — and they're ravenous. At these odd-hour weddings it's important to have heavy hors

d'oeuvres — cheese, crackers and fruit won't do. It's also critical that food be *replenished* during the cocktail hour. Many times caterers will put out *one* salmon, or *one* plate of cheese, or *one* plate of fruit and when it's gone, it's gone. Their clients, on the other hand, should have had it written into their contracts that the hors d'oeuvres be replenished until the end of the cocktail hour.

Have a light cocktail hour for a sit-down lunch or brunch. Serve champagne, punch or Mimosas (a combination of orange juice and champagne) when guests arrive. Simple hors d'oeuvres should also be available. Food and drinks should be replenished until brunch or lunch is served. Write this into your contract.

Be leery of catering businesses that don't offer separate rooms for cocktail hours. This happens in Florida quite often, where many clubs offer cocktails and hors d'oeuvres by the pool, which is fine provided there's no hurricane or the mosquitoes aren't swarming. Their solution to this dilemma is to move the cocktail hour into the room where the dinner will be served (which wasn't large enough to handle the cocktail hour in the first place). Guests having nowhere to put empty glasses and dirty plates will put them on dinner tables. This isn't a pretty sight. Make sure your contract specifically states you are to have a back-up room in case of inclement weather.

Food may be served three ways at the cocktail hour. It may be passed (butlered), or put on a buffet table for guests to help themselves (displayed) or both. For 150 or more guests, it's essential that the food be butlered and displayed, especially if the ceremony is in the same place as the reception. This will help prevent 150 people attacking a buffet table *all* at the same time.

The Structure of the Traditional Reception

The order of the traditional reception is as follows:

— Introduction of the bride and groom, families and bridal party.

— At gentile weddings, the first dance. At Jewish weddings, the Motzi, or blessing over bread.

— At gentile weddings, ethnic dances (if any). At Jewish weddings, the first dance.

— At gentile weddings, the blessing before dinner. At Jewish weddings, the horah.

— The first course (or salad).

— The toast (although it may come at a different time depending on the catering director).

— *Salad.*

— *Main course.*

— *Dessert.*

— *Ceremonial dances — bride with father, etc.*

— *Cake cutting.*

— *Garter and bouquet toss.*

— *More dancing.*

During dinner soft music should be played, not dance music that confuses everyone — "Should I be eating or should I be dancing?" At no time should the music be cut completely. Silence can ruin the party mood.

In between courses dancing should resume. It's up to the captain or maître d' to stay on top of this and to direct the band or D.J. This also means that the communication between the kitchen and the person supervising the affair must be continual and flowing. The salad should not be coming out of the kitchen while the bridal party is being introduced.

The Late-Morning Brunch, Lunch and Early-Afternoon Receptions

Many couples have late-morning or early-afternoon, semi-formal weddings with receptions immediately following. Morning and afternoon affairs are easier to reserve and are usually less expensive. Don't forget Sunday if Saturday is booked.

You may have a sit-down lunch — turkey amandine with scalloped potatoes, for example, or a sit-down brunch including eggs Benedict and potatoes Diane for 50 guests or more. In either case, the guests are served by waiters at the table. Arranged seating is a must.

Precede the sit-down lunch or brunch by a light cocktail hour serving Mimosas or punch, along with light hors d'oeuvres that should be butlered. The optimum situation is to have cold hors d'oeuvres displayed — cheeses, crackers and fruit — and light, hot hors d'oeuvres passed. Always make sure that food is available to your guests if alcohol is being served. And put it in your contract that the hors d'oeuvres be replenished until lunch or brunch begins. Wine, Mimosas or Bloody Marys may be served with lunch or brunch, and afterward you may have an "open bar" provided there's dancing.

If you have 50 to 150 guests you may have a "brunch-buffet" and decide to skip the cocktail hour. According to Michele Richardson, Catering Director at Boca Pointe Country Club in Boca Raton, Florida, "To offer an hors d'oeuvre cocktail hour before a brunch-buffet is redundant. Timing becomes an important factor. A brunch-buffet allows everyone to be fed within an hour or two, because food is made available to the guests when they enter the room. To go from a cocktail hors d'oeuvre hour to a buffet is overkill. It's just not needed." This is a good suggestion provided that pictures are taken *before* the ceremony. If not, you may choose to have a light cocktail hour before the brunch-buffet.

If you decide to skip the cocktail hour, open the cold section of the buffet to your guests. It should feature cheeses, fruits and other light hors d'oeuvres. At the same time you may butler hot ones. Put it in your contract that these are to be replenished.

Later on, the hot buffet (that has been readied) may be stocked with waffles, creamed chicken over biscuits, ham and assorted rolls. A chef might be assigned to cook eggs (any way the guests choose) and wine may be served. There should be at least two buffet lines (or a double-sided buffet) to keep people moving.

Use place-cards because *arranged* seating for all guests is a must. Here's a good rule to follow: any time people use a knife and fork, there must be a place for them to sit and eat.

Wine, Mimosas or Bloody Marys may be served with brunch. Afterward, you may have the bar open for a couple hours if there's dancing.

A wedding lunch or brunch without dancing will usually last as long as the food and drinks do. Sometimes brides will hire a strolling violinist or guitarist to provide music. Be prepared, however, for a short reception if your guests can't dance.

Most late-morning and early-afternoon receptions are over by 4:30 or 5:00 p.m. This gives the catering director a chance to book the room for an evening affair.

The Cocktail-Hors d'Oeuvre Reception for the Semi-formal Wedding

A cocktail-hors d'oeuvre reception may be the answer for those who want a semi-formal affair, but can't afford a buffet or sit-down dinner. This reception should be held around 1 p.m. or slightly later. There is no cocktail hour.

After the ceremony, guests go to the reception where they are fed simple hors d'oeuvres, crudité (vegetable platter), cheeses, wine and champagne (or the bar may be open). After the bride and groom arrive, heavy hors d'oeuvres are passed and displayed for guests to help themselves — these may include meatballs, chicken fingers, shrimp or miniature quiche, spears of fresh fruit and vegetables wrapped in pastry. The hors d'oeuvres are displayed for the remainder of the party (until dessert is served), and the buffet table is kept replenished with a varied selection of finger-food. Make sure this is stated in your contract. The bar remains open for the remainder of the party. You should have a band or D.J. for dancing.

Not everyone is seated at cocktail-hors d'oeuvre receptions. If 100 people are attending, the catering director will probably suggest seating for 60. The food does not require a knife and fork to eat or a place to sit down. By the same token, place-cards are not used. The idea is to keep everyone up mingling and dancing.

It's my suggestion, however, to have tables reserved for the bride, groom, bridal party and families because a wedding day is long and tiring. The catering director also should be aware of the number of elderly people attending who also will require seating.

These types of receptions work well whether you're having 100 or 300 guests. It's important that food be displayed as well as passed if more than 150 people are attending, or your guests will spend your reception in food lines.

There is one drawback to this reception. As Ms. Richardson states, "Anytime you limit seating no matter how great the music or entertainment, or how enthused your guests are, you will find the reception not lasting more than three to three-and-a-half hours. When people can't sit down, they leave. Considering all the traditional wedding rituals — introduction, first dance, toast, cake cutting, and bouquet and garter toss — this doesn't allow much time to mingle, visit and have fun with your guests."

Even with this disadvantage, I feel the cocktail-hors d'oeuvre reception to be a pleasant, fun way to celebrate your wedding no matter what your budget. It might be the kind of reception you'd like to consider.

The Sit-Down Dinner and the Formal and Semi-formal Reception

A sit-down dinner preceded by the cocktail hour is usually the first choice of most brides having a formal wedding and the choice of many having a semi-formal, late-afternoon or evening reception. A sit-down dinner is advisable if there are more than 150 guests (buffets take up too much room and are too time consuming).

Sit-down dinners are priced *inclusively* with everything from the cocktail hour to dessert in the package. The packages offered for the sit-down dinner are not etched in stone and can be upgraded for a price. For example, if you're having the "Sterling Package" at your club featuring chicken Kiev, potato, vegetable and salad, with soup as the first course, you might want to upgrade to a shrimp cocktail appetizer that will cost you more per person. Clubs, restaurants and hotels are usually very flexible in this regard. Write down all additional charges so there are no surprises when it comes to paying the bill.

The length of your reception will depend upon the number of guests. A sit-down dinner for 150 or more people will require a five-hour reception — one hour for cocktails and hors d'oeuvres, four hours for dinner and dancing. A four-hour reception is acceptable for 150 or less, but you won't have much time to party after all wedding events are completed — the first dance, toasts, the horah or tarantella, dancing with your father, etc. Be sure to give yourself enough time to have fun — it's the most important day of your life.

The Buffet - For the Formal or Semi-Formal Wedding

Buffets are appropriate for both semi-formal and formal weddings but their *look* is not as formal. The fact that guests serve themselves detracts from the formality of the occasion. If you want a sophisticated reception it's best to go with a sit-down dinner.

Buffets (like sit down dinners) also come in packages. The difference lies in how the food is served and how it's itemized. Brochures will list all buffet food items available, the number of people they feed and the cost of each item. This makes it easy to choose the food you're going to have from salads to desserts, and to determine the total cost of the reception.

For example, you may have your choice of meats — ham or tenderloin of beef or turkey. Your choice of salads may be tossed, fruit or shrimp — all varying in price. You may have your pick of numerous side dishes from potatoes to rice and a variety of vegetables. You may decide to have a pasta station with a chef creating on-the-spot pasta selections for your guests. The choices are numerous but don't make them alone. A buffet is a tricky thing. Let the catering director help you to make the right selections. For example, they may say, "If you're having a pasta station, don't have too many starchy side dishes, rice or potatoes." Or, "Don't go overboard on the cheese. It doesn't take long for it to get warm and greasy." All of these tricks-of-the-trade are important to know. A good catering director will steer you in the right direction.

Most people don't think that you need place-cards or seating for everyone at a buffet but that's not so. When people enter the reception they should know where they're going to sit. People milling about trying to decide where they want to sit wastes time and makes the reception look unstructured. Besides, your parents might end up seated next to the exit doors.

Buffets are more expensive than sit-downs because of waste, maintenance and help. If a chef serves a sit-down dinner of chicken Kiev, rice pilaf and string beans amandine for 100, he knows exactly how much food goes on a plate and how much to buy. A buffet, however, is a different cup of tea. How much chicken Kiev, rice pilaf and string beans will 100 people eat if they help themselves? He must make more food for a buffet because he can't take a chance that he'll run out. Lisa Coccoli, Catering Director at the Boca Raton Resort and Club in Boca Raton, Florida, describes it simply as "portion control." You have it with a sit-down meal, but not with a buffet.

If the bride decides she wants a pasta or carving station, a cook must be assigned to prepare the pasta and slice the beef. The buffet lines must be maintained. If a chafing dish is half-empty, it must be removed and filled. Servers should stand behind hot dishes and serve the guests. All spilled gravies, peas and olives must be continuously cleaned up. A buffet takes a lot of time, effort and maintenance — and results in wasted food.

When guests arrive, greet them with an open bar or glasses of champagne. Hors d'oeuvres may be butlered while trays of crudité and fresh fruits should be available on buffet tables. Once the bride and groom arrive and are introduced, the rest of the buffet (that has been readied), will be stocked with salads, hot foods and side dishes. (Make sure your contract states that food is replenished until dessert is served.) The guests may then help themselves.

The success of a buffet reception depends on the number of guests and the number of food lines. There should be at least two lines, or a double-sided buffet for 150 guests.

Buffet receptions for 150 guests, with dancing, should last five hours. Less than 100 people, four hours, although you might not have much time to party after the first dance, bouquet and garter toss, and the cake cutting, etc. Give yourself enough time to have fun.

The Station Reception and the Formal and Semi-formal Reception

The station reception is somewhere between the heavy buffet and the cocktail-hors d'oeuvre. It has a terrific advantage over the buffet, however, because there are so many stations that guest lines are kept to a minimum. One station might feature a ham or beef, another pasta, one might contain cheese and fruit while a fourth features side dishes.

The cost is about the same as a buffet. The type of food served requires arranged seating for all guests. You can't expect people to balance plates of linguini and drinks at the same time. Place-cards are a must.

The success of the station reception depends on the number of guests and the number of stations. The more people you have the more stations you'll need. This will ensure lines are kept to a minimum.

A Twist on the Traditional

Many clubs, hotels and restaurants offer *theme* parties for those that want a reception slightly askew of the traditional. Boca Pointe Country Club in Boca Raton, Florida, for example, offers a Luau Party, a Southern Buffet, an Oriental Buffet and Across America — featuring foods from all corners of the USA — New England Clam Chowder, Louisiana Blackened Fish, Prime Rib Eye of Beef and Idaho Baked Potatoes.

Although your guests don't have to look like Scarlet O'Hara or Rhett Butler, or wear muu-muus at such receptions, your decorations as well as the food should reflect the theme you're trying to convey. Don't do one without the other.

It's also important to know your crowd. A "Southern" or "Across America" buffet shouldn't offend anyone's taste buds, but there might be people who don't like Oriental cuisine or the type of foods served at a luau — like little roast pigs with apples in their mouths. Analyze your crowd before deciding on a theme reception.

Also, request a tasting. It's fine to have an Oriental buffet for Oriental guests at a county club. But if the chef is Italian you may experience difficulties. Always have a tasting when you have a theme party or when you serve ethnic food, even if you have to pay for it.

Cakes, the Cost and the Cutting

There are many ways to buy wedding cakes. Many hotels, clubs and restaurants that provide cakes charge by *the person.* Others, however, throw the cake into the package and offer several designs and flavors from which to choose. Look at pictures of their cakes to see how you'd like yours decorated, and always ask to taste the cake (if possible) you'll have at your reception.

Make sure the cost of the cake includes the "cutting". Many places will charge you to slice a cake you've bought elsewhere. This could double the cost. In these instances, it might be better to take their cake. Whatever the policy of the club, hotel or restaurant, I think it's ridiculous to be charged for cake cutting. If you're having an expensive reception, they should be more than glad to include it in the package. Make sure all details are written into your contract.

Dessert Before Cake and the Viennese Dessert Table

Dessert is always served with dinner at a formal or semi-formal affair. Many brides ask if the cake may be served as dessert. As mentioned previously, some catering directors regard the cake as traditional and ceremonial, to be cut and served long after dinner is over, hence the necessity of dessert served with the meal. Dessert is usually included in most packages.

An alternative to dessert is the Viennese Dessert Table, which is an expensive and extensive display of pastries and cakes, served buffet style, with cordials or without. It's expensive because it's a buffet that has to be maintained and replenished, and because of the variety and amount of pastries, pies and cakes. If served with cordials it costs more. Ask if there's a pastry chef on the premises and if not, don't choose a Viennese Dessert Table. The club or restaurant that doesn't have a pastry chef becomes a middle-man, selling you pastries bought elsewhere. Chances are you're going to pay more than if the goods were made on the premises and the quality may be lacking.

Viennese Dessert Tables also take time. They're often moved onto the dance floor because of their size so that guests have easier access. This stops the dance music and the party.

How to Save Money on Food

Save money at the cocktail hour by having hors d'oeuvres butlered instead of displayed. Have a packaged sit-down dinner that includes everything from cocktail hour, to champagne toast, to dessert. For the main course, serve chicken rather than seafood or beef. At a semi-formal, day reception, you may skip the appetizer and start with the salad. Make sure the package includes *all* those "superfluous" charges (see page 165).

THE CATERED WEDDING - LIQUOR

The Cash Bar and Weddings

Many clients ask me about having a "cash bar" (guests pay for their own drinks) at their receptions. No! A reception is no different from any party that you and your family are hosting. When you attend a party at a friend's home do you expect to pay for the drinks? I think you'd be insulted. I know I'd be. If you're considering a cash bar because money is a concern, there are a few alternatives on the next page.

How to Buy Liquor

There are a number of ways to buy liquor for a reception:

— *By the drink.* One system requires the bartender to write down every drink that's served. He keeps a chart beside the bar listing the liquor. He puts a slash mark beside the appropriate liquor each time he serves a drink. The other method involves dividing the bottles into tenths before the reception begins, and counting the number of bottles opened and the number of

tenths served after the party ends.

— *By the bottle.* This system counts all *open* bottles at the end of the reception. You're charged for each open bottle.

— *By the head.* This system charges a flat fee for each person of drinking age.

The trouble with systems one and two is control. How many drinks did the guests really drink? How many bottles were actually opened? Before I got into this business, I encountered this problem at the first wedding I planned, my stepdaughter's.

My husband and I bought the liquor, per drink ($4.50), and the wine to be served at dinner by the bottle ($20.00). We had 90 people attending. When we got the bill for the liquor it was close to $5,000. That meant that each person had approximately eight drinks and one bottle of wine. We had many family members attending that didn't drink, and we also bought a keg of beer for our younger, college-age guests. When I brought this up to the catering director, her answer was, in effect, "It's your word against ours." I protested vehemently, but we signed the contract and we paid the bill.

The best way to buy liquor is by the head. A hotel, club or restaurant will charge you a flat fee for each guest of drinking age, for a four- or five-hour open bar. In this way, you'll know in advance the cost of the liquor. Also, ask what the overtime charge is (per hour, per person), if you go over the four- or five-hour limit. Have this put in your contract.

TIP: If you're paying for liquor "per head" I advise having one bartender for every 50 guests during the cocktail hour (although many places advise one for every 70 guests). After the cocktail hour, I advise one for every 70 guests. Countless brides have told me that they only had one bartender for 100 or more people, and doubted if their guests got more than two drinks all evening. Not only that, the lines were horrendous. If your reception place balks at this idea tell them you'll pay for the extra bartenders. It will be well worth it. *Write this into your contract.*

The Wine or Champagne Toast

Your package might also include wine for dinner and a champagne toast, but if it doesn't, serve wine and champagne at dinner this way. Write this into your contract.

Allow yourself two glasses of wine per guest for dinner and one glass of champagne for a toast. Then make these calculations:

Number of Guests	Glasses per Person	Glasses per Bottle	Number of Bottles Required
100 (wine)	2	5	40
100 (champagne)	1	6	17

You might even add a contingency factor of 10 percent if your guests are a partying bunch, and add on an additional three bottles of wine. You only need, however, one glass of champagne for a toast.

After you've made your calculations, tell the catering director that you give them permission to serve 40 bottles of wine and 17 of champagne — no more. If they run out, make sure they ask your permission before serving additional wine. Write this into your contract and the price of the wine and champagne, per bottle.

Be aware of *corking charges.* Most places allow couples to buy their own wines for their receptions

but may charge exorbitant fees to open them. This is where corking charges come into play. By the time you pay them to open your wine, it might have been more economical to buy theirs. Whatever you decide, make sure it's in your contract.

If you are positive that your guests and family are not heavy drinkers, and think it would be to your advantage to buy liquor based on consumption (a "per drink" or "per bottle" charge), inform the catering director at the time you sign the contract that you'll count all open bottles at the end of the affair. This may keep them honest but *I don't advise buying liquor this way.* For some reason, even teetotalers seem to prefer stronger drinks at weddings.

How to Save Money on Liquor

Premium liquor is considered an upgrade but is it essential? I think you'll find the difference in cost between bar liquor and premium brands is minimal. If you're paying for liquor by consumption (either per bottle or per drink), buy bar liquor. If you're paying by the head, insist on premium brands. It shouldn't be that much more expensive. Check with your catering director.

To save money at the cocktail hour serve champagne and wine, butlered (with strawberries in the glasses). At the reception, close the bar during dinner. Not only will it save money, I think it's a smart move. People shouldn't be going to the bar during dinner, especially if wine is being served or there's champagne on the table for a toast.

If this sounds chintzy, close the bar for the first half hour of the reception (when the bride, groom, families and bridal party are being introduced), and the last half hour when people should not need to consume more alcohol.

RESERVATIONS

In General

A few hundred dollars should reserve a reception place if you book it a year ahead, although many establishments will ask for 10 percent of the estimated cost. If you book them six months before, 50 percent may be required with the balance paid in cash, with a credit card or certified check a few days before the affair, some on the day of the affair. Check this with the catering director. Be sure to put your deposit on your credit card in case the place goes out of business.

The cancellation policy should appear somewhere on the contract. Read it before signing. If possible, write it into the contract that you receive credit for your deposit if the wedding is postponed and you rebook the reception with them. Many contracts also state that the place is entitled to the deposit money (and sometimes more), if you cancel or violate the contract and they can't rebook the date.

The Guarantee

At most clubs, hotels, restaurants and catering halls you must *guarantee* the number of guests (agree to pay for a specified number of people even if they don't show up). The reason is simple. A catering director knows how many occupants a room will hold. If you anticipate 100 people, he's going to show you rooms that accommodate 100. If you like the room and the catering director reserves it for you, he'll ask that you guarantee 100 guests. This is his insurance policy so he doesn't lose money in case 50 people show up.

Lisa Coccoli advises people to decrease the guarantee if they're not sure of the number of guests. She says, "Give a lower number for the guarantee. If more people decide to come than planned, you can always up the number but you can't decrease it." She also says to, "Ask the reception place what percentage over the guarantee they prepare for. Many prepare for five percent over the guarantee. This can give you some leeway."

Tax and Service Charges

Weddings at clubs, restaurants, hotels and catering halls require that you pay tax and service charges. The service charges may be as high as 20 percent plus all applicable taxes. This can be expensive. Look at your contract to see if service charges and taxes are *included.* If not, have your catering director calculate their approximate cost. Put this figure into your contract.

You may tip the person in charge of your reception for doing a superior job — for putting favors on the tables or place-cards, for example, or for making sure your rented linens are safely put away for pick-up. But never let a bartender or piano player put a cup on the bar or piano for tips — that's tacky. Besides, they're being paid enough.

Watch for Those Superfluous Charges

It is not unusual for many places to charge for cake cutting, valet parking, dance floor rental, room rental, bartender fees, chef charges, butlering charge, white glove service or a room for the bride and groom.

If you are having a large wedding (125 or more) and are having a packaged sit-down dinner, heavy buffet, lunch or brunch, these items are negotiable. In fact they should be waived (this may not be the case at large convention hotels).

If a club or hotel as standard procedure offers valet parking to their guests, why should you pay extra for it? If they are a hotel or club with guest rooms — why should you pay for a room for the bride and groom? If you're paying for drinks, why should you pay for a bartender?

Make sure that all these items appear in your contract. You don't want to let yourself in for any surprises when it comes to paying the bill. Be a tough negotiator.

M_____

_____ *Accepts* _____ *Regrets*

Please select one entree for each person attending
____ *Chicken Francaise* ____ *Beef Tenderloin*

Be aware of *choice of entree* charges. If you offer your guests a choice of entree, say chicken or beef, you should only pay for the number of chicken or beef dinners they order. For example, beef tenderloin is going to be more expensive than chicken. If you're having 100 guests, you should not pay for 100 beef dinners if only 25 are served. Yet many places will demand that you pay for 100 beef dinners.

You can easily determine the number of dinners you'll need by putting the *selection* on the respond cards of the invitations — like the sample above (for additional information, see Invitation chapter).

Catering directors usually ask for a final head count a few days before the reception. By this time your responses should be in, and you should know how many chicken or beef dinners to order.

And Finally - Don't Forget the Follow Up

Call the catering director every few weeks to see how things are progressing. The week before the reception call to verify the correct time and date of your affair. Ask them what it is — don't tell them. The proper use of follow up can save you time, aggravation and money. Use it often.

SAVING MONEY - OTHER ALTERNATIVES
The Reception at Civic Sites

Most cities offer civic sites for private parties that may include parks, museums or historic buildings. The city may charge for the rental of the facility that usually includes clean-up charges. A security deposit may be required just in case someone gets out of line and damages the property. Civic sites are usually reasonably priced and most allow you to hire your own caterer and buy your own liquor, definitely a money saver. They may not, however, provide tables, chairs, linens, etc., which you would have to rent through a party rental store or your caterer. It's my advice to let your caterer handle all rentals. You should not be worried about whether your tables and chairs will be delivered to the museum on your wedding day. Most caterers charge a small percentage over the rental fee to supervise these details. It's well worth it.

There are some drawbacks. Many civic sites have beverage restrictions, time limits and don't provide adequate electrical power. For example, they may not allow alcohol on the premises, close at midnight and if you're on the beach, where are you going to plug in the tape player? It's important to review these things with the city employee in charge.

The city, just like any other place you'd consider for your reception, will require you to sign a contract and leave a deposit to reserve the date and the place. Find out about their cancellation policy. Go over the contract, read the fine print and make sure that all details are in writing

Receptions at the Elks or Moose - or How About Women's Clubs?

Many private organizations rent their facilities for parties. Some permit you to hire your own caterer and buy your own liquor, but most supply their own which will be cheaper than liquor supplied by a private club, hotel or restaurant. If you're on a budget, it's smart to investigate them.

The Church Reception

Most churches have "social halls" where simple receptions can be held after the ceremony. These are warm, family affairs — children may be invited and light food and beverages are served (many denominations do not permit alcohol). Guests gather to offer their best to the bride and groom, stay an hour or so, have some light refreshment, and a piece of wedding cake and leave. Many times the women of the church provide the refreshments for a minimal fee. You also may have to pay for the rental of the hall that you, your families and friends can decorate.

In Summary - The Final Word

Have fun.

Celebrate with your families and friends.

Toast your future.

Eat a piece of wedding cake.

Have a Wonderful Life!

The magnificent harbor of Playas Del Colo, Costa Rica.

The Honeymoon

Many, many centuries ago, the Israelites raided neighboring tribes to obtain wives. Once a man captured a bride and fled from her vengeful family, he spent the night, or *moon,* with her in seclusion drinking mead — a liquor made from fermented honey. The mead was called *bride ale,* which later became the word *bridal* — and the night of honey-drinking seclusion became known as the *honeymoon.*

Men may no longer raid neighboring tribes to obtain brides, but the honeymoon tradition remains. Today, 98 percent of newly married couples go on a honeymoon.

The Importance of a Honeymoon

It's my advice to take a few days off for a honeymoon. Believe me, you'll need rest and relaxation, and time to enjoy yourselves after going through the rigors of planning a wedding — not to mention the wedding itself, which is one stressful, tiring day!

Many brides postpone their honeymoons until their work schedules permit vacation time. I feel, however, that *you should postpone the wedding date until you're able to go on a honeymoon.* It's essential for peace of mind. You've both been through a lot, now take a few days to be alone and have fun. Schedule and budget a honeymoon into your plans from the beginning. You'll be glad you did.

The Groom's Responsibility

The groom should plan the honeymoon. The bride will have enough on her hands with the wedding (since the bride does the majority of the work), even if she has help from her mother or future mother-in-law. I hate to say this, but most future grooms don't seem to get too involved. It's always left to the bride, who usually must balance the enormous task of planning the wedding with holding down a full-time job. It's not easy. The groom, therefore, should take the honeymoon by the horns and plan it in conjunction with his fiancée. He should not take her to Alaska in winter if she hates snow, for example, nor should he take her to the Cayman Islands if she doesn't like to swim.

Sunset in Playa Hermosa

Where to go should be a joint decision — one that's made after all possibilities are researched and discussed. After the destination is determined, the groom should handle the details.

Financing the Trip

Start making financial arrangements for your trip early — put a few dollars away from your paychecks every week and budget for it. Don't deny yourselves the romance of a honeymoon.

Maybe you'll even be one of the lucky brides receiving your honeymoon for a wedding gift. Or, you may get engagement gifts, or wedding or shower gifts (checks) from family and friends,

that you may want to put away for your honeymoon — but be realistic. Don't think in terms of spending *all* your money on a honeymoon or running up those credit cards. You'll be paying for it for months after you return, and that's not a happy way to start a marriage.

When to Make Arrangements

Make arrangements for your honeymoon as soon as your wedding date is set, and your ceremony and reception places are reserved. "Seasonal" places, like the Caribbean or skiing resorts in winter, for example, fill up fast. Get your reservations in as soon as possible.

Honeymoons and Travel Agents

Most couples book honeymoons through travel agents. Travel agents, whose commissions are paid by suppliers, make all reservations from air and ground transportation to rooms, and can save you time and aggravation. Tell them when and where you want to go, how much you have to spend, and let them do the work.

It's best to have a travel agent referred to you. Once you have a name, call, and make an appointment to meet them. At the first interview, a travel agent should make an effort to understand your wants, needs and personalities. The agent must also know your budget, which will affect the type of honeymoon he or she can plan for you. It's also essential that the bride and groom meet together with the travel agent.

Joseph Vendi, owner of "Travel Is Fun" in Kendall, Florida, and in business for more than 33 years, says, "Honeymoons are a delicate thing, because a good travel agent must put reality into the honeymoon without eliminating the fantasy. A couple from New York City, for example, might think that a secluded island is romantic, but in fact it's so different from their lifestyles, that they would drive themselves crazy by the end of a week. A good travel agent will recognize this and steer them in the right direction — a beautiful island, yes, but maybe one that's not so secluded." A good travel agent also will try to get you a honeymoon spot in which you feel comfortable. A honeymoon is a unique experience — maybe you've never been intimate before, and having other honeymoon couples around will relax you. On the other hand, you might be living together, and the last thing you need is to be around starry-eyed kids who can't keep their hands off one another. The travel agent should

Volcanic stream, Costa Rica.

make an effort to know your needs. This will help guarantee the success of your honeymoon.

After the initial visit, give the travel agent some time to research "types" of honeymoons for you from cruises, to formal hotels, to informal beach clubs. He should be able to give you plenty of options in all price ranges. Ask for brochures so you can study and compare honeymoon spots.

An agent should follow up with you on a regular basis. Think twice about hiring an agent if it seems you're always the one who makes the call.

Be Prepared

Once you have brochures from a travel agent, go to the library and bookstores and research destinations. This is the best way to ensure that the places you're considering are right for you.

Newlywed Referrals

When you visit a travel agent, ask for *referrals* — newlyweds (and only newlyweds) who recently planned their honeymoons with the travel agent. If possible, the travel agent will provide you with names. Call and ask these couples if they were happy with the travel agent and the service provided. Ask if their honeymoon lived up to their expectations — the way the travel agent envisioned the trip for them.

If these "referrals" were happy with the travel agent and their honeymoon, you should be too. If they expressed complaints, look for another agent.

Trip Referrals

Once you decide on a specific place, have the travel agent give you the names of newlyweds (and only newlyweds), who have recently honeymooned there. I've had many brides return from their honeymoons and say, "Well, it wasn't exactly what we wanted — it was nice — but we'd never go there again!" This is your honeymoon. You're only going to do this once, and you want it to be as perfect as it can be. By talking to people who have been there, you'll get first hand information. For example, "The place was gorgeous, but we were on the 'American Plan' (food included), and was it ever lousy! We each lost 10 pounds!"

Deposits and Trip Cancellation Insurance

Once you've made all the arrangements for your honeymoon, you'll need to leave a deposit, that may be a minimal cost per person, or be as high as 25 percent of the trip's total cost. When you make the arrangements for a trip, be sure to ask about the cancellation policy. Some vendors will return your money if you cancel a month before, others will charge a service fee no matter when you cancel; others will not return the deposit.

If the trip you're contemplating does not have a lenient cancellation policy, it's important to safeguard your money with trip cancellation insurance, available through your travel agent. This will cover you if there's "just cause" for the cancellation — sickness or a death in the family. It will not, however, cover you if you break up. Always *read the fine print* of the cancellation policy before you purchase it.

Credit Cards, Travel and Your Budget

Credit cards are not only plastic money, they are valid proof of identification. Most rental car companies will not rent cars without them, nor will hotels rent lodgings. It's important, however, not to abuse them.

If you're on a budget, it's best to pay for your trip in advance. This includes the airfare, hotels, etc. Put these reservations on a credit card to protect yourself if a vendor should go out of business (do not pay for reservations with a check or cash, which offers no liability protection), and pay them off as soon as you can. By the time your trip rolls around, these expenses should have been paid.

When you travel, take limited cash, and make sure you get traveler's checks. Take a credit card with you that has a "limit" — and have fun spending whatever you can afford. That way, you'll have no regrets later.

Checking Reservations

One month before you leave on your honeymoon, call and confirm all reservations. If you employed a travel agency, they should do it.

Copacabana, Rio De Janeiro, Brazil.

When you receive the tickets and itinerary for your trip, check them thoroughly. Make sure the reservations are made for the right days, the right flights, right destinations and the right hotels.

Documents Necessary for Domestic and International Travel

If you're traveling within the United States, the bride and groom must carry a current driver's license and one other form of identification. I strongly suggest that this be a valid credit card. As mentioned before, it's often impossible to rent cars or lodgings without one. Also, be aware that many rental car companies will not rent cars to people under the age of 25 because of insurance requirements. A passport is required when traveling outside the United States, except in Canada, Mexico and some Caribbean countries —

A lush beach in Hawaii.

although *proof of citizenship* is required. This includes a voter's registration card, or birth certificate and a photo I.D. — a driver's license with your picture on it. Be sure to check your destination's identification requirements with your travel agent. You may even need a visa.

Don't be careless with your passport. It is a valuable document that should be kept on your person at all times — not stored in your luggage. Don't leave it in your hotel room if you're not going to use it. Keep it in the hotel safe. *Always make a photocopy of the inside cover of your passport.* If it's lost or stolen, you'll have all the information you'll need to help the authorities trace it, or to get temporary assistance.

TIP: To avoid unnecessary confusion, have your airline tickets reserved in your maiden name. That way, the name on the tickets will be the same one that's on your passport.

Make a Checklist

Before you leave, make yourselves a personalized checklist like the one following, and check off the items as you pack them. I am going to list a few unforgettable essentials. You add to the list the things you need to take:

— *Tickets, reservations, and itinerary.*
— *Passports or necessary I.D.*
— *Traveler's checks (avoid carrying a lot of cash).*
— *Credit cards.*
— *Medications — (visit your doctor if traveling to a place where dysentery is common to get preventive medicines to take along).*
— *Glasses or hearing aids.*
— *Sporting equipment — skis, tennis racquet, golf clubs, etc.*
— *Sports clothes — bathing suits, scuba suits, golf shoes, etc.*
— *Cameras and film.*
— *Adapters for razors and hair dryers if traveling abroad.*

Before you leave, count the number of suitcases you have, including overnight bags, carry-on luggage *and your handbag.* You should have this same number in the car when you leave, at the airport (if applicable), and at your hotel, etc. when you check in.

Leave a copy of your itinerary with your parents — your flight numbers, where you'll be staying and pertinent phone numbers.

A Memorable Memento

Don't waste money on useless mementos — salt-and-pepper shakers that say "St. Thomas" or that straw hat that has no purpose when you get back to Iowa. The most beautiful mementos you can have are pictures. If you don't know how to take them — learn. Cameras are so easy to use that photos practically take themselves. Take pictures of each other and the places you visit on your trip. You'll treasure them forever.

Your Head's in the Clouds - Keep Your Feet on the Ground

When you're on your honeymoon, be careful. The Caribbean and Mexico, for example, are loaded with "time share" properties and land "deals." Many employees at hotels and resorts sell honeymooners' names to these companies. Before you know it, they're calling you, wining and dining you, and 10 days later, you leave Mexico with a 10-year mortgage and a "time share" in the Yucatan. It's your honeymoon — relax, have fun, but be cautious.

How to Save Money

— The "Package Honeymoon" Deal. These trips are available through travel agents and include everything a bride and groom will need for that perfect honeymoon including air fare, airport transfers to lodgings, room, food and use of recreational facilities at the honeymoon destination. Be sure to investigate these thoroughly before signing a contract. Read the fine print and ask for referrals from newlyweds who have recently been there.

— Travel off-season. The Caribbean, for example, is much cheaper and hotter in the summer than the winter. If heat doesn't bother you and you're on a shoe-string budget, summer might be that ideal time to visit a romantic Caribbean island.

— Cities are expensive. It may be far more economical to stay in lodgings outside London or Paris, for example, and commute on a daily basis. If language is a barrier, however, this is not advisable.

— Stay at rental apartments or condos rather than hotels. They may be cheaper and you can cook your own food. Your travel agent can investigate these for you.

A word of advice concerning this last point. It might be better to stay in a more expensive place and be pampered, than have to cook and clean, which you shouldn't be doing on your honeymoon. There's plenty of time to turn into a wife later. Relax and enjoy yourselves on your honeymoon — you'll be back to the real world before you know it!

A reception in full swing.

Entertainment

For centuries, dancing has been an integral part of wedding celebrations and even today the most important part of any reception is the music. It will make or break the party. If people are dancing and having a good time, they won't want to go home. But bored guests, who tend to exit early, can put a damper on any party. Don't let this happen to you. Find good entertainment — it's the key to a happy, fun reception!

Most music for receptions is provided by bands, orchestras or disc jockeys, although smaller receptions may feature one-man-bands or small combos. A successful reception depends on how well the band or orchestra leader or disc jockey conducts the affair and their interaction with the crowd. That gets people on the dance floor. It's also their job to see that the reception runs according to schedule, so it's essential that you take time to find solid, professional entertainment.

The First Step

Referral is the key to finding good entertainment. Ask recently married friends, relatives and business associates what *type* of entertainment they had. Maybe one person had a great band or a fabulous disc jockey, while another had a one-man-band for a small or informal wedding. It's a matter of taste, budget and your wedding type.

I can't put too much emphasis on the importance of *referral* when it comes to finding good entertainment. Trust your recently married friends, family and business associates. This is one time when you shouldn't let your "fingers do the walking through *The Yellow Pages*."

Catering and Referrals

Referral fees are often paid to businesses or caterers by the bands, orchestras or disc jockeys they refer. If the band charges $3,000, for example, a $300 fee may go to whoever referred them. Although caterers will not refer bad entertainment, many will refer the same groups year after

177

year. This denies you the opportunity of seeing other entertainment that may be just as good and less expensive. Referral fees come out of your pocket, so rely on referrals from people who have nothing to gain from their suggestions.

Entertainment, Budget and Wedding Type

Orchestras and bands are proper for formal weddings. I know many brides who could well have afforded a band or orchestra for their formal weddings, but chose a disc jockey instead. But one D.J. performing with bulky equipment doesn't provide the ambiance or type of music a formal wedding requires. Formal weddings require live music with all the energy and inter-action that only a band or orchestra can provide.

You may have a disc jockey for a semi-formal wedding, but I recommend that you hire a band if you can afford it. If your budget's tight, however, it's better to go with a good D.J. than a bad band.

You don't need entertainment for an informal wedding, but a D.J. or a one-man-band may liven the festivities. The choice is yours.

Morning or Early-Afternoon Weddings

Many brides who have late-morning or early-afternoon receptions think entertainment isn't important. They hire strolling violinists or a gui-tarist and wonder why their guests eat and run. Don't expect people to have hors d'oeuvres with cocktails, or lunch or brunch with drinks, and then sit around with nothing to do but listen to a guitar or violin. It just doesn't work that way. Even if you play music on a compact disc, you'll be glad you did. People love to dance.

TIP: If you decide to have a late-morning or early-afternoon reception and want to dance,

select a reception place with a windowless room. When daylight is streaming through the win-dows, people can't seem to get in the mood. A windowless room simulates the night — and party time!

What About an Orchestra?

Orchestras play big band music from the 40's era of Artie Shaw, Harry James and Glenn Miller. Years ago, brides invariably had big bands at their receptions, which were grand affairs with hundreds of people in attendance. Orchestras were composed of anywhere from 10 to 20 pieces and their sound was big enough to carry any size room.

Orchestras play from sheet music and rely sole-ly on their acoustic instruments. Orchestras do not use electric guitars, for example, or synthesiz-ers. With the advent of rock and roll, the big band sound of orchestras were replaced by four- or five-piece bands that used synthesizers and elec-tric instruments to emulate a bigger sound. People liked rock and roll and, besides, bands were much less expensive than orchestras. Orchestras provide a beautiful, different sound for the 90s. Don't think they're for old people, or you can't dance to them. Get a good orchestra and you can really swing!

Because of their size, orchestras can be expen-sive, particularly if they have a "name". The smallest orchestra is composed of six pieces including a vocalist. If you have ample funds to spend on entertainment check out some orches-tras. You might be pleasantly surprised.

When to Book

Entertainment should be reserved after the wed-ding date is set, and the ceremony and reception

A band plays for a reception on the beach.

places are booked. If you want a certain band, orchestra or disc jockey, don't hesitate to reserve a year or more ahead to avoid disappointment.

Absurd though it may seem, in highly populated areas across the country (New York or Los Angeles, for example), it might be necessary to reserve entertainment up to two years in advance.

When you hire entertainment leave a small deposit, about 20 percent — although some bands and orchestras may demand as high as 50 percent. Think twice if your wedding is more than a year away. You never know what could happen that may cancel or postpone the affair. Bargain with the person in charge to reduce the amount of the deposit. Put the deposit on your credit card so you'll be protected if they go out of business.

Be forewarned that if you change or cancel the date and don't rebook with them, you may be sued for loss of business that is the full amount of the contract.

Beware the Booking Agent

Many times people call bands and orchestras and unknowingly speak to booking agents. Booking agents often put bands and orchestras together with musicians who have never played together before. This is why you'll often hear the criticism, "The band I booked was not the band that showed up at the reception." Michael Rose, President of Michael Rose Orchestras in Boca Raton, Florida, goes one step further, "In the industry we call these 'screamers', because when the bride and groom show up at the reception and find the orchestra isn't the one they thought they were going to get — they start to scream!" "To protect yourself," Mr. Rose adds, "always put the name of the orchestra leader and the vocalists on your contract."

Let's say you hear a fabulous band at a friend's wedding called "Show Boat". You call them to find they're available for your wedding, June 26th. The contract you sign lists the band but *not* band members' names. When you show up at your reception, Show Boat is there all right but the members of the band are not the ones who played at your friend's reception. At that point, there's nothing you can do except pray they'll be good — and SCREAM!

Be sure to get the band members' names and specify them on your contract when booking a group you've heard and liked. That way you'll know that what you saw and heard is what you'll get.

Whether you book a band or orchestra directly or go through an agent, it's important to work with the band or orchestra leader. Make sure you establish a good rapport, and that they get to know your likes and dislikes. Music at your reception should reflect your personality and tastes, and so should the band or orchestra leader's performance. You may like a band leader, for example, who's sophisticated and prefers to keep a low profile. Orchestra leaders more often fall into this category. On the other hand, maybe you're a party person and would prefer a band with a boisterous leader — one who really likes to get the party hopping! Either way, the decision is yours.

The First Call

When you first contact a band, orchestra or disc jockey monitor the "respond time " (the time it takes them to return your call), which should be within 24 hours. If your call is not returned promptly or you must call back, think twice about whether you want to hire them. If they're lax on

The groom dances with an old flame (actually his brother who "dressed" for the occasion).

returning your calls, they might be lax about showing up in time for your wedding.

Ask if your date is available. If so, speak directly with the band or orchestra leader or disc jockey who will perform at your reception.

If considering a band, ask the band leader how long the group has been in business and the *more* important question, "How long have the members played together?" Band members should play together regularly. You want experienced musicians accustomed to practicing and performing together. This isn't as important with an orchestra, but it is critical that the orchestra leader and vocalists regularly perform together.

Ask the band or orchestra leader or disc jockey at what types of functions they perform most? Do they usually play night clubs? Or do they regularly perform at parties and weddings? This is critical. A night club band, orchestra or disc jockey may not know the first thing about a reception, which is a scripted event from the introduction of the bridal party to departure of the bride and groom. They have to know what they're doing because, in conjunction with the catering director, they run the show. Your next question should be, "When can I come to see you?" Make an appointment to see the band or orchestra leader or disc jockey — no one else.

The First Appointment

Good bands and D.J.s play a mix of music. They know that a wedding is composed of people of varying ages from grandparents to friends of the bride and groom. They should know Top 40 tunes as well as old standards such as "It Had to Be You" or "I Left My Heart in San Francisco." They also should play music from the fifties and sixties — popular with people of all ages. The

band or disc jockey also should know classic dance numbers like rumbas and cha-chas.

When you meet, they should inquire about the age ratio of people attending your wedding — how many are over 60, under 30, or somewhere in between? Let the band leader or disc jockey give you advice based on the types of music you would like, and your guests would prefer.

Bruce Raye, President of Raye Stevens Music and Entertainment in Coral Springs, Florida states, "Brides and grooms have to be aware that certain types of music, even if they like it, are not appropriate for weddings. I once had a bride and groom who *only* wanted flamenco played — even for their first dance. I explained that the first dance should have words — be romantic, a song they could relate to — one that would be unforgettable! I also explained that one or two flamenco numbers would be fine, but not for the whole reception." Bruce persuaded the couple to go along with him and were they glad, because only a few people got up to dance when flamenco music was played.

Orchestras, on the other hand, feature music from another era. Michael Rose states, "Many brides and grooms today have never heard the big band sound *live*. When they do, their reaction is 'Wow! This is a great sound. This is what we want at our reception.'"

He also says orchestras create a more elegant ambiance. "When people walk into a formal dining room and see an orchestra and hear this wonderful sound, it creates a whole different atmosphere. It takes them into another era — they're surrounded by softness and beauty."

The Video Audition

At the first visit, the band or orchestra leader

Dancing the Horah.

or disc jockey will show you a video of their performance. Be sure to notice if band members are lip-synching or if it's a "live" performance. Many bands have music recorded in a studio where they sound their best and then lip-synch to the music for the video. Try to see a live video along with a lip-synched one, or a video combining lip-synching with a live performance. It's essential to know how a band sounds at a wedding — not just in a studio.

Are the entertainers in the video smiling? You don't want a miserable band entertaining your guests. Make sure the band is standing and performing together, having fun and interacting with one another. You don't want band members sitting down (aside from the drummer), looking at their watches wondering when they can leave.

The entertainers should be neatly dressed and well-groomed. For formal or semi-formal weddings, they should be in "black tie." Watch the interaction of the band leader or disc jockey with the crowd. Is he too loud, too soft, or just right? Are people dancing and laughing or are guests glued to their seats? How much is the band leader or disc jockey interacting with the crowd? Some people say, "I just want them to introduce the bridal party and play music the rest of the time. I want my guests to dance and have fun, but I don't want the band leader (or D.J.) stealing the show." Other people feel just the opposite. That's why you must find a band leader or D.J. who controls the reception your way. It's strictly a matter of taste.

You shouldn't have these concerns, however, when watching videos of orchestras. They are expected to dress formally and to look and behave in a sophisticated manner. Interaction between the orchestra leader and the instumentalists or vocalists will be subtle. His interaction with the crowd also will be low key but people

An orchestra plays at twilight.

should be dancing. That's a sign that the orchestra leader is doing his job.

Watch the video to make sure that all wedding events in which the band, orchestra or D.J. participate are recapped. Look for the introduction of the bride, groom and bridal party, the blessing over bread (Motzi) or the minister saying grace, the toasts, the bouquet and garter toss and the cake cutting. Are you seeing ethnic aspects — how does the band, orchestra, or disc jockey handle the horah or the tarantella? All of these things should be included in the video.

Make sure the band, orchestra or disc jockey does not stop between songs — people should not be left stranded on the dance floor waiting for the next number. Songs should flow one into the other without undue interruption.

Ask if the band, orchestra or disc jockey is licensed and bonded. Do not consider entertainment that isn't.

Referrals from the Band, Orchestra or D.J.

Ask the band or orchestra leader or D.J. for the names and phone numbers of the brides and grooms who hosted the last five receptions where they performed. Call these newlyweds and ask if they were pleased with their entertainment. If they had a band, ask what the names of the band members were (if they know them), or at least the names of the band leader and the female or male vocalist, the same for an orchestra. Most people hire bands and orchestras because they like a particular vocalist. A red flag should go up if their vocalist is not the one you're getting. Ask if

184

they had complaints, how many breaks the entertainers took, and if they ate, smoked or drank alcohol at the reception. Ask how loud the band or disc jockey was and if guests could hear each other talk over dinner. Inquire if they could make suggestions on how the band, orchestra or disc jockey could improve. Take notes because this should give you insight into what you don't want at your reception.

If the referrals you spoke with had complaints, find someone else to entertain at your reception.

Should You See Them Live?

Samantha and Gary Farr, owners of the band Samantha Farr & Secret Formula in Hollywood, Florida don't let prospective clients drop in at other clients' weddings. As Ms. Farr says, "A band has no right to have auditions at other people's affairs. Our business is 100 percent referral, therefore, people already have heard us or heard of us when they make an appointment. Then they meet us in person and see our video. We feel that's enough." She further adds, "Caterers don't like it either. Prospective clients may come poorly dressed to see a band at someone else's wedding. Not only that, they may show up when we're playing dinner music. It's not fair to the bride and her family."

Bruce Raye, on the other hand, feels just the opposite. "Since many bands lip-sync their videos," he says, "how's the client supposed to know how they perform live? As far as I'm concerned, it's a necessity." He also feels it's essential to determine if the band's equipment is adequate and adds, "You should see the band in a room that's comparable in size to yours to make sure their equipment is powerful enough to carry the room."

Both these arguments have merit. The choice is yours. If you feel it's necessary to see the band live, insist on it, but be forewarned that many catering directors do not permit "auditions" either.

Orchestras for the most part, are difficult to see live. If you were paying big money for a 10-piece orchestra, I'm sure you wouldn't want uninvited guests standing at the back of the room. Many orchestras, however, do play at hotels and nightclubs. When you meet with the orchestra leader be sure to ask.

The Sequence of Events

All receptions are sequenced to follow an order of events from the introduction of the bridal party to the departure of the bride and groom. All of these events, however, should not be scheduled for the first hour. The sequence also differs if you're having a Jewish or gentile wedding. I recommend the following sequence:

GENTILE WEDDING	JEWISH WEDDING
Introduction	Introduction
First Dance	Motzi (blessing over bread)
Ethnic Dances	First Dance
The Blessing, if any	The Horah

(Next)
First Course or Salad
(Dancing in between Courses)
The Toast
Salad
Main Course
Dessert
Ceremonial Dances, Bride with Father, etc.
Cake Cutting
Garter and Bouquet Toss
More Dancing

The toast must be coordinated with the catering director, who may change the sequence of the reception to accommodate the pouring of wine or champagne.

The Size Factor

Samantha and Gary Farr say that if you're having 85 to 150 people, you need a minimum six-piece band for the best sound. In their band, the "core" or pieces that are constant are the guitar, sax, bass (who also plays trumpet), female vocalist, keyboard and drums. If you have more than 150 people, they feel it's best to increase the size of the band to seven or eight pieces.

You may decide after hearing a few bands that five pieces better suits your ears and your pocketbook. Try to increase the band to six pieces if you're having a large number of guests. A large room requires a bigger sound.

The same holds true for an orchestra. The bigger the room, the more pieces required. Let your orchestra leader advise you on how many pieces are required for your reception based on the number of guests and room size.

The Band's Equipment

Technology, particularly in the form of synthesizers, has changed the course of live music. Smaller bands can now obtain a bigger sound. It also allows a bride on a tight budget to achieve a "big" sound with fewer band members, therefore reducing cost.

Synthesizers also enable bands to easily keep up with Top 40 tunes. A computer is programmed with the music and put into a synthesizer enabling the band to follow along. As Samantha Farr states, "It's O.K. to do this for Top 40 hits because they change so much — it would

be impossible for a band to keep up with them otherwise, but you don't want to hire a band that plays everything with a synthesizer."

Inquire about the band's equipment that should be state of the art and powerful enough to accommodate any size room.

Continuous vs. Non-Continuous Music

Ask that *continuous* music be played for your reception. This means that the band or orchestra breaks five minutes out of every hour. When they break, however, a member of the band or orchestra is always left on stage to play, so there's never silence at the reception that destroys the party mood. If you book a band or orchestra to play continuous music, members are not to eat, smoke or drink alcohol during the reception, although you may offer them sandwiches when the affair ends.

Non-continuous music means the band or orchestra will play for 45 minutes and then take a 15-minute break. A musician should be left on stage to play during breaks, or taped music may be played depending on your agreement with the band or orchestra leader. Remember that there should never be silence. It can ruin the party. During 15-minute breaks, members of the band may eat (but not in the reception room) their own food or you may offer them sandwiches, but they should never drink alcohol.

Continuous music played at a reception is more expensive than non-continuous and this should be specified in your contract. If employing a D.J. specify that tapes be played while he's on breaks.

Requests

Many couples will request songs for their weddings, especially for the first dance. If the band

Chamber music precedes an elegant at-home wedding.

leader does not know the selection he should learn it for your reception. Be leery of a band who refuses. Most good bands will try to learn three to four "special" songs for a wedding, but any more than that is asking too much. A disc jockey, on the other hand, should have no problem getting the music you request for your reception.

An orchestra is a different cup of tea since contemporary music is not their forte. Be aware that an orchestra will charge more for requests if they're not familiar with the music.

Bands, orchestras and disc jockeys usually have brochures or sheets listing first-dance selections, while bands and disc jockeys will also have lists of Top 40 numbers. These lists are designed to help couples make their selections so be sure to ask for them. Go over your choices with the band leader or disc jockey. It will give them a feel for the type of music you like.

The Details Sheet

Your band or orchestra leader or disc jockey should ask you to fill out a sheet specifying the details of your wedding. Names of the bride and groom, bridal party, the first dance selection, etc., should be listed. It should also include pertinent personal details — "My parents are divorced and I don't want them introduced after I dance with my husband. Just ask our families to dance and then the maid of honor, best man and other members of the bridal party." If your band or orchestra leader, or D.J. doesn't give you a details sheet, copy our sample and give it to him.

TIP: Do not change your details sheet at the last minute without informing the band or orchestra leader, or disc jockey. This may prove embarrassing at the reception.

How Long Does the Music Last?

Most entertainers play four hours. If they play longer, it's called overtime and you're charged for it. Agree to a price for overtime when you meet with them and put it in your contract. If things get carried away and you want them to stay an extra hour, there won't be any surprises when it comes to paying the bill.

Ceremony Music

Band leaders or disc jockeys will also provide music for your ceremony if you request it. A band leader, for example, will provide a guitarist, keyboard, cellist or harpist. They also have a repertoire of ceremony music from which to choose (so do D.J.s), and will be more than glad to help with the selection. You will, however, pay for the additional musicians and for the disc jockey's extra time.

The Cocktail Hour

Many band leaders and catering directors have mixed feelings about music and the cocktail hour. Some catering directors say that people talk so much that the music is wasted and that one musician simply can't be heard. This is especially true if the cocktail hour is outside. If you're planning on music for your outdoor cocktail hour have at least two musicians.

If you're paying musicians to play for your ceremony, they might as well play for the cocktail hour. There's no sense wasting musicians if they're already there. (Disc jockeys, however, must set up for the reception during the cocktail hour.)

The Reception Supervisor

The person who supervises the reception, usually the captain or maître d', must have good communication with the band or orchestra leader, or D.J. and the kitchen. If the first course is late, for example, the chef will notify the catering director who will notify the entertainment. If a band leader, for example, had planned a five-minute break, he'll skip it and play dance music until the first course is served. At a reception everyone must be flexible.

Your band, orchestra leader, or disc jockey must speak with the catering director before the wedding. They should know how many courses are being served and how the wedding is structured. It's essential that the two communicate well. This takes the stress off the bride, groom and their families who should walk into the reception knowing they're in competent hands.

Introductions

The bride, groom, families and bridal party are always introduced at the beginning of the reception which can waste valuable time. Catering directors have told me it can take 20 minutes to get everyone organized, not to mention the time it takes for the introduction itself.

It might be smarter to introduce the parents of the bride and groom, the best man, maid of honor and the bride and groom, period. If parents are divorced, don't waste time introducing their spouses or escorts. Have the band leader say something like, "And now folks, the parents of the bride, Sue and Bob " (no last names) and the parents of the groom, "Jane and Paul." Introducing three or four sets of parents for one couple can be confusing and time-consuming. If parents refuse to be introduced together skip their introduction.

Going Home Signals

When the wedding cake is cut don't let the band, orchestra or disc jockey go on a break. This will signal the guests the affair is over and they'll begin to leave. After the cake is cut and the bouquet and garter toss, there should be another hour of dancing. By the same token don't let the photographer move up the cake cutting so he can leave early. This is a sure signal to the guests that the party's over. Also, don't let the band, orchestra leader, or D.J. give the centerpieces away until the last fifteen minutes, because this also signals that the party's over. At the end of the affair, have them tell the guests that the person at each table whose birth date is closest to the wedding date gets the centerpiece.

A Receiving Line Alternative

Bruce Raye says that in the last 30 to 40 minutes of the reception, he gets all the guests in a circle on the dance floor. The bride and groom who are in the center, walk around it and thank guests for attending. When they come to the end of the circle, the band playing soft but up-beat music, breaks into a fast dance while everyone is still on the floor. It's a great way to end the party. This also could be done with an orchestra or disc jockey.

Extra Charges

Depending on your state, you may be charged a service tax or the band or orchestra may try to charge you a union tax. Don't pay a union tax — that's the band or orchestra's responsibility. Watch for other superfluous charges like administration fees. Read the fine print before you sign a contract.

Tips for Success

— According to Alyse Sands, vocalist for Ray Stevens Music and Entertainment, the bride should not feel intimidated by the female vocalist. "Watch the video," she says, "If they're dressed provocatively, simply ask that they tone it down." "The female vocalist," she adds, "is not there to compete with the bride — it's important that she keep a low profile."

— If the party's slow and no one's dancing, take the initiative. The bride and groom should visit all the guest tables and say, "Hey, come on! Get on the dance floor!" Your friends and relatives will do what you ask on *your* day. Take the lead and get out there and party if you want your guests to.

— Line dances, group dances and ethnic dances are always good to get the party jumping. Conga lines, for example, get everyone involved and guests don't need a date to participate.

Your Contract with the Band or Orchestra

This contract should include:

— Name of the band and the band members, *particularly the band leader and the vocalists.* For orchestras, the name of the orchestra leader and vocalists.

— Date, time, and place of the affair.

— Hours the band or orchestra is to play and overtime charge.

— Amount of coverage. The ceremony, for example, and cocktail hour and reception.

— Musicians for the ceremony and cocktail hour, how many and cost.

— Price, and how it's to be paid. 20 percent down, for example, balance due on or before the day of the affair.

— The type of music played, continuous or non-continuous, specifying that a band member play during breaks or that tapes be played.

— No eating, drinking or smoking while performing, or during breaks in the reception room.

— Terms of cancellation and terms for refunding deposit, if any.

Your Contract with the Disc Jockey

This contract should include:

— Name of the D.J. performing.

— Date, time and place of the affair.

— Hours the D.J. will perform and overtime charge.

— Amount of coverage, ceremony, for example, and reception.

— The type of music played, continuous or non-continuous, and that tapes will be played during breaks.

— Price, and how it's to be paid.

— No eating, drinking or smoking while performing, or during breaks in the reception room.

— Terms of cancellation and terms for refunding deposit, if any.

Sample Entertainment Sheet

Name of Bride and Groom:_____

Date of Affair: _____

Place:_____

Time of Affair:_____Time we may set up:_____

Type of Affair: Circle one:

Sit-Down Dinner   Buffet   Lunch   Brunch   Cocktail-hors d'oeuvre

Ceremony time: _____Cocktail hour time: _____

Musicians needed for ceremony or reception: Yes_____ No_____

Give details:

_____

_____

_____

Will you have the traditional: (Check one)	Yes	No
Bride to dance with father.	_____	_____
Groom to dance with mother.	_____	_____
Ethnic dances.	_____	_____
Which ones: _____		
Bouquet toss.	_____	_____
Garter toss.	_____	_____
Cake-cutting ceremony.	_____	_____
Centerpiece give away.	_____	_____
Blessing or Motzi.	_____	_____
Toast.	_____	_____

Name of best man or person giving toast: _____

Name of person giving blessing or Motzi:_____

Introduction of Bridal Party

Bride's parents:_____

Groom's parents: _____

Best man: _____ Maid of honor:_____

Bridesmaids: Groomsmen:

1._____   1._____

2._____   2._____

3._____   3._____

4._____   4._____

5._____   5._____

6._____   6._____

Flower girls: _____

Ringbearer: _____

First dance selection (should be with words, a slow song, unforgettable!):

_____

Special requests, limit the number to three (for bands only):

_____

_____

_____

Comments (anything we should be aware of?):

_____

_____

_____

The groom goes wild!

A couple attends a premarital counseling session.

Premarital Counseling

Premarital counseling should be a prerequisite of marriage just like a license. The divorce rate in the United States is over 50 percent for first-time marriages. Close to 50 percent of families headed by women with children live in poverty. A divorce affects a man financially for *one* year — a woman and her children, however, may pay for the rest of their lives. It's up to *you* to stop this trend and take control — and premarital counseling may be just the way to do it. (Also see Part III, Premarital Agreements.)

What's wrong with a little premarital counseling? Maybe you'd like to communicate better than you do? Maybe you fight too much? Maybe one of you has a drug or alcohol problem? Maybe one of you wants children — the other doesn't. The time to face these issues is *now* — not later in divorce court.

If you can spend months to plan a wedding, why not put a little effort into planning your *marriage*. It will be well worth it.

How to Find Premarital Counseling

Many churches offer premarital counseling. The Catholic Church has its Preparation for Marriage — a requirement that may take four to six months to complete. They also offer "encounter weekends," where engaged couples meet to discuss the realities of married life with married couples who talk openly about their experiences. These encounters also emphasize communication between engaged couples.

Other churches and temples offer premarital counseling for engaged couples through their family service organizations. These organizations offer top-notch counseling programs for people of all religious backgrounds. You don't need to be a member of a church or synagogue to get counseling. If you're interested call to find out what's available. Or, you may prefer counseling that isn't religiously affiliated.

"PAIRS" - For Life

One highly successful counseling program available to engaged couples is called PAIRS (Practical Application of Intimate Relationship Skills). PAIRS is internationally recognized as the most comprehensive "how to" program on sustaining intimacy in relationships. You learn innovative communication skills and receive the necessary tools that will equip you to understand your partner's emotions. Men like the PAIRS approach because it's more like taking a college course than attending a counseling session. PAIRS is like a preventive insurance policy helping those who want to avoid the hazards that often come when the "honeymoon" is over. Hara Estroff Morano, Executive Editor of *Psychology Today* magazine calls it "...the most unusual and innovative development in psychology today." For information on how to contact PAIRS, see the Appendix.

Be "Prepared"

In 1977, Dr. David Olson developed a "premarital inventory" for engaged couples called *PREPARE*. It is administered through trained counselors or clergy members and is said to predict — with over 80 percent accuracy — whether a couple will, or will not, have significant marital problems.

The couple begins by answering a 125-item questionnaire measuring their attitudes in 14 different categories such as communication, financial management, sexual relationships and religious orientation. A computer analyzes the results and comes up with the couple's compatible areas called "strengths" and areas of conflict called "growth areas".

A counselor trained to use PREPARE then works with the couple to help them recognize and resolve their areas of conflict. Once a couple recognizes a problem, they can begin to solve it. For more information on how to contact PREPARE, see the Appendix.

For Those Who Don't Have Time

If you don't have time for counseling or you live in an area where it's unavailable, there are a couple of alternatives. *Getting Ready for Marriage*, a book by David Mace (published by Abington) discusses everything that professional counselors do.

The other alternative is a set of video tapes called *Only Love* by Father Mark Connally, narrated by Joe Garagiola. Father Connally is a marriage counselor, whose tapes will give you a realistic look at all facets of marriage through the experiences of married couples. The tapes show you how to deal with everyday problems and how to live together and work as a team. These tapes are for couples of all religions. As Father Connally says, "It's not finding the right partner, it's being the right partner."*

* Footnotes, see page 356.

The bride and groom pose after the ceremony, an example of "environmental portraiture".

Photography and Videography

Wedding photography is unique because the photographer must capture the mood and feeling of two people in love, using only a camera. He also must be able to make his subjects feel at ease and relaxed in front of a camera — which is no easy task.

Years ago, photography was done to record an event. The photographer lined people up and snapped their photos, period. Through the years, wedding photography has grown into a highly specialized field requiring talent, creativity and expertise. A bride today wouldn't consider a photographer who was not an expert.

Wedding photography also requires diversity. For *formal* shots of the bride, groom, bridal parties and families, the photographer must be able to pose his subjects so they appear relaxed and happy — he must make them feel the mood he wants to convey in his photos. He must work well with people and have technical skills, too.

Photos also must be taken *unobtrusively* at a wedding. These are the ones that capture the mood — the bride crying uncontrollably before she walks up the aisle or the groom smearing her face with a piece of cake. This is called *candid* photography. Candid shots of a wedding tell a warm, romantic story — unposed, natural.

Somewhere in between is *casual* photography that includes posed, but relaxed shots of the bride and groom taken before the wedding. They may be shot in the studio or in natural surroundings. Photographers call this *environmental portraiture.* Once again, the photographer must be an expert at getting the couple to relax. He must be able to capture their love and feelings for one another. You should see emotion in his photos. It's the mark of a good photographer.

All three types of photography take talent, creativity and experience. The wedding photographer you choose must be a master at each.

Shopping for a Wedding Photographer

Ask for referrals from recently married friends, relatives or business associates. If they were happy with their photographer ask to see their wedding albums. If you like what you see make an appointment.

It is essential that the photographer be referred to you. Nothing can ruin wedding memories like bad photography. If the pictures are inferior there's nothing you can do — you can't get married again next weekend.

It's very difficult to shop "price" when searching for a photographer because talent, creativity and experience are intangible factors. How do you put

The bride, groom, and bridal party pose after the ceremony.

a price on them? But they're essential for beautiful wedding photos. That's why it's imperative to take the time and make the effort to find a good photographer — one who will work within your budget.

Most photographers sell their wares in "packages". Basically, the more photos the greater the cost of the package. Many times clients choose a photographer by comparing numbers in packages. "He's going to give me ten 8 x 10s, seven 5 x 7s and twenty wallet photos. The other guy's the same price but he's giving me half that." This is *not* the way to choose a wedding photographer.

It's the *quality* of the pictures that count — not the numbers. Says Tim Roberts, President of Roberts Photographics in Boca Raton, Florida, "What's the point of having an album with 20 bad pictures when you could have had an album with 10 beautiful ones? If you're on a budget find a premium photographer and select a small package. Later on, you can add more photos to your album as you can afford it."

The First Visit

When you first meet with a photographer he'll show you wedding albums containing the best examples of his work. The photos in these albums may be a mix of different sizes — 5 x 7s, or 8 x 10s, or 5 x 5s, or 10 x 10s. As the bride and groom, you may select your album pictures from proofs (pictures taken before, after and during your wedding and reception) that may later be enlarged for your album.

Photographers often mix the size of their pictures. They may use enlarged shots for close-ups of the bridal couple, while smaller photos may show crowd shots of people dancing or seated in church before the ceremony. Photographers who use this method equate size with importance. The larger the picture the more important the subject. On the other hand, you may find a photographer who prefers to use photos that are all the *same* size. At this point, it's up to you to decide which you prefer. Make your opinions known to the photographer. It's important to see wedding albums covering the event start to finish — and not two or three good pictures selected from various weddings. If the photographer doesn't show you wedding albums, ask to see them.

The photographer may also show you bridal portraits (blown-up, poster-size pictures of the bride or the bride and groom) that may be included in a premium package.

The Photographer and Control

Wedding photographers must be in control. It's difficult to get people organized for pictures during the frenzy of a wedding. The photographer must be disciplined, fast and able to get the job done in a polite, courteous manner. If the band leader at the reception forgets the first dance the photographer must remind him. If the best man forgets the toast, the photographer must find him

and get it done. At the same time, he must be in the shadows, clicking away. The best photographers are unobtrusive. Chances are you'll know if the photographer is in control when you meet him. He should have command of his work, taking you through the sequence of a wedding with his albums, highlighting the importance of certain pictures and why specific techniques were used. He should explain the types of photos he'll take before, during and after the wedding and reception. He should clearly explain his packages and what they include. He should not hesitate to put anything he says into a contract. When you leave his studio, you should feel confident that he's an expert, and you're comfortable with him.

Photojournalism and Wedding Photography

According to *The New York Times*, Denis Reggie is considered among America's hottest wedding

The bride with her maids and flower girl.

photographers. He is the Kennedys' photographer and has reportedly covered every one of their weddings since 1980.

Mr. Reggie considers himself a photojournalist. He doesn't pose people at weddings nor does he take formal shots. Instead, he takes candid shots as the wedding unfolds and lets his pictures tell the story. Says he, "I want to watch and document rather than pose and fictionalize."* The renowned Marcus Studios in New York also use a photojournalistic approach when snapping the rich and famous. Patty Davis, whose wedding was photographed by Marcus, calls the studio "the best in New York" because they work unobtrusively and

A romantic pose on the beach.

* Footnotes, see page 356.

their pictures "reflect the event."* Most wedding photographers use a combination of candid and posed photography. They "pose" the couple, families and the bridal party before or after the ceremony — when the bride dances with her father, for example, or when the couple cut the cake. They take candid shots at other times — the father of the bride crying when he first sees his daughter in her wedding gown, or the ring-bearer as he throws a tantrum and stomps on the pillow.

You might opt for a photojournalistic approach or you might want a combination of formal posed photography with candid photography. When you interview photographers, however, you'll be able to see what type of photography they prefer by looking at their albums. Is there a pleasant mix of style, or is one type of photography more prevalent than the other? Maybe you found a true photojournalist and there are no posed photos. You should, however, select a photographer who does the type of photography you prefer. Put the emphasis on what you want.

THE PHOTOGRAPHS

Formal Shots

Before the wedding the bride will pose for *formal* shots in her wedding gown or the bridal couple may choose to have a photo session together that will include casual but posed shots. These are normally taken in the photographer's studio, although to make a bride and groom more comfortable or to take advantage of beautiful natural surroundings, they may be taken elsewhere — on a beach or in a park.

Before the Wedding

Shots often are taken of the bride and her attendants, mother and father, and other members of the immediate family as they prepare for the wedding. These should take no longer than 30 minutes to complete and should include a mix of candid as well as posed shots. If the photographer charges extra for these photos, then a bride who's trying to economize may skip them.

Pre-Ceremony Photographs

Before the ceremony, pictures of male members of the bridal party are taken along with those of the immediate family arriving for the ceremony and the arrival of the bride. There should be photos of the processional and ceremony (if permitted) and recessional. The photos should be candid as well as posed.

The bride, groom, and bridal party pose after the ceremony.

Posed Full-length Formals - Before or After the Ceremony

These include posed shots of the bridal couple, their attendants and immediate families at the altar or under the chuppa, taken either before or after the ceremony. There should also be photos of the couple leaving for the reception.

The Cocktail Hour and Reception

Candid photos taken at the cocktail hour and reception must include all key events — the first dance, the toast by the best man, the cake cutting, etc. Guest tables should be included if the bride and groom request them. There may be some posed photos but the majority should be candid.

There should also be shots of the bride and groom leaving the reception that should be a combination of posed and candid photos.

RECOGNIZING GOOD PHOTOGRAPHY

The Formal Shots

Look for *variety* in the posed shots of the bride in the album. There should be head-shots, full-length, three-quarter and shoulder-and-head photos. Pictures should highlight the bride's gown including the front, back and train. If you can't see the detail of the bride's dress, chances are the pictures were shot with improper lighting, bad film or equipment, or by an unskilled photographer.

The bride should be posed both sitting and standing. You should see her at all angles. You shouldn't notice prominent features if she has them. Her makeup should be natural. If you notice extreme makeup, be leery. Photographers always take test shots before a photo session. If the makeup was over done, he should have told the bride or the makeup artist to tone it down. Look at the background. Is the bride photographed against a dark color that emphasizes the color and detail of her gown, or is she photographed against white, providing a heavenly almost mystical look? Either is correct. Watch for cluttered pictures filled with floral arrangements or candelabra, things that detract from the bride and the beauty of her dress. The same holds true if the bride is photographed outdoors. The scene should be simple but memorable — the sunrise or sunset on a beach, the beauty of an old stone monastery. She should not be photographed in a field of bright red poppies, for example. Nothing should upstage the bride and her gown.

A bride should be photographed outdoors in the early morning or late afternoon when the sun has direction — not in the middle of the afternoon when the sun is brightest. If you see photos in which the bride's face looks washed out or her dress looks like a big white blob, you'll know the lighting was improper, the photographer was unskilled, or the photos were shot at the wrong time of day.

When you have your bridal portrait done, ask your photographer to take a few black-and-white photos that later can be given to the newspaper for the wedding announcement.

Casual but Posed Formal Shots

The bride and her fiancé, whether posed in the photographer's studio, their homes or outdoors, should look happy and comfortable in the pictures. Posing is difficult, and men feel especially silly and nervous. A good photographer will get the couple to relax before he takes their pictures. He knows the success of his photos depends on

After the ceremony, a romantic setting makes for a romantic picture.

his ability to capture their happiness, their feelings for one another, their intimacy — on film. According to Tim Roberts, "Most pictures that tell the warmest story — show the most interaction — are those where the couple is *not* looking at the camera. An inexperienced photographer, on the other hand, will say, 'Look at the camera and smile.' Serious, pensive expressions are the most dramatic and the most difficult to pose. Watch for them. They're the mark of a good photographer."

There are different ways to photograph in a studio. Pictures taken against a light background conveying an up-beat, happy feeling are called *high key*. Those taken against a dark background conveying a deep and dramatic mood are called *low key*. Either is correct — it's a matter of taste and preference. Check studio photos to make sure the lighting is good, that the faces don't shine (it's not a bad idea to put some translucent powder on the face of the future groom) and that you can clearly see them. Look at the couple's clothes. The bride and her fiancé should wear the same type of clothes whether formal, informal or somewhere in between. They also should wear clothes in the same color family or the same color. Their attire should be plain to emphasize their faces (not bright checks, stripes or plaids). The pictures should be uncluttered. You should notice the bride and her fiancé first — not the Victorian sofa on which they're sitting.

If the pictures are shot outdoors make sure their faces are illuminated and that you can see detail. Look at the backgrounds which should be memorable but simple.

FEEL THEIR ROMANCE through the photos. You should feel warmed by their intimacy. They should be touching, relaxed and happy. That's the most important part of all.

Before the Wedding and Reception

The next sequence of photos in the album will be those of the bride, attendants and family members preparing for the wedding. These may be taken at the bride's home, at a hotel or at the church or temple.

Pictures may include the bride getting dressed, putting on makeup or her veil in front of a mirror, or with her mother or maid of honor fussing over her. There should also be individual photos of the bride in various poses. There should be pictures of the bride with her mother, her father, her brothers and sisters and grandparents. There should be photos of the bride with her bridal party and if she has one, her favorite cat or dog. There should be candid as well as posed pictures that should take the photographer no longer than 30 minutes to complete.

Are the backgrounds of these posed shots interesting? Maybe taken in front of a fireplace or a family portrait, or in front of a big picture window — or perhaps outside in front of a gazebo or a brook? Are the groupings of attendants and family members interesting? Can you see everyone's face clearly? Does the lighting maximize the details of their clothing? Make sure there are photos of the bride leaving for the ceremony with her parents.

Before the ceremony, the guys pose for a few shots.

Photographers often take portable backdrops to the reception to photograph the bride, groom and bridal parties. This replaces the formal bridal sitting in the studio. As Tim Roberts says, "Why should a bride play make-believe, get dressed in her wedding gown and carry an awful, silk bouquet for a formal portrait in the studio when I can photograph her on her wedding day — with fresh flowers when she looks the most beautiful."

This is an interesting touch, provided you have the time and the room to do so before the reception. This added extra, however, is usually not included in the photographer's package.

Before the Wedding or After?

There's much controversy created by photographers who insist on shooting formal shots before the wedding. They say there's more time to take photos before the ceremony than after. They also say that the bride, groom, bridal party and families are more relaxed and patient and look their best.

Timing, however, may also be a critical factor. If another ceremony is scheduled directly after yours, there might not be time for formal photos. Besides, the bride and groom who have their pictures taken before the ceremony can go directly to the reception and enjoy the party.

This may be a drawback for those who feel it's bad luck for the groom to see the bride before the wedding. Many brides also feel this makes the ceremony anti-climactic. If your photographer suggests taking your formal photos before the wedding, think about the pros and cons. The choice is yours.

The Ceremony Photographs

Be aware that many churches and temples prohibit photography during the ceremony. Some prohibit the flash, making the photographer's job that much harder because he must use *available* light.

The first photos taken at the ceremony are of the groom, best man and groomsmen. Most of these shots will be posed — the guys shaking hands or the florist pinning on their boutonnieres. Look at the backgrounds. Are they taken in some dingy little waiting room provided by the temple or church? If they are, the photographer should have known to move the groom and his party to more pleasant surroundings. There should also be candid photos of the groom with his friends and family before the start of the ceremony.

The big event is the arrival of the bride. Here's where you should see raw emotion — a mother

or father in tears, the bridesmaids offering handkerchiefs. Photos should include those taken in the limo before the bride exits, her father helping her from the car, her mom primping her gown. The four-year-old flower girl dancing around in a super-hyper frenzy, while the ringbearer plays "frisbee" with the pillow, are unscheduled moments that make for poignant pictures — watch for them.

When the procession starts, the key photos are of the bride with her father — or in a Jewish ceremony, the bride with both parents. Photos should also include the father kissing the bride when he gives her to the groom or, in a Jewish ceremony, the father and mother kissing the bride.

Mr. and Mrs. after the ceremony. The ride to the reception and a toast to life.

TIP: During the processional, hold your head high, your flowers low — and smile! You want your pictures to be happy and beautiful.

Ceremony pictures should be romantic: the bride and groom looking mistily into each other's eyes as they repeat their vows, their first kiss as "husband and wife," the groom breaking the glass in a Jewish wedding. The camera should record it all.

If you are not permitted to take pictures during the ceremony you may re-enact it afterward. Your

The bride and groom recite their vows.

photographer will take some key photos (the first kiss, the rings, etc.) that should take no longer than 10 minutes to complete. The recessional is next. There should be pictures of the bride and groom walking down the aisle arm in arm followed by the bridal party. The photographer, however, should *never* stop the recessional to photograph. This ruins the spontaneity.

Heart-warming, candid shots can be taken after the recessional is over when the bride, groom, bridal party and immediate families congregate at the back of the room. For a few minutes they let their hair down, hug and kiss, cry, laugh and savor the moment. Watch for these pictures when inspecting an album — capturing these moments is the mark of a good photographer.

At this point there may be a receiving line. The album may include a few photos of the bride, groom and their families greeting their guests.

Full-length "Formals"

Before the ceremony begins — or afterward — the bride, groom, bridal party and immediate families will have *formal* photos taken. Examine these pictures closely when reviewing photographers' albums. These should include photos of:

The Bride — photographed full-length with her entire dress shown. Her face should be photographed at different angles, looking up, looking down at her flowers, toward the camera or tilted to the side. No matter what the photo, the bride's face should be clearly seen.

The Groom — photographed full-length, should have one foot slightly in front of the other with his shoulders angled inward. A good photographer will make sure the groom's hands are properly positioned. He should have one hand in his pants'

pocket and the other on the back of a chair, or he may even fold his arms across his chest. Many times men, not knowing what to do with their hands, will drop them at their sides, which makes for a boring picture.

The Bride and Groom — posed romantically. The couple may be touching or kissing or the groom may face the bride and look at her, while touching her bouquet. He may put his hands on her face and gaze deeply in her eyes. The poses should be interesting, varied and at all times you should see their faces.

Family Shots and the Bridal Party — include photos of the bride and groom with respective families, alone and together and with their bridal party. Watch for "spaghetti line" photography that occurs when the photographer lines everyone up side-by-side. The result is you need a magnifying glass to see the faces. Watch for interesting groupings on stairs, for example, or with some people seated or standing, but with the bride and groom always the focus of attention. All faces should be illuminated so you can see them clearly. And all bodies and limbs should be correctly positioned.

It's extremely important for these pictures to have light backgrounds. According to Tim Roberts, "Dark backgrounds are the sign of a photographer who was too lazy to use a tripod. To ensure proper background light the picture must be shot at a slow shutter speed. The camera must be kept steady — and this requires a tripod."

Pictures Before the Reception

Once the formal pictures are completed, the photographer will take a few shots of the couple entering their car or limo destined for the reception. Make sure these photos are in the album.

Photographers often take the bride and groom to a park or the beach, any memorable place where he can photograph them — capturing their romance, their love for one another in natural surroundings. If this is standard procedure with the photographer he'll mention it to you. These photos should be taken on the way to the reception and should take no longer than 20 minutes to complete.

Cocktail Hour - Reception Photographs

Cocktail hour photos should be minimal — a couple pictures of the bride and groom with their guests, an overall picture of the room and the buffet centerpiece or ice sculpture.

Key reception events must be recorded. These include the introduction of the bride and groom, bridal party and families. The couple's first dance (these should be isolated photos of the couple), and the parents dancing together and dancing separately with the bride and groom — especially the bride dancing with her father. Members of the bridal party also should be photographed dancing. A picture must be taken of the clergy blessing the food or the bread, preferably with the bride and groom in the picture. When toasts are made the bride and groom also should be in the photo. A good photographer might say to the best man as he prepares to make the toast, "Hey, why don't you call the bride and groom up here! Say what you have to say to them." This can make for wonderful photos. Watch for these in an album.

Other *musts* are the cake cutting, the groom removing the bride's garter and the toss, the bouquet toss and the woman who catches the bouquet having the garter placed embarrassingly on her leg by the man who caught the garter. In Jewish weddings, the bride, groom and parents being lifted on chairs and the traditional folk dances must be photographed.

You also should see pictures of the bridal table. If it is a long dais and the shot is formal, the group must be positioned behind it so that all are properly seen — again watch for spaghetti-line photography. Look for interesting groupings. Photos also should be taken of family tables.

If the bride and groom want formal photos of their guest tables, it becomes necessary for the photographer to physically position the guests so that everyone is seen. This may be difficult to accomplish since he must photograph everyone when they're seated.

There also should be lots of action-packed candid shots. Are people dancing, having a good time? Does the photographer capture the happiness of the bride and groom? Are they laughing? Are there pictures of stolen kisses? Do the guests look relaxed and unposed? You should feel happy when looking at these pictures. If you do, you're looking at something very special.

After the Reception Photographs

When the bride and groom leave the reception, you should see plenty of emotion in the photographs. The bride in tears, or beside herself with joy as her parents and friends say good-bye, everyone laughing and crying as she and the groom drive off in their funny, decorated car.

THE TECHNICALITIES
The Photographer, Restrictions and Set Up

It's up to the photographer to speak to the officiant before your ceremony to find out about restrictions and set up times. If you're being married at a club, hotel or restaurant, the catering director will supply the photographer with this information. The photographer, however, should make the effort to talk directly with your officiant, because many have their own idea of "what is" and "what is not" proper during their ceremonies. Many officiants will not allow photography during the ceremony no matter where it's held.

If the bride and groom want formal shots taken before the wedding, it's up to them or the photographer to clear this with the person in charge. They must also get permission to bring a backdrop or extra equipment to the reception, and a place must be set aside in advance where photos can be taken.

These details should be arranged well before the wedding. Unreasonable demands should not be made to the officiant or the catering director on the wedding day.

One Photographer or Two?

Naturally, two photographers can be better than one provided you're having a large wedding. There's less chance of missing any action. But two photographers cost more. For a small wedding one should do.

The Equipment

While the photographer is *the* ingredient that makes for beautiful, successful wedding photography, his equipment is crucial. Some photographers use 35mm cameras, but a medium-format camera (2 1/4 inch) is preferable for wedding photography because of the size of the negatives. They're bigger, sharper and clearer which means better enlargements. 35 mm negatives are so small

they can't be retouched. If anything must be corrected, it must be done on the print.

Many top photographers like Denis Reggie and Monte Zucker use *square format* cameras that produce square pictures. Mr. Reggie finds the square "...the ultimate shape. It's pleasing, it looks balanced, it composes well." He further adds, "...when I look through rectangular-format cameras now, it's as if they're missing half the picture."* When interviewing photographers look at the differences between rectangular photos and square ones. Decide which you prefer.

Ask the photographer if he has a back-up for his equipment, not just the camera. "The photographer's flash broke and he had to go back to the studio to get another..." is a lament I've heard all too often.

A good photographer will try to make you feel comfortable and will make an effort to get to know you and your tastes — he'll work hard for you. If you interview one who says, "I stay four hours, that's it. You decide where you want me to be and when." Politely excuse yourself and leave.

Ask the photographer if *he* is the one who took the pictures in the sample albums and portraits he's shown you. If not, get another photographer.

Is retouching available? Almost all couples will find a picture or two that they want enhanced — a blemish removed from a face or the removal of an exit sign above a door. Bridal portraits almost always are retouched to remove facial lines. Does the photographer have an assistant? He must have someone to help with the equipment, the lighting and to get people assembled. A wedding is too big a task for one person to handle effectively. Ask the photographer if *he* is the one who will be photographing your wedding. I can't tell you how many clients have told me that the

* Footnotes, see page 356.

photographer they booked was not the one who showed up at the wedding.

The Photographer and Special Effects

Did you ever see pictures with a soft, ethereal look and wonder where it came from? It came from a *diffusion* filter used by many photographers to give a different dimension to their photographs. If the photo looks out of focus, however, you'll know that the photographer used too strong a filter. Another filter used in wedding photography is the *starburst.* Look at some ceremony photos. If candles at the altar seem to be emanating light beams, you'll know a starburst filter was used. These filters give pictures a striking, beautiful, surreal appearance.

Other special effects include the *multiple exposure.* An example would include a photo of the bride and groom with a "madonna" floating overhead, who looks like she's part of the picture. Or the happy couple photographed *in* a brandy snifter. These types of photos date an album and are distracting. Special effects have their place, but avoid photographers who overuse them. Photos in an album should be classic and timeless.

Photography and Makeup

All photographers stress the use of good makeup to ensure beautiful photographs. Makeup enhances a face and defines its features — emphasizing the best and down-playing the worst. Faces without makeup, on the other hand, appear washed-out and blah when photographed, especially if the photographer used a flash.

Makeup evens skin-tones and emphasizes the color and features of the eyes, lips and cheeks. It also can trim a prominent nose or hide blemishes and other imperfections. Beautiful makeup is essential for beautiful photography and will reduce the cost of retouching bridal portraits.

You should not wear makeup heavier than normal for photographs. The most important thing is to look like *you.* If you usually don't wear much makeup, wear it minimally on your wedding day. You want friends and family to recognize *you* when you walk up the aisle. Use products with a matte finish to avoid shine. Don't use shimmering makeup (especially eye shadow) that may not reproduce well in photos.

Many brides employ makeup artists for their posed photos at the photographer's studio, while others use them only on their wedding day. If you decide to hire one, you must have a trial run first. Be sure the makeup isn't too heavy. You don't want to look like Cleopatra in your album. If the makeup artist doesn't please you, find another.

DETAILS

The "Group Liaison"

Assign a family friend or relative to the photographer on the day of the wedding. Tim Roberts calls this person the *group liaison,* or one who acts as an intermediary between families, friends and the photographer. It's up to the group liaison to point people out to the photographer and herd them up if necessary, eliminating the photographer's frantic attempts to run after everyone to take their pictures either before or after the ceremony.

Flowers and Photos Before the Wedding

Nothing enhances wedding photography like the beauty of fresh flowers — but they are fragile. I have seen bridesmaids throw their bouquets around like dish rags at the bride's house, only to be wilted and bent out of shape by the time they reach the ceremony.

Photographers often choose outdoor locations for pre-wedding shots but be warned that bouquets, corsages, boutonnieres and a hot summer's day don't mix. By the time you get to the ceremony your flowers may be dead. Whether you have flowers delivered to your home well in advance of the ceremony (which is the choice of most photographers), or delivered directly to the ceremony beforehand, the choice is yours.

Should You Feed the Photographer?

Traditional weddings are long. Seven or more hours may elapse from the pre-wedding shots to the end of the reception. For that reason it's a good idea to provide food for the photographer and his assistants and they'll appreciate it.

Tell the catering director to set up a small table at the back of the reception room and to supply sandwiches for the photographer and his staff. (You are in no way expected to give them the same meal you give your guests.) Be aware that some photographers stipulate in their contracts that food be provided. At no time, however, should the photographer or his assistants drink alcoholic beverages.

PRICE, DEPOSITS, AND CONTRACTS

Photography Packages

Most photographers sell wedding packages. These vary in price depending on the amount of coverage and the number and size of photos provided. Naturally, a small, informal wedding with 50 guests and two people in the bridal party is not going to require the time or effort of a formal wedding with 200 guests and 20 people in the bridal party. This should be reflected in package prices.

Maybe you want a leather album filled with 8 x 10s, 10 x 10s, 3 x 5s and 5 x 7s, albums for your

The bride and groom light the "Unity Candle."

parents, a bridal portrait, portraits for your parents and wallet photos. You may even want "thank-you photos" (a combination "thank-you note" and photo of the bridal couple). The problem is, it usually takes the photographer weeks to get them and you should be sending thank-you notes within three weeks of receiving your gifts.

You also may want a "flush" mounted album (pictures are permanently bonded to the pages of the album and finished with a lacquer spray). Flush mounts are expensive, but if you desire them, the photographer should be able to provide the service for an additional fee. They also may be included in a premium package.

On the other hand, you may be on a limited budget and want a vinyl album. You may want ten 5 x 7 photos, no albums for your parents and some wallet pictures. There also should be a package for you.

Basically, the cost of the package is based on the number of photos, their sizes, the way they're mounted and the composition of the album, whether leather, vinyl or cloth. You might also want a bridal portrait. If it's not included in the package, you'll have to pay an additional fee. These portraits can be displayed at the reception.

Packages also are based on the amount of coverage and the number of photographers. You might want the photographer to bring a backdrop to the reception to stage posed, studio-type pictures of the bride, groom and bridal party before it begins. You might want him to take a trip to a romantic hide-a-way to shoot informal pictures of you and your fiancé before the wedding. You may want two photographers at the reception so that none of the action is missed. The greater the coverage the more the cost.

The First Meeting

Don't be pressured to sign a contract after your first meeting with a photographer. Interview several and see their work before making a decision. Then go home and review what you've seen and heard. Base your choice on the quality of their photography, your comfort level and the package they structure for you. If you don't feel relaxed, find someone else. It's essential that you feel comfortable with your photographer.

The Next Meeting

Once you decide on a photographer, it's time to discuss details. Let him know the types of photos that most interest you and your families. He should know where *you* want the emphasis to be. Plan the photos with the photographer but don't let him dictate to you. He may give you a worksheet like the one following, or discuss the format with you and hand you a detailed computer printout when the meeting is over.

He should tell you how long the formal shots and the environmental portraiture will take. He will also tell you when he'll arrive and when he'll leave. If there's a divorce among parents and remarriage, the photographer should be informed. He'll arrange his schedule to include more time for formal photos, including step-parents, so that no one is left out.

The photographer should discuss all family members and how they'll be grouped for formal pictures before or after the ceremony. This should be discussed in detail. After the ceremony, time is limited. The photographer may have less than one hour to get everyone photographed. It's important that no one be left out. In the frenzy after a wedding, there's the risk that it could happen. At

Before the reception begins, the bride and groom together.

The bride before the ceremony.

one wedding I attended, the grandmother who paid for the affair was included in only one photograph. She was very upset. The bride should have told the photographer in advance of her grandmother's generosity and more pictures should have been taken. Step-parents must be included and the feelings of divorced parents should be respected if they choose not to be photographed together. If the photographer does not give you a "family work-sheet" copy the one in this chapter and give it to him. It will enable him to call people by name, get them assembled in a fast, orderly fashion and take their photos without risk of leaving anyone out. Make sure you assign a *group liaison* (see information in this chapter) to the photographer.

LIST FOR PHOTOGRAPHER:

Wedding of:_____Date:_____

Time:_____Place:_____

These photos are in addition to photographs of the bride and groom, and the photographs of the bride and groom with their bridal parties:

Bride and groom with her parents _____

Bride and groom and her grandparents_____

Bride and groom with her step-parents_____

or: _____

Bride and groom and her step-grandparents_____

or: _____

Bride and groom with her parents:

and her brothers_____

and her sisters_____

and her brothers and sisters_____

and her grandparents _____

and her sisters & husbands_____

and their children _____

and her brothers & wives_____

and their children_____

Bride and groom with his parents _____

Bride and groom with his grandparents_____

Bride and groom with his step-parents _____

or:_____

Bride and groom and his step-grandparents_____

or: _____

Bride and groom with both sets of parents_____

Bride and groom with his parents:

and his brothers _____

and his sisters _____

and his brothers and sisters_____

and his grandparents _____

and his sisters & husbands_____

and their children _____

and his brothers & wives_____

and their children_____

Bride with her sisters_____

Bride with her brothers_____

Bride with her brothers and sisters_____

Groom with his brothers_____

Groom with his sisters_____

Groom with his brothers and sisters_____

List any special relatives and friends of the bride and groom with whom you'd like photographs taken. Also list those, if any, who don't want to be photographed together:_____

_____

_____

_____

The Contract, Deposits and Cancellations

After the details are finalized, you should sign a contract with the photographer. It should include the date, time and place of the wedding and reception. The name of the photographer shooting the wedding should be on the contract and it should state that *no one else* will be photographing. The package should be outlined in detail: a pre-bridal session, the ceremony, the reception, etc. It should also state at what time the photographer is permitted to leave, after the cake cutting, for example, or when the bride and groom leave for their honeymoon. Photography preferences should be detailed whether candid or posed, or a combination of the two (for example, 80 percent candid, 20 percent posed).

The number of photos, albums, portraits, etc. you're to receive should be in the contract — ten 10 x 10s, five 5 x 7s, one bridal album, two parent albums, retouching for the bridal portrait. Leave nothing out.

Your contract should state delivery dates. You should have your proofs within three weeks of the wedding and your completed album (including retouching) within 90 days after you select your proofs.

Photographers normally ask for a 50-percent deposit to hold the date and reserve their services with the balance due *before* the wedding day. However, if booking the date more than a year ahead, I feel a 30-percent deposit to be more reasonable. Whatever deposit you give a photographer, put it on your credit card so you're protected if the photographer goes out of business. If the wedding is canceled, the photographer is entitled to the deposit. If you've taken the precaution of wedding cancellation insurance, you'll be protected. What if the wedding is called off? Put it in the contract that you receive credit for your deposit if you schedule another date, or a refund if he rebooks the date. Be forewarned, however, that most photographers will not agree to this.

If you change your mind and decide to hire someone else, the photographer is entitled to the deposit. In fact, *no matter what the reason for the cancellation, he may attempt to sue you for loss of business,* so be very careful with your deposit and the contract you sign.

AFTER THE WEDDING

The photographer will develop the film and select the best photos for the bride and groom to review. These are called proofs. The proofs are in chronological order and will take you through your wedding beginning to end. When looking at proofs you should not see duplicate poses or fuzzy pictures, or people with their eyes closed. Those shots should have been removed by the photographer.

Your job is to choose the best photos from the proofs for your album. Make sure all wedding events are represented — the bride and her father walking up the aisle, the first dance, cake cutting, etc. Your album must tell the story of your wedding. Keep that in mind. Do not choose a bunch of random shots that you think are good.

The photographer may show you proofs in a number of different ways. He may put them in a proof book (album) or he may make slides of the photos and show them on a screen. Tim Roberts enlarges all his photos, eliminating standard proofs. His reasons are simple. "Many times a bride and groom will like a small picture — until it's blown up. In my case, the first thing they see is the finished product, so they know what they're going to get. They can also tell if the photo needs to be retouched. Sometimes that's impossible to see on a small picture until it's enlarged. This eliminates a lot of extra work."

Many photographers explain that proofs are not corrected in any way and are often not centered. These adjustments, they claim, are made later when the photos are enlarged and cropped for the album. Tim Roberts says this is an excuse for poor photography, "A good photographer will compose his shot *in* the camera and cropping should be minimal."

Photos also may be corrected (if you don't like the background, for example, or someone has a skin problem) by touching up the negative, or if need be, the print.

Some photographers sell their proofs, others include them in the package, some won't part with them. If you didn't purchase the proofs, you may want to do so after seeing them. The choice is the photographer's and yours.

Couples often select the photos for their albums at the photographer's studio, because many photographers don't allow proofs to be taken from the premises. Others allow couples to take the proofs for a reasonable amount of time to select the photos for their albums. If you didn't buy the proofs, however, they're the property of the photographer.

Most photographers protect their proofs with a copyright stamp or seal. This means they can't be reproduced. If you decide to take photos from a proof book you may get in trouble. All proofs are numbered and missing proofs are easily found. Possession of a proof doesn't mean you have the right to reproduce it.

Albums

Your album should take you pictorially through your wedding start to finish. Emphasis should be on the bride and groom, their families, bridal party and guests in that order. Pictures should equally represent your families — one family should not dominate another.

The albums your parents choose (called "parent albums") are usually different from the bride and groom's because of bias and personal taste. You wouldn't expect the groom's family to choose photos of the bride's family and friends for their album. But just like your album, your parents' albums should tell the story of your wedding start to finish.

Albums come in all different sizes, shapes and materials. If you decide to upgrade your album after you select your photos — or upgrade your package — it should be no problem. The photographer should be more than glad to accommodate you.

Now, on to:

VIDEOGRAPHY

The Essence of Videography

The essence of videography, capturing both *action* and *sound* on film, distinguishes it from still photography.

Videography is candid, although the videographer may pose the bride and groom before the ceremony, asking them what they did that morning or if they're nervous or scared. He might also record the bridal party's good wishes and advice for the soon to be married couple, and he'll tape guests as they arrive at the ceremony location.

Imagine the action in this shot captured on video.

He'll then videotape the wedding and reception start to finish and edit several hours of tape into a polished, professional, one-to two-hour movie. A top videographer must not only possess the skills of a good photographer and be a good camera-man, he must also be a superb editor — an art unto itself.

A Word of Advice - Videotape!

Clients are forever asking me, "Should I spend the money to videotape my wedding?" I give them a resounding "Yes!" because I've yet to have a couple tell me they didn't enjoy their video. In fact, newlyweds often watch them over and over again — especially the *highlight* tape (a 20-to 30-minute video that captures the main events of the wedding). Their parents seem to enjoy it as much as they do.

On the other hand, many couples regret they did not videotape their weddings. Wedding albums tend to get thrown in a closet while videos are kept next to the VCR. My advice: spend the money to videotape your wedding.

Shopping for a Videographer

Most photographers work with videographers, but it is not uncommon for a bride to employ a photographer from one studio and a videographer from another.

Again, referral is the key to finding a good videographer. Ask recently married friends, relatives and business associates who they employed. If they were happy with their videographer and the quality of the tapes, ask to see their wedding videos — the full-length video as well as the highlight tape. If you like what you see, make an appointment with the videographer.

Use Your Common Sense

Many videographers first show prospective clients a sample highlight tape, because a full-length wedding video may last well over an hour. But also insist on watching a full-length video (fast-forward it to speed things up). If you don't have time, you might ask for a sample, full-length tape to take home to view and study at your leisure. If he won't agree to this, make another appointment to watch a full-length tape in his studio.

Use your common sense when watching demonstration tapes. If you went to the movies and the picture was fuzzy and out of focus and the story was boring, you'd walk out. The same holds true for wedding videos. They should be fast moving, with clear, crisp pictures, and they should tell the warm, intimate story of a wedding.

Most people think that "more means better"

when it comes to wedding videos, but that's not so. The "Godfather" Part I, for example, won the Best Picture Oscar in 1972. This movie spans generations and details the rise of a powerful mafioso and the calamities that befall him and his four children. It's considered one of the finest movies ever made and lasts 171 minutes. A wedding video, in contrast, tells the story of one couple's wedding day. The finished, edited video of *one* day in the lives of *one* couple should not be longer than an Oscar-winning movie that spans generations.

A wedding video should not run longer than two hours. Optimum time is one-to one-and-a-half-hours depending on the length of the ceremony. According to Don Sheff, President of the New York Institute of Photography, long tapes are unnecessary because the value of a tape lies in how often it's watched, shorter tapes being enjoyed much more than longer ones. Mr. Sheff also says that the ceremony *must* be taped in its entirety but not the reception. "How many *Alley Cats* can you watch?" he asks. After you interview a few videographers and watch a couple of full-length tapes, I think you'll agree with the experts. Long wedding videos can become tiresome. You don't like to be bored. So why bore others with a drawn-out video of your wedding?

Details

To recognize good videography follow this simple check list:
— The opening should look professional and be titled. It should also be romantic, exciting and personalized — "The Wedding of Susan Roberts and Daniel Smith" — not, "Our Wedding". The title should be made interesting and romantic by the

use of special effects and editing, and should be so professional that you feel you're about to watch a movie on HBO.

— The picture should be clear and sharp. The demonstration video you're shown should be as crisp and clean as the videos you see on the six o'clock news.

— Watch for jumpiness. The picture should be steady.

— Lighting should be even and natural. People should not look illuminated by the videographer's lighting. (They shouldn't squint their eyes or point their fingers toward the camera.) The picture should not be too dark or too light. Colors should look natural.

— There should be even transitions. A wedding glides from one event to the other and that's what the video should do. You shouldn't see a blackout, for example, as a way of moving the couple from the ceremony to the reception. What you should see is a waving and smiling bride and groom getting into a limo, driving away as the picture fades out — fading in once again as they pull up at the reception. But there shouldn't be too many "fades". Watch for more innovative special effects — the couple, for example, seemingly frozen in stone as they wave goodbye at the ceremony, only to show up at the reception and thaw before your very eyes. Or how about when they seem to turn into little blocks called "mosaics". Special effects are an imaginative way to smooth transitions.

— Special effects should be limited. They are often times used to open wedding videos. That's what you see when an animated Cupid flies across the screen announcing the wedding of Susan and Daniel. They also smooth transitions

from one scene to the next and may be employed to make the recap of the wedding (normally at the end of the tape) more interesting. And special effects may be utilized to give a video more dimension. A *split* or *multiple screen,* in which endless images of the bride and groom appear, for example, will add scope to any video. Animation, graphics and slow motion may also be employed. But be aware that too many special effects can be distracting and tasteless.

— The sound track should be clear and good quality, not muffled or cracked. It should also be loud enough and pleasing. (Remember that the background music chosen for the video is normally the choice of the bride and groom.) The music you hear at the ceremony and reception should be clear, of good quality and audible. All unnecessary noises, like a loud cough or sneeze at the ceremony, should be edited out of the tape.

Make sure all wedding events are covered:
— The groom and groomsmen at the ceremony before the wedding (may be candid, posed, or both — the choice is yours).
— The arrival of family and guests.
— The arrival of the bridesmaids (may be candid, posed, or both).
— The arrival of the bride.
— The processional, ceremony, recessional.
— The families, bride and groom and wedding party after the ceremony (may be posed or candid shots).
— The bridal couple leaving for the reception.
— The cocktail hour.
— The introduction of the families, bridal party, bride and groom at the reception.
— The first dance.
— The blessing of bread or food by clergy.

— The best man's toast (preferably with bride and groom in the picture).

— Overall shots of guests dancing, traditional folk dances, etc., the bride dancing with her father, the groom with his mother.

— At Jewish weddings, the bride, groom and their parents lifted on chairs.

— The cake cutting, the bride and groom feeding each other.

— The garter and toss.

— The bridal bouquet and toss.

— The winner of the garter toss placing it on the leg of the woman who caught the bouquet.

— The bride and groom leaving for their honeymoon.

— The ending: strong scene, the bride and groom in a passionate kiss, for example, or waving goodbye from their car.

Overall Composition

Unsurprisingly, the principles that make for good photography make for good videography. You shouldn't see jumpy frames or pictures that leap from one scene to another. Lighting is also critical. People shouldn't appear washed out or so dark you can't see their faces. Lighting also should appear natural. People shouldn't appear illuminated.

Scenes should be varied and interesting. There should be a combination of close-ups, not to mention full and wide-angle shots. There shouldn't be too much "panning," often utilized at the reception to show a large crowd dancing, or at the church to show its size and beauty, or to show the guests, seated before the ceremony begins. There should not be too much "zooming," which occurs when the camera moves in on a subject (close-up).

Zooming may be done fast or slow but it shouldn't be overused. If there's too much panning or zooming — you'll know it. The effect is nauseating. Observe the videographer's interpretation of the action. In one tape I saw, a reader was standing at a pulpit reciting scripture. To the far right was the maid of honor kneeling at the altar. Upon viewing it I thought, "What's she doing there?" The videographer should have focused exclusively on the reader. According to Don Sheff, there should be nothing in a frame that's distracting. The rule is "simplify!"

When watching demonstration tapes always check to make sure the bride and groom are not blocked, especially during the ceremony. I have seen tapes of couples whose faces are permanently marred by candelabra because video equipment was poorly angled.

Are you straining to hear the bride and groom during the ceremony? If you are, the videographer probably didn't use a wireless microphone. A wireless microphone attached to the groom's lapel or the lapel of the officiant provides the most audible sound. *Make sure the videographer uses wireless mikes.* They are the best technology has to offer (so far).

Cameras are critical to the overall quality of a video. While broadcast-quality, industrial cameras ensure the sharpest, clearest videos, they're expensive — not many videographers can afford them. (If you're paying thousands of dollars for your video, however, make sure your videographer uses them.) For that reason, many videographers use *prosumer* equipment (coined from the words professional and consumer) that is steps above the camcorder but less expensive. Make sure your videographer uses prosumer equipment if he can't afford broadcast-quality, industrial cameras.

A video will capture the action that a photo misses.

Super VHS film also is essential. The first tape the videographer puts together is called the *master*. From this tape he makes copies for the bride and groom, and families. These copies will be clear and sharp provided the master was made with Super VHS film.

Watch that good action isn't cheapened by special effects. I saw one video where guests at the reception formed a wild conga line and were dancing uproariously from one end of the room to the other. The groom was having a great time hanging on to the bride's bustle, lifting her skirts while she danced with a panama hat over her veil. I laughed as I watched until the videographer switched to slow-motion. It ruined the spontaneity of the action.

Photojournalism and the Video

In the last chapter I discussed photojournalism as a viable alternative to formal photography. But when it comes to videography, I feel it's *essential* to create a meaningful, interesting, fast-paced wedding movie. Your video should tell the story of your wedding start to finish — unposed, natural. You have a photographer for still, formal shots. Make your video different.

Most videos I've seen look contrived or canned. The videographer posing the groom and the groomsmen before the ceremony, asking corny questions, taping their uneasiness and their nervous, silly answers. Wouldn't it have been more intriguing to tape them being "naturally" nervous — playing catch with a boutonniere or *endlessssly* straightening a bow tie? Or how about those beautiful moments directly after the ceremony when the newlyweds, their families and bridal party congregate at the back of the room hugging, kissing, letting their hair down — savoring the moment. These shots make for a great video. Or how about the videographer taping the photographer as he struggles to arrange the euphoric bride, groom and their bridal party and families for formal shots — instead of taping the formal shots themselves? These funny, warm, exasperating, candid moments are the kind that the videographer should capture.

Videos can be boring, especially if the bride and groom want shots of each of their guests at the reception. The videographer goes from table to table, turns on his lights and hands each guest a microphone as he tapes them offering their "best" to the couple. Guests are aware of the videographer. Their faces are illuminated by his lights and they're pointing their fingers at him while they wait for the microphone. How many comments like, "Good luck, Sue and Dan" can one video

tolerate? Wouldn't it be better to see candid shots of your guests at their tables — talking, laughing, having fun together? Don't forget — the best photographers are unobtrusive. This rule should also apply to videographers.

If you want a photojournalistic video of your wedding, make the effort to find someone who's experienced. See samples of their work and make sure they follow the rules of good videography.

If you want a mix of posed and candid videography, tell your videographer where *you* want the emphasis to be. You may want 75 percent candid, for example, and 25 percent posed.

The Importance of Editing

Besides sound and action, editing is another major difference between still photography and videography. When the still photographer presents your proof book, it will contain many photos following the chronological sequence of your wedding, start to finish. With the help of the photographer you choose the photos for your album. In effect, you are the editor. Not so with the video. The videographer may have several hours of tape that he must edit into a succinct one-to one-and-a-half-hour movie and a 30-minute highlight tape. It's up to him to decide what should and shouldn't be included in the tapes. He alone is the editor.

This is why your input is so important. You must stress to the videographer — before your wedding — where *you* want the emphasis. Inform him, for example, that you want a candid video with a few posed shots and that you don't want a lot of panning or zooming. Direct him to focus on you, your families, the bridal party and guests —

in that order. Furthermore, you might add that you don't want each guest's remarks recorded, although you do want him to tape your families' wishes for your wedding day. Be specific with your requests. You may say for instance, "When you edit the video we want special effects at the beginning and end for transitions. We want the video to last one to one-and-a-half hours." (This will depend on the length of the ceremony.) List all these things in your contract.

Watch sample full-length wedding videos to determine the editing skills of the videographer. If the editing is good, the tape will keep your attention. It shouldn't drag. There should be interesting transitions, and all key wedding events should be included to tell a fast paced, engaging story start to finish. The emphasis should be on the bride and groom, their families, bridal party and guests in that order. Annoying scenes should be removed, including people's backs and irritating or loud sounds. Special effects should enhance and diversify the tape, not overpower it.

Be aware of *in-camera editing*. Many videographers tell brides that they edit as they shoot, which is absurd. A tape can't be edited while it's in the camera. In-camera editing means that the videographer turns his camera on and off at key moments, and hands the bride and groom the tape at the end of the evening. Good editing takes a lot of time and isn't cheap. To determine how you want your video shot and edited, watch sample videos closely. Make notes about your likes and dislikes and discuss them with your videographer. If he doesn't agree with what you want, find out why. There may be justified technical reasons for his reluctance. If not, look for another videographer.

Two Videographers or One?

Are two videographers better than one? According to Don Sheff, it's not the number of videographers that's important but the number of cameras. At the ceremony, for example, one videographer can be stationed at the altar while a second camera runs continuously from the balcony. The videographer will catch the action as the guests enter, and the procession as it makes its way up the aisle. The "balcony" camera will capture a different perspective of the ceremony — and the recessional.

At the reception it isn't necessary to have two videographers or two cameras. As Mr. Sheff says, a wedding is a "scripted" event. The videographer knows the sequence of the action. He's not going to miss it. Editing becomes a bigger and more expensive job, however, because two tapes must be edited into one succinct, interesting, fast paced movie. Two cameras will give you more coverage and different perspectives, but it's also a matter of budget. Having two tapes edited into one movie costs more.

Video "Packages"

Just like photographers, videographers sell "packages". Their price is based on the amount of coverage and editing, the number of cameras and videographers, and the number of tapes purchased.

You may, for example, want the videographer at your house before the ceremony to videotape the preparations. Or you may only need him to tape the ceremony. Maybe you desire two cameras at the ceremony, maybe just one. You may wish the tape edited with childhood pictures of you and the groom. For the grand finale to end your video, you may prefer it edited with pictures taken on your honeymoon. Or you may not want the tape edited at all. You may require a highlight tape for you and your parents and two full-length copies. Whatever you need, the videographer should be able to offer you a package that meets your requirements and your budget.

Before You Sign a Contract

Meet with a few videographers before making a decision. Make sure you feel comfortable with the videographer. Don't be pressured into signing a contract after the first meeting. It's important that you interview many videographers, study their work and compare their packages before making any decisions.

The Next Meeting - Details

Make sure that the videographer makes arrangements to visit your ceremony and reception sites. This will enable him to better judge lighting and will also give him an idea of where and how he can set up his equipment. He should also call the ceremony officiant to ask if there are any restrictions on filming.

Ask the videographer if he has backup equipment. If he has only one camera, it's better to find someone else. Also ask if he has an assistant. This is important. Video equipment can be cumbersome and is too much for one person to handle effectively.

Ask the videographer if he's *the* one who shot the demonstration tapes he's shown you as samples of his work. If he didn't take them, drop him. Make sure the videographer is willing to work with you. If he's one of those who says, "I stay four hours, no matter what, take it or leave it." Leave it.

Ask the videographer if *he* is the one who will be shooting your wedding. Put this in your contract. Too many clients have told me that the person they booked wasn't the person who showed up at the wedding.

The "Group Liaison"

The same friend or relative you assigned to assist the photographer should also be there to help the videographer. This person is called the "group liaison" — or the one who acts as a liaison between the videographer and the friends and families of the bride and groom. You don't want the videographer wasting valuable time running around trying to find Aunt Mary or Uncle Al before the ceremony or after. Leave that to the group liaison. It's especially important to have a group liaison if the families are large or the wedding is.

Should You Feed the Videographer and His Assistants?

A wedding means a long day for a videographer and his assistants. That's why it's advisable to provide food for them at the reception. Ask the catering director to set up a small table at the back of the room (where the photographer and his assistants are seated), and to provide sandwiches for them. You aren't expected to provide them with the same meal that's offered to your guests. At no time should the videographer or his assistants drink alcoholic beverages.

The Contract, Deposits and Cancellations

Once you decide on a videographer, it's time to sign the contract. Just make absolutely sure that

A video will capture the romantic moments of the bride and groom.

the following items are included:

— The date, time and place of the wedding and reception.

— The name of the videographer shooting the wedding.

— What the video coverage includes — shots at the bride's house, the ceremony (including two cameras), and full coverage of the reception.

— How you want the video shot and edited, for example, a few posed shots but 90 percent candid. Emphasis on bride and groom, families, bridal parties and guests, in that order. No table shots of guests and their "well-wishes", family members only. Special effects for the beginning, end and transitions only.

— What the package includes, for example, two full-length tapes completely edited with special effects, one highlight tape.

— The time the videographer is permitted to leave the reception.

— The date you can expect the finished product.

Most videographers want a deposit to hold the date and reserve their services. If you reserve the videographer more than a year ahead, a 30 percent deposit is reasonable, although many will ask for 50 percent, with the balance due before the wedding date. Always put it on your credit card so you're protected if the videographer goes out of business.

If the wedding is canceled the photographer is entitled to the deposit, unless it's written in your contract that you are to receive a credit or refund. Most videographers, however, won't agree to this. A more logical suggestion would be that he agrees to a refund if he rebooks the date. This should also be written into your contract. If you change your mind and decide to hire someone else, however, the videographer is entitled to the deposit.

The Camcorder and Uncle Chuck

It seems that everyone has an Uncle Chuck with a camcorder who wants to videotape your wedding — for free! As Don Sheff pointed out to me, "Everyone also has an Aunt Emma with an oven — but would you let her make your wedding cake?" Of course not. Good videography requires a professional with good equipment, lots of talent and years of experience. To make sure you will not be disappointed with your video, hire a professional and stay on good terms with Uncle Chuck.

A bride and her maid hold beautiful colorful bouquets.

Flowers

Flowers — their beauty, colors and quantities — make a wedding different from any other occasion that a woman celebrates. It's unlikely she will ever again carry a bouquet, or choose boutonnieres or corsages for her family, or bouquets for her dearest friends. Maybe she will never again be so frivolous when it comes to buying centerpieces. Flowers make weddings special. For centuries, flowers have made brides feel beautiful and happy. They remain an integral part of the festivities.

The first bridal bouquets were not flowers, but herbs. Ancient cultures believed herbs, like garlic, had the power to cast off evil spirits and to grace a bride with their attributes. If a bride carried sage, the herb of wisdom, she became wise. If she carried dill (the herb of lust), she became "lusty". Later flowers replaced herbs in bouquets — thank goodness — and acquired a symbolism all their own.

Orange blossoms trace their history to mythology. The goddess Juno gave them to Jupiter on their wedding day and ever since orange blossoms have been carried in bridal bouquets. Teddy Roosevelt's daughter, Alice, carried a bouquet of orange blossoms when she married. When Jacqueline Kennedy wed Aristotle Onassis in a traditional Greek Orthodox ceremony, crowns of orange blossoms were placed on their heads symbolizing happiness and fertility. The beauty of flowers, their symbolism, and the important role they play in weddings has never waned throughout the centuries.

Fresh Flowers and Bridal Parties

Fresh flowers are a requirement for all weddings — no matter how large or small, formal or informal because they make a wedding festive. Every bride should carry a fresh floral bouquet (even a simple nosegay will do), whether she is marrying for the first time or the third. All brides-maids should carry flowers. The flower girl should carry a basket of flowers, the ringbearer should wear a boutonniere, and all members of the immediate families should have corsages and boutonnieres.

The flowers you require for your wedding will depend on its size and type. A large, formal wedding with a regal bride and six bridesmaids resplendent in ornate gowns, would require full-floral bouquets styled to match the formality and design of their dresses. A simple corsage worn by this bride or a single rose carried by these brides-maids would look out of place. At an informal wedding, on the other hand, the bride may wear a simple corsage and the maid of honor may carry a single rose flanked by decorative ribbons or pearls. It would be perfectly appropriate.

I stress fresh flowers for a wedding because it's the *one* day of your life when you should carry them. They don't need to be elaborate or expensive, but a bride and her bouquet should go together just like "...love and marriage."

Silk Flowers and Weddings

To save money, many brides consider using silk flowers for weddings. They're under the erroneous impression that silk flowers are cheaper than fresh. This isn't the case. Good "silks" that look real, are fine in texture and soft in color, can cost three times more than the real thing. If you use inexpensive silks in your bouquets or for centerpieces at the reception, they'll look it! Silks have no place at weddings. If you want to save money, use fresh flowers.

Floral Components

Flowers, depending on quantity and type can be expensive, but their beauty makes the day. They should figure significantly within your budget. Wedding flowers can be broken down into three specific areas:

1. Flowers for the ceremony — these may include altar bouquets or arrangements, and flowers or bows for the pews or chairs along the aisle. Flowers may also be placed at the entry, in the foyer or behind the altar. Your florist, after visiting the ceremony site, can advise where flowers can be used to their best advantage within your budget.

a. Ceremony accessories — these may include trees (usually fichus or palms) that fill "dead" areas at the ceremony site or provide color or camouflage — to hide a dull beige wall, for example. These trees may be decorated with tiny white lights, providing a soft, romantic glow for an evening wedding. Florists may also rent kneeling benches, aisle runners, candelabra, chuppot, arches and pedestals that elevate arrangements (which may be placed on either side of the altar or along the aisle).

2. Bridal party flowers — these include flowers for bridal party members and the immediate family.

3. Reception flowers — these may include centerpieces for the cocktail hour and dining tables at the reception, flowers for buffet tables and arrangements for the place-card table and ladies room.

a. Reception accessories — these may include mirrors that the centerpieces are placed on, votive candles and risers (lucite or glass pedestals or

An elegant, dramatic presentation bouquet.

vases used to elevate centerpieces). Again, rental trees (with or without lights) may be used to fill space, provide light, color and camouflage.

The Basic Minimums and Wedding Type

The chart on page 234 shows basic flowers required for each wedding type, whether formal, semi-formal or informal. You may add more if you choose depending upon your budget. For example, if you're having an informal wedding, you may wish to have a couple of simple bouquets for your ceremony placed on either side of the altar. Or, you might want to have a flower girl basket for your pre-school niece. On the other hand, you might be having a formal wedding and want the ceremony site decked with flowers top

A boutonniere doesn't always have to be a rose.

A live Calla lily sprayed gold and flanked by stephanotis makes a unique corsage.

to bottom. If your budget allows this is perfectly acceptable. Just remember to keep your flowers in line with your wedding type.

Florists and Production Companies

Many brides with unlimited budgets choose to have ceremonies and receptions resplendent in flowers, satin, lace and bows — weddings made in wonderland. Who can forget the ceremony or reception in *Father of the Bride?* A perfect example of what money CAN buy.

These "magic" weddings require the skill and expertise of "production companies" as well as florists. The production company provides the tent, for example, draping it in yards and yards of tulle, bows and lights. Meanwhile, the florist provides the trees, potted flowers, and centerpieces. Such a team may design a theme wedding — "A Night with Ali Baba", for example. Many large florists double as production companies. They're able to structure and design all facets of a "wonderland" wedding. If you have an unlimited budget and visions of a show-stopper wedding, hire a bridal consultant or a party-planning company who makes them their specialty. To be sure that you're hiring a reputable, experienced consultant or company, ask for references, check them thoroughly and see samples of their work. Don't attempt this type of wedding on your own.

Wedding Dates that Cause Problems

Christmas, Easter, Mother's Day and Valentine's Day are the biggest "floral days" of the year, and they can play havoc on a wedding. Wholesale florists stockpile flowers for weeks before holidays in anticipation of high-volume sales. The flowers are usually not fresh but prices can be exorbitant. The cost from the wholesaler to the retailer can double, or even triple, and this is passed on to consumers. If you are considering being married on or near one of these days, increase your flower budget accordingly and book the florist well in advance — a year or more might be necessary.

I don't advise being married on or near a holiday or floral day if wedding flowers are important to you. No matter what your budget, the quality is not good and the price is too high.

Follow the "three-week rule" to ensure that your flowers will be beautiful for your bridal party, ceremony and reception. Plan your wedding three weeks before the holiday or three weeks afterward. Then you'll know your flowers will be fresh, beautiful and reasonably priced.

This bridesmaid takes a much needed break. She leans against a chair while holding a bouquet of red roses, accented with gold lamé ribbon and pheasant feathers.

Flower Minimums for an Informal, Semi-Formal or Formal Wedding

	* INFORMAL	SEMI-FORMAL	FORMAL
BRIDAL PARTY:			
Bride's bouquet	X	X	X
Toss Away		X	X
Maid of Honor	X	X	X
Bridesmaids		X	X
Flower Girl		X	X
Ringbearer		X	X
Groom	X	X	X
Best Man	X	X	X
Ushers		X	X
Mother of Bride	X	X	X
Mother of Groom	X	X	X
Father of Bride	X	X	X
Father of Groom	X	X	X
Grandparents	X	X	X
Special Relatives (optional)			
Friends, "Readers" (optional)			
CEREMONY FLOWERS:			
Altar Arrangements		X	X
Bows or Flowers for Pews			X
Aisle Runner			X
Chuppa — Plain or Decorated	X	X	X
RECEPTION FLOWERS:			
Flowers for Cocktail Hour			X
Flowers for Buffet Tables			X
Centerpieces for Dinner Tables		X	X
Cake-top Flowers, (if preferred)		X	X
Flowers for Cake-table		X	X
Flowers for Place-card Table			X
Flowers for Ladies' Room			X

LIST ADDITIONS: (for example, unity candle, kneeling bench, rental trees)

_____

LIST FLORAL FAVORITES: (for example, roses or snap dragons)

_____

LIST FLORAL EXCEPTIONS: ("I don't like carnations, etc.")

_____

* Floral minimums for informal weddings are only applicable if the bride and groom are married in temple or church. The only attendants are the maid of honor and best man.

An elegant cascade of white roses and Dendrobium orchids.

Friends and Flowers - Take Heed

If a close friend is an amateur florist who decides to give you flowers for a wedding gift, or your friend is a florist who does not specialize in weddings, politely decline. Tell your friend you wouldn't dream of having them work on your wedding day. Weddings are too risky for amateurs or for those florists who don't do weddings regularly.

FLOWERS AND BUDGET
How Flowers Are Priced

Florists base their prices on the types of flowers utilized and their quantities. Let's assume you want to use white carnations exclusively for your wedding — the ceremony, bridal party and centerpieces. A friend, on the other hand, wants to use white roses for her wedding. You have the same number of people in your bridal parties, two altar arrangements for the church and 10 on-the-table centerpieces. The cost difference? Your friend will pay approximately seven times more for her "rose" wedding.

But if you doubled the number of centerpieces and put them on risers, placed candelabra decorated with bows and carnations on either side of the altar, and doubled the size of your bridal party, you would pay as much for your "carnation" wedding as your friend who's having the smaller rose wedding.

Note that rental fees also are included in the price. Candelabra, chuppot, pedestals for the aisle, risers, mirrors and votive candles, kneeling benches, and arches, for example, are rented by the florist and added into the cost. These rentals can dramatically increase prices.

Some florists may charge for delivery and set up. Be sure to ask and make sure all fees are included in your contract.

Expensive Flowers

Most bridal books mention lilies-of-the-valley, Casablanca lilies, Calla lilies, orchids, stephanotis and gardenias as common choices for bridal bouquets. These flowers are so costly that most times I don't even suggest them. If you hear the words "orchid" or "lily" you'll know the flowers are going to be expensive.

Gardenias are the Rolls Royce of flowers and are extremely perishable, as are stephanotis. Dendrobium orchid blooms, while not cheap, can give a look similar to stephanotis. They are also less money and are heartier. If you're on a budget be aware of the flowers listed above.

Seasonal Flowers and Price

Many brides mistakenly believe it's less expensive to use flowers in season. Years ago this was true. But now flowers are flown daily to wholesalers from all over the world. Almost every flower is available year round. I receive roses summer and winter from Colombia, and the price never varies except near holidays and floral days. In summer, the cost of locally grown flowers like snap dragons is only slightly less than in the winter, so season is no longer a pricing consideration.

Beware - "Packaged" Flowers

Be leery of clubs, hotels and restaurants who offer "packages" including centerpieces. Nothing is free. They merely include the cost of the centerpiece in the package. Always see the centerpieces offered before signing a contract. If you don't like them, get your own florist — one who suits your

Casablanca lilies, roses and freesia make an exquisite arrangement.

needs, taste and budget. Then ask the catering director for a reduction in the package cost.

The Importance of Budgeting Early

Many clients tell me "I've blown all my money. I'm going to cut the flowers." They've spent a ton on gowns, entertainment, food, liquor and limos. Now they're tempted to use single roses in bud vases for centerpieces at their receptions?! It doesn't occur to them how ridiculous a single rose in a bud vase will look on a six-foot round or rectangular dining table. Bud-vase centerpieces and formal or semi-formal weddings don't mix. Bud vases are for diners, not wedding receptions.

The mistake these women are about to make — and regret — could have been avoided if they did the proper legwork and budgeting. At a reception, people sit at large, round or rectangular tables. They look at each other and the centerpieces. The beautiful, floral arrangements they see on the tables should be a constant reminder of how special *this* occasion truly is.

TIP: If you get into a bind and funds become tight, cut back on the ceremony flowers (for instance, rental trees). The ceremony lasts anywhere from 15 minutes to an hour. The reception lasts four to five hours. Put your money in the centerpieces.

How to Budget

Meet with a few florists and show them the *flower minimum chart* in this chapter. Relate it to your wedding. Be sure to add extras you're considering — rental trees for the reception, for example, or a unity candle for the ceremony. Based on this chart and including your floral *favorites, exceptions,* and *additions,* ask what your approximate budget should be. The florist should be able to give you a ballpark figure of the cost based on flower types and quantities.

Once you have a few estimates, average them to come up with your flower budget. If your "averaged" estimate is too high, it's time to think about cutting back. Maybe you can use less expensive flowers, maybe you can drop the rental trees, maybe you can change the centerpieces from risers to the on-the-table variety that are less expensive. Maybe you're planning too many flowers for the ceremony site. Discuss this with prospective florists who should be able to get your flowers in line with your budget.

BRIDAL PARTY FLOWERS

Taped and Wired vs. Oasis

An age-old disagreement between florists is, "Do we 'tape and wire' the bouquet or do we use an 'oasis' holder?" An oasis holder is composed of a block of foam surrounded by a plastic cage that has a handle. When soaked in water the foam becomes wet and pliable. The florist creates a bouquet by sticking flowers into the foam which provides them with a constant water source. Once completed, the bouquet is placed in a cooler or refrigerator. The combination of water and cool temperatures help to keep the flowers fresh.

The disadvantage of an oasis holder is that an inexperienced florist may abuse it. Sticking too many flowers into an oasis can cause the foam to crumble and the flowers to fall out. My partner and designer at Floral Concepts, Tim Berry, uses oasis all the time. He wouldn't consider using anything else because he feels the water source keeps the flowers looking their best. It's his opinion and mine that taped-and-wired flowers never look as good, and our flowers don't fall out of the foam.

Before the advent of oasis, florists wired each flower and wrapped the stems with green floral tape. Then the flowers were wired together to create a bouquet. After the taped-and-wired bouquet was completed, it was stored in a cooler. This didn't always prevent the flowers from wilting, but this type of bouquet never fell apart.

The Princess of Wales carried a taped-and-wired bouquet when she married Prince Charles. It's said that the enormous bouquet took many florists days to complete. If you choose to have a bouquet like Princess Di's, be aware that taped-and-wired bouquets (because of the labor involved) can double or even triple the cost.

Gowns, Bouquets and Style

Formal wedding gowns and bridesmaids dresses require formal bouquets. I'm amazed when women with ornate, formal gowns ask for loose, casual bouquets saying, "I want it to look just like it was picked from the garden." The two simply don't mix.

A casual, loose, straight-from-the-garden bouquet is fine for an informal or semi-formal, linen, taffeta or cotton wedding gown or a simple suit. It's also appropriate for cotton or floral printed bridesmaids dresses. It's not appropriate for a

A festive centerpiece of frosted birch branches and colorful flowers will add beauty to any table.

heavy, beaded, satin wedding gown where the flowers require a tailored, deliberate look. Nor would it be appropriate for long, iridescent taffeta bridesmaids dresses where the mere formality of the fabric requires a more formal floral design.

Don't get scared and equate "formal" with dollar signs. A daisy can be formal if *styled* formally. It's all in the design. Find a florist who cares about what you and your maids are wearing. It's critical that your bouquets be styled to your gowns.

A centerpiece perfect for a fall wedding composed of fresh fruits, pheasant feathers, flowers and fresh ivy.

Bridal Bouquets and Your Wedding Gown

The three basic types of bouquets are the *presentation* (arm bouquet), the *nosegay* (round), and the *cascade* (long and flowing). Your florist should work with you to design a bouquet best suited to your gown and your size.

The presentation bouquet should only be carried if the bodice of the wedding gown is plain. An arm bouquet rests in the crook of the arm. If the top of your wedding gown is embroidered or appliqued with lace, a presentation bouquet — because of its size and bulk — will hide detailing and detract from the gown. If the dress is plain, however, a presentation bouquet of white Calla lilies or roses can be dramatic and elegant and complement the gown's simplicity. If you decide on this type of bouquet, make sure the florist considers your size. If you are tall and of medium build, for example, the bouquet should be fuller than if you were short and slight.

The nosegay is a round bouquet lending itself to any type of wedding gown. It may be composed of any type of flower or a combination of flowers. It's usually six to eight inches in diameter and therefore would not be appropriate for a large bride. If the bride is tall, stocky — or both — and wants a nosegay, the florist should increase its size proportionately.

Tim Berry designs many bouquets that are variations of the nosegay that we call "artsy colonial". He simply makes the basic, round nosegay more free-form. Many brides seem to prefer this bouquet over the tailored look of the nosegay.

The cascade is the choice of most brides. It's a bouquet that falls from the waist covering the front of the gown. It may be large or small, loose or tailored. It may be shaped as a crescent or teardrop or be free-form in design. If the skirt of your gown is heavily embroidered or appliqued, a cascade might not be a good choice because it will cover the front of the skirt.

The secret to a beautiful cascade (besides fresh, quality flowers) is that it must relate directly to the size of the bride and the size of her gown. A small woman wearing a huge gown should have a fuller, shorter cascade than if she wore a sheath. A good florist will see a picture of the bride's dress and measure her for the cascade. If the florist is unable to do this, have a friend measure the inches across the front of your waistline. The cascade should be no wider than this measurement. Then measure the number of inches from your waist to where the appliques on the skirt begin. This determines the cascade's length. If there are no appliques on the skirt, the bouquet may fall to the hem. The decision is yours, based on the advice of your florist.

The Toss-Away Bouquet

Because bridal bouquets can be large and heavy, it's advisable to have the florist make up a toss-away bouquet. This is a small nosegay that the bride throws at the end of the reception. Tradition has it that the person who catches the bouquet is the next to be married. Many women ask for a toss-away bouquet because they want to keep their bridal bouquet as a cherished memento.

Bridesmaids Bouquets

Any type of bouquet — a nosegay, cascade or presentation — is appropriate for bridesmaids. It all depends on the style of their dresses. Read the criteria above, The single-flower bouquet that's made up of an individual flower decorated with ribbons, etc. is acceptable only for a semi-formal or informal wedding.

Bridesmaids bouquets do not have to resemble the bride's. In fact, I think the contrast is pleasing. The bride may carry a cascade of white roses and Dendrobium orchids, while the bridesmaids carry nosegays of white roses or vice versa.

The bride also may choose to have the style of her bridesmaids bouquets match hers. They may all carry nosegays or cascades, for example. The bride's bouquet, however, should be larger and more important. She may carry a cascade of Dendrobium orchids and roses, while the bridesmaids carry small cascades of roses, gerbera daisies and Star of Bethlehem.

The Flower Girl - An Alternative

Most wedding sites do not permit flower girls to throw petals when walking up the aisle. People tend to slip on them. For that reason, it's advisable that a flower girl carry a basket filled with flowers.

Another alternative is to have her carry a fireside basket (one without sides) filled with individual flowers like roses that have been decorated with ribbons. As she walks up the aisle, she pauses occasionally to hand roses randomly to women guests. This can be a show-stopper, but I don't advise trying this with very young children.

For the Immediate Families - Corsages and Boutonnieres

Corsages and boutonnieres are always given to members of the immediate families including grandparents. Women usually receive pin-on corsages composed of elegant flowers such as orchids or roses, but these have their drawbacks. Fresh flowers are heavy. A corsage pinned to a light-weight dress may tear it. I always advise my clients to use wrist corsages or hand-held corsages instead. A hand-held corsage is composed of one or two flowers trimmed with pearls, rhinestones or ribbons that match their dress. It has a handle and is carried, not worn. Many women prefer this type of corsage.

Boutonnieres come in many shapes and sizes, and can be made up of any number of small flowers or a single rose or carnation. Boutonnieres, however, should always match the type and color of flowers used in the bouquets of the bride and her attendants. When the bride carries a bouquet of roses and Dendrobium orchids, for example, the groom's boutonniere may be a white rose and a Dendrobium orchid bloom. If bridesmaids carry bouquets of roses or carnations, my staff makes the groomsmen's boutonnieres from roses or carnations. We may even make special boutonnieres for the fathers of the bride and groom by using a few Dendrobium orchid blooms.

Flower choices for boutonnieres are endless and they don't have to be ordinary. If you want something different, discuss it with your florist.

The Designated "Pinner"

Most florists leave corsages and boutonnieres at the ceremony before it begins and don't stay to pin them on. For this reason, it's best to designate a *pinner*, a close friend or relative who will distribute the corsages and boutonnieres before the ceremony and help pin them on. Make sure that your florist labels all pieces, "Mother of the Bride," for example, or "Uncle Henry." The pinner should not get stuck guessing "who gets what" corsage or boutonniere.

THE IMPORTANCE OF COLOR

It's very important to relate color to your wedding season. Are you being married in summer or in winter? A garden look for a winter wedding would look out of place, as would a "frosted" look for a summer wedding. Flowers like daffodils, snap dragons and tulips are synonymous

This bouquet of mixed flowers and colors is the perfect centerpiece for a formal wedding.

A unique on-the-table centerpiece of Dendrobrium orchids, Cattleya orchids and Delores roses.

with spring; as holly and poinsettias are synonymous with Christmas and winter. Autumn brings to mind vibrant colors — oranges and rusts, deep reds and golds. Don't rule out cornucopias filled with fresh fruits and greens for centerpieces, especially around Thanksgiving. By contrast, summer evokes memories of fresh-cut garden roses, snap dragons, asters and peonies.

Are the flowers you visualize congruent to the season you've chosen for your marriage? Begin by blending the two in your mind before you meet with a florist.

Background Color and Ceremony Flowers

Background color is a critical consideration in floral design. Before the florist chooses the colors for an arrangement he must know where the arrangement will go. Will it sit on a large, glass dining table flanked by mauve chairs or be backed by a grey wall? The grey wall and the mauve chairs provide the *background* color for the arrangement — and the colors of flowers selected must relate to those colors.

He may choose colors that contrast with the background color giving a bold, dramatic look. Or he may choose flowers that are all the same color — called *monochromatic* design. Your florist also may choose different flowers whose colors seem to blend together, or he may select opposite but compatible colors, such as red and green.

Let's begin by relating background color to weddings. At the ceremony the background color *is* the walls, windows or stained glass behind the altar or the chuppa. Not the walls on either side of the room or the carpet. Let me give you a couple of examples:

Example 1: You're being married in church. Behind the altar is a huge, vibrant stained glass window. You'd like a large bouquet to stand on each side of the altar in front of this window.

It's summer and the bridesmaids are dressed in lime green, their bouquets white, pink and lilac. They'll stand next to the altar arrangements during the ceremony. What colors should the altar flowers be? White. White flowers with their lack of color will not antagonize the colors in the stained glass window, and will blend harmoniously with the cool lime of the bridesmaids dresses and their multicolored bouquets. It's the obvious choice.

Example 2: You're having a Jewish wedding at a hotel. The walls of the ceremony site are beige, which you detest. Your florist suggests placing rental trees, fichus or palms, along the length of the wall for camouflage. Your background color has just changed from beige to green. The chuppa will be placed in front of the trees and draped with white tulle. Your bridesmaids are wearing black Watters and Watters gowns with white, off-the-shoulder collars. What color for flowers? Since you obviously are having a black-and-white wedding, the obvious choice is white bouquets for the bridesmaids and white arrangements for either side of the chuppa. Had the dresses been totally black, on the other hand (black being neutral), any color of flowers would be appropriate for the ceremony as well as the bridesmaids bouquets.

Background Color and Your Bridal Bouquet

Your wedding gown *is* the background color for your bridal bouquet. Your gown may be ivory, white or blush, or you may wear a brightly-colored dress or suit for a second or informal wedding. Whatever color you choose, the color of your flowers must relate to the color you're wearing.

Wedding Gown and Bouquet Colors - The White Wedding Gown

White is compatible with all colors but this doesn't mean you can choose purple, red and fuchsia flowers for your bridal bouquet. A bouquet should complement the wedding gown just like the right pair of earrings or the perfect pearl necklace. A bridal bouquet should be part of the total picture and shouldn't stand alone. A bride dressed in white from head to toe carrying a fuchsia, purple and red bouquet draws attention from herself to the flowers. This bouquet screams, "Look at Me!" That's why I always advise white flowers, or a combination of light pastel and white flowers, for a white wedding gown.

White flowers are not stark white. Look at a white rose. It may look slightly pink, creamy or even yellow. The different shading of color evident in a white rose is one factor that makes monochromatic design beautiful. The other is texture.

Different flowers produce different textures. A bridal bouquet made up of white Dendrobium

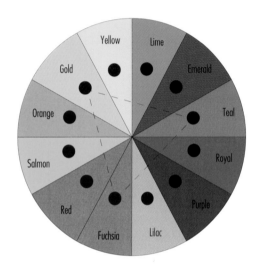

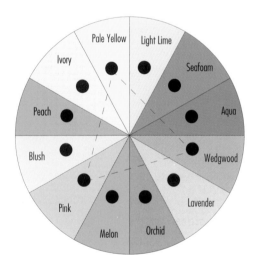

Color Wheels.

orchids and white roses will produce two distinctly different shades of white — and their petals will be two different textures. White Monto Casino or baby's breath (small flowers used as *fillers* in bouquets) also add different shades of white along with varying textures and dimension. Ferns or any type of greens and their varying shades and textures are a suitable backdrop for white flowers, providing the contrast necessary to separate the white bouquet from the white wedding gown. (See illustrations in this chapter.)

The Ivory Wedding Gown

White and light-pastel flowers may also be used against an ivory wedding gown, because white flowers are never stark white in color and will blend harmoniously with any shade of ivory or candlelight.

The Colored Wedding Gown

If your gown is blush or pink, or you're wearing a brightly colored suit or cocktail dress, it's best that your bouquet pick up the color of your dress. If your gown is blush or pink, your bouquet should be white with a few pink spray roses to pick up the color. Or you may have a pale pink bouquet of spray roses, Livia roses, gerbera daisies and mini-carnations with just a hint of baby's breath as a filler. Once again, I opt for pale colors and white which won't detract from the wedding gown. The bouquet should complement the dress.

If you are wearing a brightly colored suit or dress, match one of the colors in your bouquet to your dress. If you decide to use bright, colored flowers add other blooms that are less bold in color to temper the bouquet. Add neutral flowers like baby's breath and Monto Casino to achieve perfect balance.

Bridesmaids Dresses

The colors of your bridesmaids bouquets depend upon the color of their dresses. You've already related the color of their gowns to the background color of the ceremony site. Now relate the color of their flowers to their gowns to assure perfect harmony.

Determining Floral Colors with Color Wheels

The diagrams on the opposite page contain two color wheels. The first shows bold primary, secondary and intermediate colors. The second depicts variations in these colors called "tints." I've taken the liberty of changing the names of the colors on the wheels to those commonly used to describe the colors of bridesmaids dresses. To determine compatible floral colors for your bouquets look at the wheels. Put your finger on the color that matches your bridesmaids dresses. The four colors to the right — or left — of this color will be compatible with the color of your gowns. Let's say your bridesmaids dresses are fuchsia. Look at Wheel One and put your finger on fuchsia. The four colors to the right — the ones that range from violet, to blue, to teal — are compatible with fuchsia. Your flowers may be in any of these colors. On the other hand, the four fall colors to the left — fiery reds and oranges — are also compatible with fuchsia. You may, if you prefer, choose flowers in these colors (but don't mix the four colors on the right with the four colors on the left). The rule of thumb is: the four colors to the right — or to the left — of the color of your bridesmaids dresses are compatible with it.

Because all these colors are bold, however, they should be blended with neutral filler flowers, baby's breath, white statice or Monto Casino. And always include a flower in the color of your dress — in this case fuchsia. Flowers that come in this "hot" color include gerbera daisies, roses, asters and mini-carnations.

A second way to choose colors is by selecting

opposites on the color wheels, especially if you like the bold and dramatic. Think opposites and strong, unflinching words come to mind — fire and ice, or war and peace. It's the same with color — green and red being the most familiar example. How about salmon and teal? Or purple and gold?

Let's say your bridesmaids dresses are purple

A centerpiece encircled with gold grape vines, Calla lilies, grapes, pears and apples (real fruit) sprayed gold.

and you want bold, colorful flowers. Look at Wheel One and put your finger on purple. Directly opposite purple is bright gold. Your dresses are purple so you want the gold (or deep yellow) color to dominate with a splash of purple to pick up the dress color. (When using bold colors, always have one color dominate the other.) With the florist, you choose deep yellow roses, gold gerbera daisies, gold alstroemeria (a small lily), golden aster, and — for a filler to add that touch of purple — purple statice. These bouquets will be bold, dramatic and colorful, but at the same time, that touch of statice is *the* ingredient that makes the flowers and the purple dresses come together.

Another way to select compatible colors is the *triangle* method. Let's assume your bridesmaids dresses are pale yellow. Find pale yellow on Wheel Two. Count four colors to the right of pale yellow, and you have Wedgwood blue. Count four colors to the left of pale yellow, and you have pink. Connect the dots and you have a triangle. The colors designated by the triangle — blue, pink and yellow are compatible. Let's try this again. Pretend your bridesmaids dresses are teal. Count four colors to the right, and you have fuchsia, count four colors to the left, and you have gold. Connect the dots and you have a triangle. Teal, fuchsia and gold are compatible. Once again, you have bold colors that should be tempered liberally with soft, neutral fillers. Be sure to have at least one flower pick up the color of the dresses.

THE RECEPTION
Coordinating the Reception

The proper blend of color is essential if you want your reception site to look well coordinated and beautiful. The first step is selecting the linens. These must relate to the background color of the room, *not* the colors of the bridal party. Assume your wedding colors are hot-pink and white. If your reception room is dull beige, it's best to go with white linens. A dozen tables covered in hot-pink cloths against the backdrop of a dull beige room could be nauseating. Introduce the colors of your bridal party with accents — hot-pink napkins and matches, for example. And be sure to pick up the bridal-party colors in the flowers you select for your centerpieces.

If you choose on-the-table centerpieces, the background color will be provided by the white tablecloths. Your centerpieces should be composed of pink and hot-pink flowers, white flowers and greens. This will pick up the color of the linens and your bridal party and won't clash with the beige room.

If your centerpiece is on a riser, the colors of the flowers should blend with the background color of the walls and incorporate the colors of the bridal party and the linens.

For a black-and-white wedding, it's best to go with white linens and black accents, which are the most festive. Black tablecloths can overpower a room and look dismal. White flowers should be used for the centerpieces, which may be sprinkled with black bows, or ribbons or accented by black curly willow (thin flexible branches).

Requirements for Receptions

Centerpieces are a *must* for a semi-formal or formal wedding, even though they don't need to be elaborate or expensive. Guest tables should look festive, and nothing can make a room look more joyous than pretty table cloths and fresh flowers. Once again, it's important that you don't equate "formal" with dollar signs. Even a carnation can be formal. It's all in the design.

Floral Concepts once designed the flowers for a formal, Southwestern wedding. The bride wanted "cacti" centerpieces. Tim bought good-quality fake cacti and placed them in rough-hewn wooden baskets that he pickled with white paint. Then he braided curly willow into handles and trimmed them with fresh ivy. Sprouting from the baskets were a few white roses, several white Dendrobium orchids and assorted greens. The bases of the baskets were covered with Spanish moss. To make the arrangements festive and bridal, he sprinkled them with Diamond Dust, an opalescent powder which makes everything sparkle. The baskets were placed on mirrors surrounded by votive candles — their light flickering against the dusted flowers and cacti. The bride later told us that the centerpieces were the hit of the reception. Even better, they weren't expensive.

Minimums for the Formal Reception

There are no limitations on flowers for formal weddings, but there are minimums (see chart in this chapter). These should include arrangements for the cocktail hour, for buffet tables, for dining tables and flowers for the ladies room and place-card table. These arrangements may be as elaborate as you'd like. You may also have flowers for the cake top and cake table.

Minimums for the Semi-formal Reception

A semi-formal reception requires arrangements for the dining tables, whether simple or elaborate. You also may have small centerpieces for the cocktail hour and for the hors d'oeuvre buffet.

Many times catering directors offer small, decorative hurricane lamps for cocktail-hour tables.

Minimums for the Informal Reception

Floral centerpieces are not necessary for informal weddings. If you want them, however, keep them informal, colorful and festive. Buy pretty, flowering plants, for example, that can be placed on the tables. Cover the pots in satin, or colored fabric, or colored foil paper and enhance them with ribbon or tulle bows.

Cake Top and Cake-Table Flowers

Many women don't like to place ceramic brides-and-grooms on top of their wedding cakes. They prefer a "cake crown" — a bouquet of fresh flowers coordinated to the colors of the cake. It's a refreshing, delightful alternative to that good old, ceramic bride-and-groom. Tell your florist if you also want flowers decorating your cake table.

THE FLORIST

How Far in Advance?

Finding a talented, affordable florist can take time and effort so begin your search early. It requires diligent legwork and research to find a good florist who suits your needs, tastes and budget. If the florist is extremely popular, it might be necessary to reserve as far as a year ahead. Once you find one, leave a deposit to hold the date.

How to Find a Florist

Price, although a factor, should not be a primary consideration in your choice of florist. The florist who arranges your flowers is selling you more than posies, they're selling you *talent* and *expertise.* You may, for example, buy a gown or invitations cheaper at one store than another. You may even haggle with the catering director and get "white-glove service" thrown into the deal, but talent and expertise have no price. These two intangible factors, more than any other, will make your wedding flowers beautiful. That's why it's so difficult to find a talented florist who won't break the bank.

Ask your recently married friends, business associates or relatives for referrals. If you don't know any newlyweds, call the organist at your temple or church. I've found these people very observant. They know who is dependable and who isn't, who shows up on time or doesn't show up at all. They also know beautiful flowers when they see them, since — after all — they attend a multitude of weddings.

Ask for recommendations from your catering director at the hotel, restaurant or club where you're having your reception. But be careful. Many are paid referral fees by the vendors they recommend. One catering director at a country club in our area refers a particular florist, even though this florist has been sued repeatedly by many disgruntled brides.

At receptions, entertainers set up their equipment at the same time florists decorate the rooms. So ask your band or orchestra leader or D.J. for a referral.

Flowers are too important to a wedding to trust to the *Yellow Pages.* Start making inquiries of friends, relatives and business associates, now!

Make a List

List names of florists referred to you by recently married friends, business associates or relatives along with referrals from your organist, band leader or catering director.

Florists who are duplicated on your list should have top priority. Call them first. Most floral shops employ at least one person who specializes in weddings. Ask if your date is available. If so, ask how many weddings are booked on the same day as yours. If the number seems excessive try someone else. Next, ask if they charge for a consultation. Some florists do and this can be expensive. If you reserve them, however, you should not have to pay for the consultation. The charge should be deducted from your bill.

Facts the Florist Needs to Know

Before you meet with florists to discuss details and finalize the cost, know the following information. It will save everyone a lot of time and make the florist's job easier:

1. The Ceremony

— Know the dimensions of the room and the length of the aisle.

— Know how many rows of pews or chairs extend down the aisle.

— Know how high the ceilings are.

— Know the color of the walls.

— Take snapshots to show the florist.

2. The Reception

— For the cocktail hour and reception know the dimensions of the rooms.

— Know the height of the ceilings.

— Know the color of the rooms.

— For the cocktail hour, know the size of the tables if you plan on having arrangements for them. If you need flowers for the hors d'oeuvres tables, know their sizes also.

— For the dinner, know the dimensions of the

tables where the guests will be seated, for example, 72-inch rounds or four-by-six rectangles. If you're going to be seated at a long table with your wedding party or only seated at a small table with the groom, know the dimensions.

— Know the sizes of buffet tables.

— Know the size of the place-card table if you'd like an arrangement for it.

— Know the size of the top layer of your cake if you'd like a cake crown. If you want flowers to decorate the cake table, tell the florist.

— If you want an arrangement for the ladies' room, know where it should go and the size it should be. Know the color of the linens you've selected. Ask your catering director, caterer or party rental store if you can borrow a napkin to use for a color sample.

— Know all restrictions, for example, no candles at the ceremony or reception sites, no aisle runners, and no taped bows on pews.

Discussing Details and Cost

It's now time to meet with prospective florists to discuss details and cost. At this meeting, you should see pictures of their wedding flowers. These pictures should include bridal and bridesmaids bouquets, boutonnieres, corsages, altar bouquets, church decorations and chuppot. There also should be pictures of centerpieces, either on the table or on risers — from the simple to the elaborate. If you like what you see, discuss your wedding flowers further with the florist. If you don't, excuse yourself and leave. *Do not look at professional floral books that do not contain actual pictures of weddings the florist has done.* If professional floral books are all they have to offer, go elsewhere.

If you like the pictures, however, discuss your wedding flowers in detail with the florist. Make sure these points are covered:

1. The date, the time and place of the ceremony and reception.

2. The formality of the wedding: Formal? Semi-Formal? Informal?

3. The ceremony:

   a. The restrictions of the church, ceremony site or synagogue. Wax candles and aisle runners, for example, or bows taped on pews or chairs may be prohibited.

   b. Flowers and decorations for the ceremony site. Do you want two altar arrangements? Do you want bows for the pews or chairs? Or, bows and flowers? Do you want an arch, and if so, do you want it decorated with tulle, flowers or both? Do you want candelabra at the altar or do you want to extend them down the aisle with flowers, bows or both? Do you want the first chairs or pews on either side of the aisle designated for the immediate family with bows, flowers or both? Do you need a chuppa? How do you want it decorated? Do you want an aisle runner? How long should it be?

   Are there any "dead" spots at the ceremony site that need flowers or trees? Are there any ugly walls or doors that need camouflage?

   c. The time allotted for set up before the ceremony and rip down once it's over. This tells the florist if the amount of decorating you want for the ceremony is feasible.

   d. When can we visit the ceremony site?

4. The bridal party:

   a. The bridal gown and its color. Bring a picture of the dress from a magazine or a Polaroid photo, so the florist can effectively style your bouquet.

b. The number of bridesmaids.

c. The bridesmaids dresses — their style and color(s). Bring a picture of the dress from a magazine or a Polaroid snapshot.

d. The flower girl(s) and ringbearer. How old are they? What are they wearing? What colors? Would you like the flower girl(s) to have a floral halo?

e. Besides the groom, the number of male attendants.

f. The color and type of dress the groom and male attendants are wearing?

g. The number of parents and grandparents (including step-parents and step-grandparents) attending.

h. Your flower preferences. For example, many women say, "I hate carnations," or "I love tea roses and snap dragons."

5. The reception:

a. Are you having a cocktail hour? Do you need floral arrangements either for the tables or the buffet?

b. How many guests do you anticipate? Most catering directors seat eight to 10 at a table. If you were having 100 people at your wedding, seating eight at a table, you'd need 13 centerpieces. If you sat 10 at a table, you'd need 10 centerpieces.

c. What type of centerpiece do you prefer? One that sits on the table? Or one that's on a lifter or riser?

d. What are your flower preferences?

e. Do you need any rental trees (with or without lights) for the reception room to fill the empty spaces, camouflage others or to brighten the room?

f. When can we visit the reception site?

After these questions are answered, the florist should be able to give you a price. If it's agreeable, ask if you can visit them on a day they're preparing for a wedding. Don't sign a contract or give them a deposit at this time.

If the price of the flowers is way over your budget, it's best to look for someone less expensive. If the price exceeds your budget by a couple hundred dollars, however, ask where you can cut. Many times you can get the "look" you want by substituting less expensive flowers. For example, altar bouquets for the ceremony need not be made of roses and orchids. Carnations, Star of Bethlehem, pompons, gladioli, curly willow and baby's breath will do the same job for a lot less money.

Let the florist make suggestions on how to cut the price. If you like his suggestions you're ready for the next step.

Visit the Florist on a Wedding Day

The next step is to visit the florist on a day they're preparing for a wedding. Look at the corsages, boutonnieres, bouquets, arrangements for the ceremony and centerpieces. Then ask yourself these important questions:

1. Do the flowers look fresh? Or are they drooping or wilted?

2. When I look at the bouquets and centerpieces, do I see a lot of flowers or do I see a lot of greens? It's important to notice the flowers, not the greens.

3. How big are the flowers? Smaller varieties are less expensive than larger varieties.

4. Are the corsages trimmed with pretty laces, pearls, rhinestones or ribbons?

5. Are the bouquets filled with flowers or a lot of

greens? Once again, it's important to see the flowers first.

6. Are the designs of the flowers — both bouquets and centerpieces — pleasing to me? Do I like them?

7. If you're seeing more than one wedding at the same time, are the designs of the bouquets and centerpieces different? Are the flowers varied? This is extremely important. Many florists who specialize in weddings tend to "package" them. Every week they use the same types of flowers and designs for the bouquets and centerpieces and change only the colors. If you think a florist is packaging the flowers, drop in a second time to make sure they're not. If you're happy with what you've seen, however, you may have found the florist of your dreams.

Booking the Florist and Deposits

If you like the florist's work, it's time to book him. This means leaving a deposit that will reserve your wedding date. Many florists ask for a 50-percent deposit with the balance due before the wedding. Be very leery of a florist or any vendor who demands early full payment, especially for a discount. If you give a florist a deposit put it on your credit card to protect yourself in case the florist goes out of business. But be sure to read the fine print of the contract. You might see the phrase, "Deposits are not refundable for any reason." If you see this clause in the contract, insist the florist give you credit for your deposit if the wedding is canceled and you agree to rebook the date with them. If the florist won't make the change, give him a small advance to hold the date, then three months before the wedding give him the balance of the deposit.

Hopefully, nothing will occur three months prior to the wedding that will cancel or postpone it.

The Role of the Florist on the Wedding Day

On the day of the wedding, the florist is responsible for bringing the flowers to the ceremony and decorating the site according to contract provisions. He is also responsible for delivering the flowers to the reception and decorating the site if contracted to do so.

After the ceremony and reception is over, he is responsible for retrieving all rental items, the chuppa, kneeling bench or rental trees, mirrors and votive candles.

He should make sure that all corsages and boutonnieres are labeled — Mother of the Bride, for example, or Uncle Henry — no matter how large or small the wedding is. If you're spending a bundle with this florist, it's advisable that one of his employees be at the ceremony to pin on corsages and boutonnieres, and show the bridesmaids and bride how to carry their bouquets. It's also important to have the florist at the ceremony in case someone is left out, a favorite aunt, for example. I can't tell you how many weddings I've been to where the bride will say, "Oh my God — there's Aunt Hilda — I completely forgot about her!" A florist on the scene can whip out a corsage or boutonniere in no time. If not, you've got an embarrassing situation on your hands.

The Contract

Make sure the contract lists:

1. The date of the wedding, the time and place of the ceremony, and the time and place of the reception. The time the flowers will be delivered to the ceremony and reception.

The wedding of my mother-in-law and father-in-law, Agnes Ventimiglia to Mr. Francesco Gallo, October 8, 1921.

2. All the bridal-party flowers (including flowers for the immediate families) and flowers and extras for the ceremony — candelabra, rental trees, chuppa, etc.

3. All the flowers and extras for the reception, including arrangements for the cocktail hour, the buffet tables and the dining tables, and all extras, including mirrors, for example, and votive candles.

4. All *types* of flowers used and their colors. If the centerpieces are to contain pink and white roses, pink and white snap dragons, pink alstroemeria, pink mini-carnations and baby's breath, make sure the *colors* and *types* of flowers used are stated in the contract. Watch wording like "pink and white flowers" or you might end up with pink and white carnations.

5. All decorations for the ceremony and reception. Make sure they are listed in detail on the contract.

6. All delivery and set-up charges if any.

7. Cancellation policy.

And Finally - Preserving the Bridal Bouquet

Today's bouquets can be freeze-dried, although it's very expensive. If it's your intention to have your bouquet freeze-dried after the wedding, tell your florist in advance. Such bouquets can't be prepped with preservatives. A cheaper method is to wrap the bouquet in a brown paper bag and leave it on the bottom shelf of the refrigerator. Don't make the refrigerator colder since icy temperatures damage flowers. Leave the bouquet for three weeks. Then take it out of the bag and hang in a dry, cool room.

There's no guarantee that your bouquet will dry beautifully preserved. Some flowers take well to drying, others don't. But it's fun to give it a try.

SAVING MONEY

— For a Catholic ceremony, have one bouquet on either side of the altar. For a Protestant ceremony, have one large bouquet on the altar. If you're having a Jewish wedding use a traditional chuppa — four poles covered with a cloth — preferably one that has significant meaning to you and your fiancé, or have the florist cover a chuppa in tulle or satin. Put one bouquet on each side of the chuppa.

The flowers for ceremony arrangements should be inexpensive — carnations, pompons, Star of Bethlehem, gladioli, fuji mums — and for a touch of the dramatic, curly willow. At the ceremony, the "look" is the most important factor. It can be achieved inexpensively.

— Ask your church, hotel or temple if it has candelabra that you can use for your ceremony. If so, make large bows and drape them on the candelabra. Place them on either side of the altar or chuppa.

— Make your own bows. Place them the entire way down the aisle, skipping every other row, or every second or third, depending on the length of the aisle. Rubber bands are an easy way to attach bows to pews or chairs.

— If your ceremony site has a center aisle (with aisles on either side of the pews or chairs), an inexpensive aisle runner can be used to achieve a dramatic effect. Before the ceremony, have a friend pull the runner down the center aisle and cut and tape it where the chairs or pews end. Then rope off the aisle with a piece of tulle or satin ribbon. Guests enter and are seated from the sides.

Imagine your friends and family entering the ceremony. They're greeted by a beautiful, elegant aisle framed by chairs or pews decorated with white-satin or tulle bows. The graceful aisle runner has been extended, and the center aisle has been roped off for the exclusive use of the bridal party. After all the guests are seated, an usher removes the "rope" and the mothers of the bride and groom are escorted up the aisle. Then the procession starts.

TIP: If friends are decorating your ceremony site, be sure they start at least an hour-and-a-half before the ceremony begins. Make sure there are enough people decorating to finish the job in time.

— Bridal-Party Flowers. Don't skimp on the bridal bouquet. Design it with the florist to match the style of your dress and your size. Use a rose

A formal blooming orchid "tree" — an incredible centerpiece for the formal wedding.

boutonniere for the groom, fathers and grandfathers. Use roses for corsages for the mothers and grandmothers. Use carnations for the groomsmen. Have the bridesmaids carry one rose, flanked by ribbons, greens and baby's breath, provided their dresses aren't formal. If they are, have them carry an orchid or two framed by greens such as aspidistra and dotted with rhinestones or pearls. These bouquets give a very formal look but aren't expensive. Have the flower girl carry a basket of mini-carnations or pompons decorated with ribbons to match her dress.

— Flowers and Decorations for the Cocktail Hour. Many clubs, hotels and restaurants provide their own decorations for the cocktail hour. These may include ice sculptures or a fountain for the buffet, or large, potted plants or trees which are placed around the room. Many places also provide small hurricane lamps for the cocktail tables. When meeting with your catering director or caterer be sure to ask.

— Flowers and Decorations for the Reception. Centerpieces are a must for a semi-formal or formal reception. Whether they be flowers, plants or candles, *something* should be on the tables to make them look festive. Flowering plants can be bought from nurseries or even your local discount department store. These can be placed in colored "foil hats" purchased from florist supply companies. (Found in your *Yellow Pages* under "Floral Supplies, Wholesale," many of these companies sell to the public.) The plants can then be placed on mirrors (rented from any number of party rental companies found in the phone book) and surrounded by votive candles, once again rented

from a party rental store. When you're at the floral supply company buy a can of "leaf shine." This stuff can turn any dirty leafed plant into one of shining glory. Just spray the leaves with it.

In Conclusion

Flowers make a wedding beautiful. Do your legwork and budget your floral dollars from the beginning. Put time and effort into planning your flowers for your ceremony, the bridal party and the reception. Flowers are a matter of taste and preference. They should relate to your personality, and their style and color should be just like you — either bold and beautiful, soft and subtle, or somewhere in between.

That's why it's so important to shop diligently for a good, talented florist; one who meets your needs, tastes and budget. The results will be worth it.

The Romantic Meaning of Flowers:

White Carnation — remember me
Carnation — pure love
Daisies — share your feelings
Holly — domestic happiness
Honeysuckle — faithfulness
Ivy — fidelity
Purple lilac — first love
White lilac — innocence
Lilies — purity
Orange Blossom — fertility, happiness
Orchid — you are beautiful
Red Rose — I love you
White Rose — you're heavenly
Red and White Roses together — unity
Violet — modesty

A bridesmaids bouquet of Cattleya orchids, Dendrobium orchids, roses, aspidistra and bear grass make a unique, elegant, colorful bouquet.

Wedding Gowns and Bridesmaids Dresses

*M*ODERN BRIDE once conducted a survey of engaged women. The majority stated that the most enjoyable thing about planning their wedding was shopping for their gown.

Selecting the right gown is a unique, personal experience, and for many, one to be shared with a mother. Many mothers of brides burst into tears when their daughters try on the "perfect" dress. One bridal shop in Fort Lauderdale, Florida, gives mothers of brides (in the business called M.O.B.s) a little card that says, "When the mother of the bride cries, you know her daughter has found the perfect gown."

Shopping for a wedding gown should take thought, time and effort. It's important to find the best gown for your figure and one that fits your personality. It's also imperative that the style of gown you choose is appropriate for your wedding type.

Few wedding gowns and bridesmaids dresses are purchased off-the-rack. Instead, they are *ordered*. Stores carry one dress per style, usually in a size 10. If you're not a 10, shopping for a wedding gown or bridesmaids dresses can be difficult. To make your task easier, pay close attention to the information in this chapter *before* you begin to shop for your wedding gown and bridesmaids dresses.

IN GENERAL

The Time Factor

Most wedding gowns and bridesmaids dresses are delivered within three months. But some take longer. For that reason, give yourself enough time when ordering them. If your wedding gown or bridesmaids dresses arrive only a couple of weeks before the wedding, in the wrong color or in the wrong size, the manufacturer might not have time to make replacements. I advise ordering a wedding gown at least six months in advance. This allows you plenty of time for alterations and the selection of your headpiece, veil and accessories.

Order your bridesmaids dresses at least five

This simple, elegant gown is perfect for a semi-formal wedding.

months in advance, especially if they must be shipped to women living out of town. This gives them ample time to have the dresses altered.

Selecting the Right Wedding Gown

Buy all *current* issues of the following bridal magazines: *For the Bride by Demetrios, BRIDE'S, Modern Bride, Elegant Bride, Bridal Guide* and *Brides Today.* All major manufacturers advertise most of their latest styles in these magazines — wedding gowns as well as bridesmaids dresses. Mark the pages of the wedding gowns that appeal to you.

Next, analyze the gowns you've selected. What do you like about them? Start with the neckline. Do you prefer it high, low, or off-the-shoulder? What about sleeves — short or long — with a *pouf* or without, inset, or no sleeves at all? (Illustrations that define terms are found in this chapter.) Look at the waistline. Do you like a dropped waist — one falling approximately three inches below the waistline? Or do you prefer the waistline falling into a graceful "V" at the center of the gown where the bodice meets the skirt? Do you like an empire line? Or princess?

Next look at the skirt. Do you prefer a full skirt, A-line, mermaid (a straight dress which flares at the knee), or sheath? Now focus on the trains. Do you prefer them short (sweep), medium (chapel), or long (cathedral)? And what about the beading? Do you like a dress heavily beaded — or with moderate or minimal beading?

Next, cut the pictures out of the magazines. Label each one with the magazine's name, the issue, date and page number, i.e. *BRIDE'S,* April-May, 19__ , page 235. If there is no page number, find the numbered page closest to your picture.

Count backward or forward to your picture to get the page number. This is extremely important. If the retailer doesn't have the dress in stock or information about it on hand, he can call the manufacturer and simply ask for the style number and price of the gown advertised in that issue.

Your Wedding Gown and the Season

Look at pictures of gowns you've cut from magazines. Are the styles you've chosen appropriate to your wedding season? A winter wedding in New York would require a long-sleeved gown. A short, capped sleeve would look and feel out of place. By the same token, a high-necked, long-sleeved, heavy-satin gown would be inappropriate for a summer wedding in San Antonio.

Many clients ask if tulle or organza gowns are proper for fall or winter weddings. They are if they have long sleeves or the bride wears long gloves.

Your Wedding Gown and Your Wedding Type

If you are having a formal wedding, your gown should be formal. It may be a traditional gown with fitted, ornately beaded bodice, full skirt and chapel, cathedral or "royal" train — one more than six feet in length. Or it may be a simple but elegant designer gown — perhaps a sheath made of fine silk with minimal beading, but with a train.

A semi-formal gown requires a simpler look. It shouldn't be as heavily beaded or ornate as a gown worn for a formal wedding. For a morning or afternoon wedding, the gown should be made of raw silk, or taffeta, or light-weight satin. Beads and glitz should be kept to a minimum. The train should be chapel length.

An informal wedding requires a look that suits the occasion — whether in a church, a penthouse apartment or on the beach. You may wear a simple gown with sweep train, or a cocktail dress, or for a beach party, you may decide to wear a swimsuit with wrap skirt.

Your Wedding Gown and Your Ceremony Site

Your ceremony site should figure significantly in your choice of a wedding gown. For a formal wedding in a small chapel, you might choose an ornate wedding gown *but with chapel-length train.* For an informal wedding in this same chapel, you might wear a simple tea-length lace dress, or a long dress with a sweep train, or no train at all.

No matter where you marry — in a restaurant, hotel, temple or church — the formality of the wedding dictates the style of the dress. An afternoon brunch would indicate a light-weight dress with minimal beading and chapel train. A semi-formal evening wedding at a hotel or restaurant would suggest a gown with more glitz — with chapel train. And for a formal, evening affair the sky's the limit — although the length of your train should be in proportion to the length of the aisle. A cathedral train could look ridiculous at a hotel or restaurant if the aisle is only twenty-five feet long. Your catering director should be able to advise you on the length of the aisle.

Your Wedding Gown and Your Body Type

It's essential to choose a wedding gown that is most flattering to your body type. Study the information and look at the illustrations in this chapter. Determine which body type you are. Then consider styles of gowns that would most flatter your figure. Do pictures of gowns you've selected from the magazines match the styles that would most enhance your particular body type?

When selecting a wedding gown use common sense. You know what type of clothes look best on you. Use your experience to your best advantage *for this most special day.* If you're thin and tall, and look terrific in fitted blouses and tight skirts, you might choose a wedding gown that's a sheath. If you're big busted and wear loose clothes to camouflage it, an off-the-shoulder dress with a portrait collar will give the illusion of a smaller bustline. If you're thin hipped, a full skirt will disguise the problem. A full skirt, on the other hand, also will hide large hips. If you're short, a sheath will make you look taller. If you're tall and well

Extended cathedral train with bustle at waist, cut-out back, Juliet sleeve.

proportioned, any style may look good. Choosing the right wedding gown will be a tough decision to make.

Your Size and The Size of Your Wedding Gown

If you're petite and thin be careful when selecting a gown. I've seen many small, thin clients insist on choosing off-the-shoulder gowns with huge skirts and trains. Heavy, off-the-shoulder gowns and small angular bodies don't mix — the dresses don't stay up. *Big* wedding gowns weigh a ton, especially if made of satin. If you're small,

Watteau train, sweetheart neck, pouf sleeve with a mitten, princess line with trumpet skirt. (Opposite): This sexy off-the-shoulder sheath is perfect for the sophisticated bride.

choose a gown made of light-weight raw silk or taffeta or light-weight satin. Avoid a cathedral train and instead select a gown with a chapel train, or a sheath with a detachable train. If you do decide to wear a *big* gown, make sure the sleeves are high on the shoulders to help keep the dress up.

Another key factor is the overall size of the dress. If you're small and thin, choose a dress proportionate to your size. Make sure it doesn't overpower you. You don't want to look like an igloo sliding up the aisle. It's important that people see you in the gown. If you're stocky, choose a simple gown made of light-weight fabrics. Stay away from heavy beading and lace that adds weight to your frame. Watch big sleeves that may broaden your shoulders. Lean toward full skirts that can work miracles by hiding large hips and avoid straight skirts that emphasize them. Once again, consider the overall size of the dress. Chances are if it's big and heavy, it will make you look bigger and heavier.

Manufacturers and Price

Many brides have preconceived notions about gown manufacturers and prices. Often they come into my store with pictures from bridal magazines asking, "Do you have something like this — but affordable?" Then they'll show me, for example, a picture of a moderately priced gown that they thought was expensive.

Be aware that many top-line designers make less expensive lines. Ilissa features the Princess Collection, Sposaeuropa, and Sposabella along with its very inexpensive but beautiful Boutique Collection. Jim Jhelm offers a less expensive line called JH, and Paula Varsalona offers In Vogue.

Even Galina has a less expensive line called Bouquet.

Buying a gown from a top manufacturer does not necessarily mean you must spend a lot, especially if you stick to their less expensive lines. What it does signify is that you're purchasing a fine dress with a premium name.

If you find an expensive dress that doesn't fit your budget, remember that most manufacturers copy each other. Shop until you find a less expensive copy.

Should I have My Gown and Bridesmaids Dresses Made?

Many people mistakenly believe having dresses made is cheaper than buying ready-to-wear. But fabrics, laces and beads used in wedding gowns are extremely expensive. Most gowns today are made outside the United States where manufacturers are able to buy yard goods, laces and beads at a fraction of the cost they pay here. That's why Mori Lee, for example, can make an elaborate wedding gown covered in lace and beads inexpensively.

And what about labor? It's no easy task to make a wedding gown. If a seamstress agreed to make your gown for $10 per hour and she estimated that it would take 120 hours to make (three weeks — not much time), your labor cost would be $1,200.

And please, consider the stress factor. Staging a wedding is an enormous task. You'll have enough on your mind, let alone worrying about the seamstress and *if* she got your sleeves on right. The same is true for bridesmaids dresses. If you're considering having them made, think about five or six hard-to-please, screaming bridesmaids calling you to complain after every fitting. You might change your mind.

THE PARTICULARS
How to Shop for Your Gown

Take the pictures you've cut from magazines to a bridal shop. Show them to the bridal consultant and ask if those particular gowns are available. If not, ask for something similar to try on.

Let the bridal consultant advise you on what she thinks might look best on you, even if it differs from what you want. Keep yourself open to

Bertha collar, long torso, intermission-length skirt. (Opposite): An intricate, unique lace turns a traditional gown into one of rare beauty.

her ideas but don't be a slave to them. Take some-one with you whose judgement you trust and who will give you an honest opinion. Perhaps your mother or your maid of honor would be ideal. Be very leery of a sales person who says you look good in everything.

Some shops do not make their stock available to their customers. The consultants choose the gowns for you to try on, based on your sugges-tions and their taste. This denies you access to their dresses. If you happen to find yourself in one of these stores, *always check the price of gowns*

Fichu collar, asymmetrical bishop sleeve, draped waist, full skirt. (Opposite): A dropped waist and illusion neckline with plenty of lace and pearls makes this the perfect formal or semi-formal wedding gown.

before you try them. If the price exceeds your budget, advise the consultant that you would pre-fer to spend your time trying on gowns within your price range. Don't frustrate yourself by try-ing dresses you cannot afford. Always try to stay within your budget.

Shop Style

The first time you shop *think style.* See what styles look best on you. Worry about beading, fab-rics and trains later. Do not buy the first gown you try on. Go to different shops and try on sever-al dresses. If you like a gown, jot down what you find appealing about it while your thoughts are fresh. Later you can analyze dresses you liked and decide which is best for you and your wedding type, your wedding season, your figure and your budget.

Not All Brides Wear White

The white wedding gown as a tradition is fairly new, originating in Victorian England where white was worn exclusively by wealthy brides to flaunt their money. Their message: "I'm rich enough to wear a dress *only* once." Dry-cleaning being what it was in Victorian England, very few people wore white. White as a symbol of purity did not evolve until much later.

At the time of the American Revolution, American brides wore red. Today, Hindus and Chinese wear red when they marry. Brides from different cultures around the world wear colors reflecting their ethnic heritage. It seems, however, that white for American brides is here to stay, although its symbolism has changed. White today means joy and celebration as well as purity and virginity.

The White Wedding Gown and You

Most women buy white wedding gowns. If your skin, however, appears sallow or washed-out in white, consider a gown in ivory, candle-light or "blush" (a soft color leaning towards pink or peach). These colors are very flattering to pale skin.

The first question to ask is, "Do I look good in white?" If not, don't buy a white dress. Ivory, can-dlelight, or blush is as beautiful and elegant as white for a wedding. (Be sure to look at swatches from manufacturers to make sure their color of ivory, candlelight, or blush suits you.) But be aware that if you choose a gown in a color other than white, there may be an additional charge for the color change.

My advice is to choose the color that most flat-ters you. If you're really intent on buying a white gown, even if it makes you look like Snow White, choose one with an off-the-shoulder neckline so that the white color is away from your face.

Fabrics

The gown's fabric affects both its beauty and price. Most medium- to low-priced gowns are made from synthetic, affordable fabrics and thank goodness they are. Otherwise, the cost of most wedding gowns would be prohibitive. A bride watching her pocketbook would be hard pressed to find a beautiful, traditional wedding gown with its yards and yards of sleek white satin, if that gown weren't made from synthetic fabric. These beautiful, man-made fabrics ensure that every bride, no matter what her budget, can afford the gown of her dreams.

When considering a wedding dress always ask the salesperson what the fabric is. A typical response would be, "satin," "taffeta," or "silk." You then should ask, *"What type of satin, taffeta, or silk?"* Most wedding gowns are made of synthetic satin or taffeta, and some are made of a man-made fabric that looks like raw silk, with its tiny lines and little bumps. Silk, too, comes in many varieties. There is silk-satin, silk-taffeta and raw silk, also known as shantung. Even tulle and organza can be made from silk. If you are consid-ering the purchase of an expensive gown, it better be made of *silk*.

Gowns made from synthetic fabrics whether they be satin, Italian satin (that doesn't have a

Jewel neck, padded shoulder, long, fitted sleeve, Watteau train, soft flared skirt. (Opposite): The pièce de résistance! An awesome sheath studded with beads makes the perfect bride.

shine), taffeta or tulle are always white-white in color. Silk gowns are always slightly off-white because silk is a natural fabric. That pure white color characteristic of man-made fabrics is not found in nature.

It's only logical that a wedding gown made of synthetic fabric should cost less than a silk gown, but this isn't always the case. A gown made from synthetic fabric that is heavily beaded may be more expensive than a simple silk gown. Silk gowns are cooler because silk breathes, while man-made fabrics don't. If it's always been your dream to have a silk gown but you thought they were too expensive, take heart! Today many companies are making raw-silk gowns at moderate prices.

Beading - Beware

If you're considering an inexpensive or moderately priced gown, be sure the beads on the dress are sewn rather than glued on. Glued-on beads tend to fall off. Dresses with glued-on beads also can't be steamed or pressed.

Trains

As mentioned before, the length of the train you select should be based solely on your wedding type. Formal weddings require gowns with long (royal or cathedral) or medium (chapel) length trains. Most sheath gowns come with detachable trains in varying lengths. A semi-formal wedding requires a train of chapel or shorter length. Gowns for informal weddings, however, don't normally have trains, although a sweep train is acceptable.

Lace and Definition

If you're choosing an expensive gown appliqued with beautiful lace, think about having the dress made in two colors. The reason is simple. If you put white lace over white fabric, the two seem to blend together, making it difficult to see or appreciate the beautiful patterns, beading and embroidery of the lace unless you're standing next to the gown. But put white lace over an ivory dress, or ivory lace over a white one, and the lace comes alive. The contrast in colors between the gown and the lace *defines* the lace and enhances its beauty. In my opinion, there's nothing more elegant. Many companies will not charge you to change the color of the lace on the dress. Others will, so be sure to ask.

Know the Manufacturer

Once you've decided on a gown, ask your bridal shop consultant who the manufacturer is, if you haven't already been told. This is extremely important. You don't want to buy a "knocked-off" gown (a copy). If the store won't tell you who manufactured the gown you're interested in, look through current and past issues of bridal magazines to find it. (Some libraries carry bridal magazines. If yours doesn't, ask recently married or engaged friends for their back issues.) Manufacturers advertise most of their gowns in these magazines.

If you don't find the dress in magazines (look through the past year's issues), go to other stores to see if they have the gown. If they don't, and you can't find the gown in a magazine, it's probably a knock-off. Be aware that stores that sell

Opposite: This wedding gown is really a sparkling mini with a wrap skirt.

knock-offs may sell them for as much or more than the original. The same holds true for bridesmaids dresses.

HEADPIECES AND VEILS

Selecting the Right Headpiece

Once you've selected your gown, it's time to select the headpiece and veil. Put your gown on — then try on headpieces and veils, because it's important that the two be coordinated. You may decide to choose a simple headpiece if your gown is ornate, one that will maximize the impact of your dress; or you may choose an ornate headpiece, one to match your ornate gown. It's all a matter of taste. Never buy a headpiece and veil in street clothes. I guarantee that what you'd choose while dressed in jeans and T-shirt would *not be what you'd buy if dressed in your gown*. It's important that the two — gown and headpiece — look like they belong together. Color should be the same. Fabrics should be the same. You wouldn't wear a silk gown and a satin headpiece, for example. One's shiny and one isn't. Beading on the headpiece also should be similar to the beading on the dress. If there are a lot of pearls on the dress, the headpiece also should be pearled. If there are a lot of crystals on the gown, your headpiece should have crystals, too. If your gown is simple, choose a simple headpiece. If you have a small face, be careful of on-the-forehead headpieces that may overpower you. A headpiece should complement your face, not overwhelm it.

Many women decide to wear crowns or tiaras. These should be worn only by those wearing formal wedding gowns. Hats also make popular headpieces. They're suitable for all types of weddings. They may be Juliet or pill-box or have large

Floor length full skirt, off-the-shoulder neckline, short capped sleeve, basque waist. (Opposite): Unique lace and beads make this wedding gown the height of sophistication and beauty.

brims with veils attached. They may also be covered in satin, silk, lace or organza to match your dress.

Selecting the Right Veil

After choosing your headpiece, choose the veil. Most headpieces come with veils attached, but these are easily changeable if you like the headpiece but don't like the veils. It's very easy for a seamstress to make a cathedral veil from tulle if you'd prefer it, or to cut a cathedral veil to shoulder length. It all depends on you and the formality of your wedding gown. Veils come in four lengths.

Shoulder Length: Reaching the shoulders and appropriate for a floor-length dress without train, or a gown with a "sweep" train.

Bow-Length: This veil reaches the bow on the back of the dress, or the waistline if the dress has no bow. It may be worn with a semi-formal dress with train or a formal dress with train. Many women who buy formal gowns don't like to hide the beautiful bows on the backs of their dresses or the beading on their trains. Either way, this veil is the perfect choice.

Finger-tip: This veil reaches to the end of the fingers, mid-thigh. I find it to be the least attractive.

Mermaid, illusion neck, high collar, draped sleeve, chapel train. (Opposite): A traditional gown with full, long sleeves and bustle, has long been the dream of brides throughout the ages.

It seems to fall in an awkward spot about a foot-and-a-half below the waistline.

Cathedral: This veil comes to the end of the train or slightly beyond and is only worn with a formal wedding gown.

The Blusher

The blusher is the veil that covers the face. It symbolizes youth, purity and virginity. *It is the prerogative of the first-time bride.* Blushers also come in different lengths. A "bird-cage" is a blusher that covers the face and stops at the base of the chin. Most blushers, however, stop at the bustline. Be careful of the length of the blusher. One that's too short, or too long, can look ridiculous.

The Importance of Poufs

A pouf is a puffy piece of tulle attached to the back of the headpiece. It's designed to give a bride height and provides a heavenly back-drop for her face and headpiece (it looks like a cloud). The pouf, however, should not be so large as to overwhelm her. If the bride decides to wear only her headpiece for the reception, it's also nice to keep the pouf. Tulle makes the bride.

Velcro and Bridal Veils

Many bridal veils are attached to headpieces and hats with velcro — many blushers also are. This makes them easy to remove after the ceremony. Cathedral veils, for example, might look beautiful for the ceremony and photos, but are impractical for the reception. Velcro solves the problem. Once you remove your veils, you still have a beautiful headpiece (with or without pouf) to wear at the reception.

If your headpiece comes with veils attached, and you would prefer to remove them after the ceremony, ask the seamstress at the bridal shop to cut them off and put them back on with velcro. This is a simple procedure.

SECOND WEDDINGS

Love and Marriage: The Second Time Around

Some beautiful sentiments about second weddings are in a book I cherish, "The Passionate Palate" by Jeanine Larmoth. I'd like to share them with you:

"Love may not be better the second time around, but the second wedding is bound to be. What the bride loses in maiden blushes, everybody gains in a good time. The big church around the corner gives place to the little white church in the country, a jewel-box chapel, a penthouse terrace, a mountain lodge surrounded by snow, every tree branch iced, or a friend's unruly garden — any number more imaginative and suitable settings. The vast hordes of unloved relatives and old family friends, who must be invited to the first wedding or be offended, are replaced by the most select gathering of the tried and true. The unflattering white dress, later to be mummified in the closet for a daughter who wouldn't wear it on a bet, becomes, rather, a flattering, outrageously expensive black silk, sprigged with flowers, that will be worn with pleasure till it falls apart, or long, flowing ash-blond crepe to match the bride's hair. The wedding is followed by a great luncheon served European-style at a long table, by a banquet *cum* picnic on the lawn, or *cum* whatever is elegant and gay… Gone the suffocation of love by protocol, the family wrangles over

Contessa neckline, three-quarter fitted sleeve, empire waist, cathedral train and veil.

precedence, the wounded vanities, the terrible, and generally regretted, expenditures…"

"A woman who has failed and gone back to try again, to whom life has come less easily, is mellower, more womanly, more likely to come to terms with herself."* My translation: the second time around — do it *your* way.

Choosing a Dress for a Second Wedding

Be yourself. Let your personality shine through. Don't wear traditional garb — the same kind you wore when you *married someone else.* Skip the

* Footnotes see page 356

white gown, the train, the veil. They are the realm of the first-time bride, as well they should be. Have a fun wedding, enjoy it and let your dress reflect your personality and the type of party you plan to have. Buy something you can wear again.

Choose a hat or simple headpiece. Or wear a beaded headpiece decorated with small poufs of tulle. But *no* veil and *no* blusher. They symbolize purity and virginity.

The same advice holds true for your attendant. A second-or-more-time bride should have *only* her best friend by her side. Her maid of honor's dress should also reflect the mood of the party, should not be a satin bridesmaid gown and should be something she can wear again

THE FINAL ANALYSIS

— Make sure gowns you're considering are appropriate for your wedding season — summer, fall, winter or spring.

— Make sure gowns you're considering are appropriate for your wedding type, whether it be formal, semi-formal or informal.

— Make sure dresses you're considering are flattering to your figure. Use your experience with clothing styles that look best on you, and use common sense.

— Make sure the color you select is the most flattering to your skin tone.

— Make sure gowns you're considering fit your budget. If they're too expensive, keep looking until you find *the* dress, the one that fulfills your dreams without flattening your wallet. This shouldn't be too difficult. There are more than one hundred major manufacturers in the bridal industry.

— Know who manufactured your gown. Be sure you're not buying a copy.

— Give yourself plenty of time. Order your gown, if possible, at least six months in advance.

— Make sure the color, fabric and beads on your headpiece match your gown.

— Make sure that your headpiece and veil match the formality of your gown.

BRIDESMAIDS DRESSES

Who Selects the Bridesmaids Dresses?

The bride! Take *only* your maid of honor or your mother with you to select the dresses. I have seen brides made crazy by bridesmaids who

High neckline, cold shoulder, asymmetrical waist, draped wrap skirt, sweep train.

couldn't make up their minds about which dress was right for them. It's your wedding and your choice.

When to Order Bridesmaids Dresses

Order the gowns at least five months in advance, especially if the dresses must be mailed to out-of-town bridesmaids.

The Season and the Color of Your Bridesmaids Dresses

You must relate your wedding season to the color you select for your bridesmaids dresses. Are you being married in the fall or winter? Look at the Color Wheels in the Flowers chapter. Wheel One shows bright, bold, primary, secondary and intermediate colors. These colors relate to fall and winter. Think of Christmas, and you think red and green. Think Thanksgiving, and you think of the rich yellow of wheat ready for harvest and the tantalizing orange of the pumpkin. The colors of your wedding should blend harmoniously with the colors of the season.

Wheel Two shows *tints*. Tints are variations of the colors found in Wheel One. These colors relate to the spring and summer — the cool lime of sherbet on a hot day or the Wedgwood blue of a perfect sky.

To properly coordinate your wedding, always relate your wedding colors to colors appropriate to the season.

The Importance of "Background" Color

Bridesmaids dresses also must be color coordinated to your ceremony site. This is extremely important. I once attended a wedding at a hotel that had walls covered with paisley wallpaper in

High neck halter, long torso, with flounce. (Opposite): Simple, elegant brocades are perfect for semi-formal weddings.

varying colors of mauve and blue. The bridesmaids wore bright blue, orchid, fuchsia and green floral prints. What a disaster. Imagine what the photos looked like.

If the walls at your ceremony site are covered in a floral print, or a Southwestern design or paisley, the best choice is a plain bridesmaid's dress in a color that won't antagonize the wall colors. Wall color provides the *background* color for your dresses. Make sure they're compatible if you want beautiful photographs. The photographer always takes posed shots of the bride and groom, bridal party and families in the ceremony room after the wedding. For this reason, your bridal party must be color coordinated to your ceremony room.

Many clients ask me about carpet color and the color they're considering for bridesmaids dresses. "The carpet at the church is red and I want orchid dresses — what are we going to do?" Put down an aisle runner and don't worry about the carpet! Your guests are going to be too busy looking at the beautiful bride and bridal party to notice the color of the carpet. For more on background color and ceremony sites, see Flowers chapter.

Bridesmaids Dresses and Formality

Nothing looks so out of sync as bridesmaids dresses that don't match the bridal gown in style

Gauntlet gloves, decolletage, four-point dropped waist, sweep train. (Opposite): Lace has always had charm and what could be more magnificent than a gown with a lace bodice and train.

or the formality of the wedding. At a formal wedding, for example, the bridesmaids dresses must be long or tea-length. They may be glitzy, or ornate, or made of rich fabrics — their colors coordinating to the season and the *background* color of the ceremony site. They may also be black or black and white.

A semi-formal wedding, on the other hand, requires a less formal look for the bridesmaids. A wedding held in the early afternoon means they can wear cotton prints or short dresses or suits. They may also wear long or tea-length gowns providing they aren't glitzy, iridescent taffeta or black. Satin, taffeta, light brocades or shantung are good fabric choices. A semi-formal wedding held late afternoon or evening follows the same rules as those for a formal wedding, except the bridesmaids shouldn't be dressed in black or black and white. Those colors are best reserved for formal weddings.

The Bridesmaids Dress That Can Be Worn Again

As weddings become more lavish and elegant, bridesmaids dresses are becoming sleeker and more sophisticated. Practicality also is entering the picture and manufacturers are producing dresses that (with a few simple alterations) can be worn for other occasions. I think this trend is here to stay.

The most simple and elegant of these designs are the two-piece suits. These suits are a great buy for bridesmaids, many of whom are accustomed to throwing money down the drain for dresses they'll never wear again. These suits are elegant, beautiful and practical, and make a welcome addition to any woman's wardrobe.

Junior Bridesmaids

Junior bridesmaids are girls between the ages of eight and 18, who are too old to be flower girls and too young to be bridesmaids. This may pose a problem, because the dresses you select for them must not be ornate or too sophisticated. The best thing to do is put them in youthful dresses in the same color, or color family, that you've chosen for your bridesmaids. If the bridesmaids are wearing fuchsia, for example, have them wear fuchsia or dusty-rose. Alfred Angelo makes many dresses appropriate for younger women in a variety of styles and colors.

Flower Girls

Although flower girls are between the ages of four and eight, a tall, gangly, eight-year-old might look out of place. By the same token, don't choose a child younger than four. Somehow they don't understand what a flower girl is supposed to do, which is walk up the aisle carrying — not throwing — flowers. Be careful when making your choice.

A flower girl may be dressed in a gown similar to the bride either in white, ivory or blush. Or, she may be dressed like the bridesmaids (providing their gowns aren't too sophisicated) or she may wear a simple but elegant cotton dress.

A Word of Advice

Junior bridesmaids and flower girls are young. Make sure they look it. Don't style their hair in "beehives" and don't have a makeup artist turn them into little Cleopatras. Don't put them in black lamé dresses. They should look sweet and innocent. They are children.

If you have a child with a skin problem, camouflage it with makeup. I once handled a wedding

Sheath, portait collar, long, fitted sleeve, basque waist, detachable train. (Opposite): A sexy but traditional tulle gown makes for a heavenly bride.

where the flower girl was so nervous she broke into a rash. Neither her mother nor the photographer did anything about it. The bride, however, was so incensed after seeing the pictures — the flower girl looked like she had measles — that she made the photographer air-brush all the photos where the child appeared — at his expense. She felt he should have *known* to put makeup on the girl before he took the pictures. Moral of the story: be prepared. You might not have a photographer who's so agreeable.

Bridesmaids Dresses and Deposits

Most bridal stores will require a 50-percent deposit before ordering bridesmaids dresses. After you select a gown, get the deposit money from your bridesmaids. Many brides advance the money for bridesmaids dresses, never to be reimbursed. This can cause hard feelings and friction between the bride and her attendants.

ORDERING GOWNS

The "Size Discrepancy Dilemma"

Ordering the correct size for your bridal gown or bridesmaids dresses can be a frustrating experience.

Sweetheart neck, padded shoulder with epaulettes, long, fitted sleeve, full skirt with reddingote. (Skirt over skirt that's detachable.) (Opposite): This Watters and Watters bridesmaid gown is perfect for a formal wedding.

Most shops carry sample gowns in a size 10. If you're not a size 10, you're going to have to use your imagination when selecting your wedding dress. It can be difficult to envision yourself in a gown that doesn't fit. Always take along your mother or maid of honor to get an honest opinion.

If you are smaller than a 10, have the consultant pin the gown on you to determine the fit. If you are larger than a 10, get into the dress as best you can. Once you've made your decision, the bridal salon will order the gown in your size. Most of the time, the size the shop advises you to buy won't be the size you normally wear and chances are (horror of horrors), they'll advise you to order a larger size. And here's where the fireworks begin.

I call this phenomenon the Size Discrepancy Dilemma, and it's caused so many problems for clients and retailers, that I feel it deserves a detailed explanation. How many times have I heard, "If I wear a size 10, why do you want me to order a 12?" The answer is simple: each manufacturer in the bridal industry has its own size chart, and individual ideas of what measurements constitute their sizes. For that reason, you must rely solely on your measurements and the manufacturer's size chart to determine the size you should order for your wedding gown and bridesmaids dresses — not on the size you buy when shopping in a department or retail store. Take a look at the size charts on page 289. One is from Ilissa, one from Bridal Originals. Notice anything unusual? They're not the same. Again, that's because each manufacturer has its own size chart.

Assume you can't make up your mind between a tight-fitting, mermaid gown from Ilissa and a similar one from Bridal Originals. Your measurements are 34-24-37.

Bridal Originals				Ilissa			
Size	Bust	Waist	Hips	Size	Bust	Waist	Hips
8	34	24	36	8	34	25.5	37
10	35	25	37	10	35	26.5	38.5
12	36	26	38	12	36.5	28	40

If you decided to purchase the Ilissa gown you'd be a size 8, although the waist will need to be taken in an inch-and-a-half.

But if you decided on the Bridal Originals gown, what size would you be? You'd be between an 8 and a 10. The size 8 gown will fit perfectly in the bust and waist but will be one inch too small at the hip. The size 10 gown, on the other hand, will be one inch too large in the bust. If you're having "cups" sewn in the dress in lieu of a bra, they'll take up some of the slack. The waist, one inch too large, will need to be taken in but the dress will fit perfectly in the hip.

TIP: If you buy the dress too small and it must be let out, a "stitch line" (caused by the needle breaking the fiber of the fabric when the gown was originally sewn) will always be visible — no matter how many times you steam it. For that reason, *it's far better to take a dress in than to let it out.*

Factors That Determine Correct Size

To ensure that you are ordering the correct size for your dresses, it's important to be measured accurately. Whether the bridal shop is measuring you, or a friend is, here's how it should be done:
— Use a plastic or metal tape measure. Cloth tapes stretch and will give you a false measurement.
— Measure the bust at the fullest part over underwear, not clothes, and pull the tape so it's snug (not loose, not tight) with the arms at the sides.

Juliet sleeve, chapel train, peblum, Sabrina neckline. (Opposite): The richness of iridescent organza is perfect for the formal wedding.

— Measure the waist the same way.
— Measure the hip at its fullest part over underwear, not clothes, and pull the tape so it's snug. Make sure feet are together. If the fullest part is at the top of the leg, measure there.

Next, ask to see the manufacturer's size chart for your particular wedding gown or bridesmaids dresses. Compare your measurements to the chart. Choose the size that most closely matches your measurements. If you are in between sizes, pick the larger size. If your weight tends to fluctuate, order the larger size. And don't get hung up over an inch. Look at the sample size chart for Bridal Originals. The difference between an 8 and a 10, or a 10 and a 12, is one inch.

Don't order your gown from any shop that doesn't follow this procedure. I've heard many complaints from clients, who swear they were coerced into ordering a larger size by a bridal shop, whose only goal was to make money on excessive alterations. These women were not measured correctly, nor were they shown the manufacturer's size chart for the gowns they selected. Also, don't be influenced by the size of the sample dress you tried on in the bridal shop. Most sample dresses will stretch out after a few months of size 16 women trying to squeeze into them, sometimes

Sabrina neckline, capped sleeve, handkerchief hem, tea-length blouson. (Opposite): The mermaid — long, low and sexy is perfect for the sophisticated bride.

by more than an inch (or one to two sizes — lace can stretch even more).

Next, examine the "seam allowance" in the sample dress. Seam allowance is the amount of extra fabric left in the side seams by the manufacturer which determines how much the dress can be let out. There is, however, a big difference between bridesmaids dresses and wedding gowns when it comes to seam allowance. In most cases, wedding gowns have a few inches of seam allowance. If a woman happens to gain a few extra pounds due to the stress of planning her wedding, the dress can easily be let out.

This does not hold true for bridesmaids dresses. Most bridesmaids gowns have very little extra fabric in the side seams, making them impossible to let out. Be sure to examine the side seams of the sample dress at the store. *The amount of seam allowance in the dress should be a major factor in determining the sizes you should order.* If you see that the dress can't be let out, and you have a bridesmaid whose weight fluctuates, or one who's in between sizes, order the larger size.

When ordering a traditional wedding gown — fitted bodice, tight waist and full skirt, it's not necessary to be concerned with the hip measurement. This is because a gown with a full skirt contains many yards of fabric that can cover any hip size. The same holds true for this type of bridesmaids dress. Determine the sizes you'll need by using the bust and waist measurements only.

If you or your bridesmaids are dieting, have the bridal store consultant take the measurements at your or their present weight and use those measurements when ordering your dress or theirs. It's been my experience that the majority of women tend to gain weight, rather than lose it through

the stress of planning their weddings — the same for bridesmaids. If you're lucky enough to lose ten pounds, however, it's nothing to be concerned about. Ten pounds usually equals one size. Taking a dress in an inch is an easy alteration.

The Pregnancy Factor

What if the bride (heaven forbid!) or one of her bridesmaids is ——— PREGNANT???? The best thing to do is order the dress two sizes larger and along with the dress, an extra yard of fabric from the manufacturer. Do this at the same time you order the dress because fabric can change color slightly from bolt to bolt, depending on how it takes the dye.

Many of my clients who are pregnant or have bridesmaids that are often want to order a dress four to six sizes larger to ensure that the dress will fit. I discourage this because the dress will be huge in the shoulders, neckline and arms. (Not only that, but you're going to pay a lot of money in "over-size" charges, see next page.) It's far more economical to order the dress a couple of sizes larger, buy the extra fabric and "gusset" the sides (add triangular panels of fabric following the lines of the dress), than it is to try to cut down, except for the stomach, the entire dress.

Ordering for the Out-of-State Bridesmaid

Because all bridesmaids dresses must be ordered from the same shop at the same time, many bridesmaids who live out of town call in their measurements to the bride so that she can order the gowns for them. Ordering the dresses at the same time will ensure they are cut from the same bolt of fabric so there won't be variations in the color. (Even black fabric can be darker or

Dolman sleeve, flared skirt, illusion neckline, high collar, padded shoulders, long torso, inverted V-waistline. (Opposite): An off-the-shoulder neckline and illusion sleeve is the highlight of this romantic, layered tulle gown.

lighter depending on the bolt of fabric from which it's been cut.)

Explain to your bridesmaids how they should be measured to ensure accuracy. This is extremely important. I have had several instances in my shop where measurements were called in, two inches shy of what they should have been. When the women came into town for their fittings, the dresses were understandably too small. Two inches means two sizes. (Once again look at the sample size charts.) In one of the cases mentioned above, it was necessary to cut off the bottom of the bridesmaids dress (thank goodness the woman was short) and piece in the sides. This major alternation was expensive. Please stress the importance of having accurate measurements to your bridesmaids. It will save them time and money, and you a lot of aggravation.

Extra Charges

If you or any of your bridesmaids are tall — 5' 7" or over, it is necessary to order "extra length" (for wedding gowns as well as bridesmaids dresses). There's always an additional charge for extra

Tiered skirt, ballet length, dropped waist, inverted V-waistline, pouf sleeve, off-the-shoulder sweetheart neckline.

length because the dress requires more fabric. (Charges vary depending on the manufacturer and the retailer.) If the store doesn't advise you to order extra length and you or your bridesmaids are tall, be sure to ask about it because they may have overlooked it. It's also important that the extra charges be noted on your receipt.

Be aware that if you or any of your bridesmaids are on the chubby side, say size 18, there'll be an additional charge. As the size gets bigger so does the charge — once again for extra fabric. (The cost will vary on the manufacturer and the retailer.) List the additional charges on your receipt.

In Case of Emergency - "Rush Cuts"

Some women wait until the last minute to order their wedding gowns and bridesmaids dresses and are unable to get them for this reason. Many manufacturers, however, do offer "rush cuts" for brides in this predicament. A rush cut means that the manufacturer will cut the dresses even though they didn't make the production schedule, and will guarantee their delivery within a few weeks — for more money. Rush cuts for wedding gowns can be hundreds of dollars — the more expensive the gown the higher the charge. The same holds true for bridesmaids dresses, although the cost is considerably less. It may also be necessary to pay for overnight shipping, if the date the dresses are to be shipped is too close to the wedding date. This can amount to a lot of money.

CONTRACTS, DEPOSITS AND FOLLOW UP

Your Receipt is Your Contract

On your receipt should be listed the manufacturer, style number, where advertised, color and size, wedding date, any additional charges — over size, extra long, charges for color change or custom changes, and rush cut charges. Look at this example:

Elva's Bridal
Boca Raton, Florida

Wedding gown for: Suzy Smith

Mfg: Ilissa, style number 2265

Where advertised: *BRIDE'S* June-July, 19 _ _ , pg. 54

Color: White with ivory lace (no charge for custom color)

Size:	18, extra long
Price:	$2,000.00
Over size:	$ 60.00
Extra long:	$ 80.00
Sub-total:	$2,140.00
Tax (6%):	$128.40
Total:	$2,268.40
Deposit paid:	$1,200.00
Balance due:	$1,068.40

Wedding Date: June 10th.

 Don't fudge your wedding date. The manufacturer won't change his schedule to get your wedding gown or bridesmaids dresses to you any faster than his schedule allows, unless you're doing a rush cut.

Deposits

The deposit on a wedding gown and bridesmaids dresses is normally 50 percent of the cost. The balance is due when the gown arrives. Many stores offer to discount the dresses if they are paid in full at the time of purchase. This is not advisable. If the store goes out of business, it's better to be out 50 percent than 100 percent.

The Check System that Avoids Disaster

Two days after placing your order for your

Bishop sleeve, Queen Anne neckline, basque waist, full skirt with a flounce.

wedding gown or bridesmaids dresses, call the shop and have a consultant read your order as placed to the manufacturer. Make sure their order contains the same information as your receipt. In this way, you'll know that the store correctly ordered your bridal gown and bridesmaids dresses.

The Confirmation

Approximately three weeks after the order is placed, the store will receive a *confirmation* from the manufacturer acknowledging the order and specifying sizes and colors. It also will include the approximate date the dresses will be shipped. This is called the "ship date".

Leg-of-mutton sleeve, panniers (poufs at waist),
basque waist, Queen Elizabeth collar, full skirt.

Three weeks after you order your wedding gown or bridesmaids dresses, call the store and ask if they received the confirmation. Also, ask for the ship date of your dresses so you'll have an idea of when to expect them. If the confirmation wasn't received, make sure the store calls the manufacturer to find out why.

If the dresses haven't arrived by the ship date, demand that the store call the manufacturer to check on the delay. If they're running late and the wedding date is close at hand, you may choose to have the dresses overnighted to you.

Cancellation Policy

Once an order for a wedding gown or bridesmaids dresses is placed with the manufacturer, the order cannot be canceled, and the store is obligated to pay for the dresses. If the wedding is postponed or canceled, or one of the bridesmaids drops out, you or your bridesmaid is responsible for payment.

FITTINGS AND ALTERATIONS

When your wedding gown and bridesmaids dresses arrive they may have to be altered. The most common alterations include making the hem shorter or longer, or adjusting the seams to make the gown bigger or smaller. If your dress, for example, fits you perfectly in the bust and hips, but the waist is two inches too large, the seamstress must take it in at the sides. She will "un-pick" the dress at the seams (take it apart) and move the fabric in one inch on each side (for a total of two inches), and sew it back together. Conversely, if the waist of your dress is one inch too small, she will follow the same procedure but will move the fabric out one-half inch on each side (for a total of one inch) and sew the dress back together. Both procedures take the same amount of time and the alteration costs should be the same.

TIP: If the wedding gown comes in too small or the bride has gained weight, the gown will have to be let out. The only thing the seamstress can do to hide the stitch-line is applique it so it can't be seen. Appliques (small pieces of beaded and sequined lace) and the time it takes to apply them can be an expensive procedure.

Wedding gowns, as well as bridesmaids dresses, can be gusseted if they need to be let out more than the seam allowance allows. Use the fabric from the hem of the wedding gown or bridesmaids dresses. If you don't have enough, try to find it at your local fabric store because most satins and taffetas are easy to match. If the dress is silk, brocade or any other atypical fabric, it will be necessary for the bridal store to order the fabric from the manufacturer. If time is a factor — the wedding is two weeks away, for example — have the fabric sent by overnight carrier.

Fitting Your Wedding Gown

At your first fitting, you need the appropriate bra or "bustière" which is a lacey, strapless, long-line bra that stops at the waist or lower. Bustières are essential for off-the-shoulder wedding gowns giving much more support than a strapless bra. They are also wonderful for women on the chunky side. They cinch the waist and hold the body firmly in place giving a more stream-lined look.

If your dress is low-cut in the front or back, the bra you choose will need to match the cut of your gown. If you are small busted, you might decide to have cups sewn into the dress in lieu of a bra. These are also very comfortable. Many bridal shops carry bustières, bras and cups for wedding gowns. Before your first fitting be sure to ask.

You also will need a slip. Bridal shops normally offer these to brides in a variety of sizes from slim to very full. Try on a variety of slips to see which fullness you prefer — the look you like the best. Once you decide on a certain slip, make sure you wear it at every fitting. Different slips, with their various layers of tulle or crinoline, can change the length of your gown.

You also will need shoes to match your gown. If your gown is silk or taffeta you need to buy shoes made of *peau de soie*, a non-shiny fabric. If your gown is satin, buy satin shoes. If your gown is simple, buy plain shoes. If your gown is ornate, buy plain shoes and add beaded shoe-clips, or buy shoes that have a small amount of beading or lace on the toes, but don't go overboard. If your dress is ivory, candlelight or blush, it will be necessary to have your shoes died to match. Ask the bridal shop for a swatch of material. Buy good shoes. It's so important to wear comfortable shoes on your wedding day.

The Bustle

Any wedding gown that has a train (unless it is detachable) will need to be "bustled". The bustle was designed so that a bride doesn't need to carry her train — which can be very heavy and cumbersome — folded over her arm when she attends her reception, as her mother had to do when she was married.

Bustling can be done in a number of different ways, but the idea is to make the train the same length as the skirt at the front. This is accomplished by gathering the train into beautiful loops or folds, and attaching those loops or folds to the waistline at the back of the gown.

Bustling can be expensive, but it's essential that it's done properly. Many stores use hooks-and-eyes that aren't strong enough to hold the weight of a heavy train. Buttons are the best choice — sewn underneath the bodice-lace at the waist. At my shop, we crochet heavy silk thread (the same color as the dress) into loops that are then crocheted into the skirt. The loops are then placed over the buttons holding the weight of the train secure. For a heavy train, it's advisable to have at least four buttons on each side of the zipper.

TIP: Always take large safety pins with you to the wedding. If anyone steps on the back of the gown after it's been bustled, the buttons may rip out.

Fitting Bridesmaids Dresses

Each bridesmaid needs the proper bra or bustière to match the cut of her dress and the proper slip. They also need shoes that match the color and fabric of the dresses. If they're wearing taffeta or shantung, their shoes should be made of peau de soie. If their gowns are satin, their shoes should be, too. If the shoes need to be dyed, have them all dyed at the same place because dye lots may vary.

Altering the Two-Piece Suit

As elegant and practical as the two-piece suit is for today's bridesmaid, fitting them may be a problem. If you have a woman who's a size 12 in the hips, for example, but a size 8 in the bust (according to the manufacturer's size chart), you have no choice but to order the 12 and take in the jacket. Such a major alteration can be expensive. Many of the jackets are lined, which requires taking the lining apart before you can start the alterations. These jackets also are "tailored" or fitted, have more seams than a traditional bridesmaids dress and many have long sleeves. They require more time on the part of the seamstress to ensure they fit properly and *time is money.*

If a bridesmaid, on the other hand, happens to be a size 12 in the bust and a size 8 in the hips, she's lucky. It's easy to make the skirt smaller by simply taking in the side seams. Many of these suit-skirts are not lined, an added plus. This is a far simpler and far more economical alteration.

If the majority of your bridesmaids have figures that are not well proportioned (as the examples above), don't choose a two-piece suit. The alteration charges can be staggering. A more traditional look may be better suited to both their figures and their budgets.

Dress Length and Photographs

Most brides want their maids dresses to be the same length for photos. If the dresses are long this is an easy task. The skirt should come to the top of the shoe, no matter what heel height the bridesmaids are wearing. If the dresses are tea-length or mid-calf, however, it becomes more complicated.

Have the bridesmaids buy their shoes in the heel height they prefer. Have the tallest woman try on her dress *with her shoes on,* and hem her dress to the desired length — for example tea-length (which is about three inches above the ankle). After the dress is hemmed, have the seamstress measure the distance from the hem of the skirt to the floor, with the bridesmaid in her dress, *with her shoes on.* Let's say this measures ten inches. All your bridesmaids dresses should then be hemmed ten inches from the floor *with their shoes on.* This will ensure that all hem lengths will be identical, no matter the heel-height of their shoes.

A romantic brocade highlighted by sweet, soft roses at the neckline makes this an elegant wedding gown.

PRICING PITFALLS

Money Upfront - for a Discount

A newspaper in our area recently reported that a bridal shop went out of business leaving many frantic brides stranded. The owner had told clients that if they paid for their gowns upfront, in full, he would discount them 20 percent. Many women did just that, only to find they had neither a wedding dress nor their money when the store closed.

The manufacturers in this case worked with the frantic brides to provide gowns in time for their weddings. They charged them cost price for the dresses. One woman who brought her gown to me to be altered had given this shop $2,000 for a Jon Bradley gown. She then paid $1,250 for a replacement. A gown that originally retailed for $2,500 cost her $3,250. She got the gown in time for the wedding, but the stress and added expenditure did not make for a happy time.

The "Such a Deal" Bridal Shop

Beware of "package" deals at bridal shops. Many clients come into my store and tell me, "They're going to throw everything in with the dress — the headpiece and veil, the shoes, the slip, the alterations, the bustle — it's fabulous!" If it's thrown into the package — you're paying for it. Nothing is free or "thrown in." One woman came into my store with a picture of a lovely , traditional gown. For $1,800 everything was included. The problem was the gown retailed for $800. She was paying $1,000 for all those little extras she thought were free.

Another shop in our area offers their clients gowns at cost — if they take their photography and floral packages. When women come into my shop and tell me this, my answer is, "Now think about it. If you owned a business, would you sell gowns for what you paid for them? How would you make any money? You would have to make a profit somewhere." In this case, that *somewhere* is excessively priced photography and flowers.

Be an educated consumer to avoid problems. *Never sign a contract* at your first visit to a bridal store (or any store). It's important that you shop and do research first — then make an educated decision.

Consignment Shops and Bridal "Outlets"

Today many brides who pay for their own weddings, and others who are cost conscious, think it a good idea to turn to consignment shops or bridal "outlets" to buy their gowns. Every woman wants her wedding to be beautiful. Many also want it to be affordable — and the allure of saving money at an outlet or consignment shop may sound appealing. The problem is, however, that gowns purchased from these vendors often carry hidden liabilities that don't become apparent until it's too late.

Consignment Shop Gowns

When shopping for a gown in a consignment shop, the first thing to do is find the label inside the dress that will tell you the gown's style number and manufacturer. If there are no labels or tags inside, ask the consignment shop to get this information from the owner. Once you know the manufacturer and the style number, call a bridal shop and ask if the dress is still "running" or if it's been "discontinued". Then ask the bridal shop to give you a ball-park figure of what the dress cost, i.e. "Around $700." If the dress was discontinued, ask how long ago. By knowing how old the gown is and what it originally cost, you can determine if it's a good buy. A good rule to follow: you should pay no more than half of what the gown originally cost.

Do your homework. Know the manufacturer of the dress, the style number and the original price to avoid problems. One woman was told by a consignment shop in our area that the dress she paid $600 for was an exclusive gown that had originally cost $1,200. When she came to my store to have the dress altered, she noticed that I had the same gown in stock. The cost of the dress, new, was $540. The bride was heartbroken.

Most women who sell their gowns through consignment shops exaggerate the original price because the shop usually splits with them 50-50. If they paid $800 for a gown, they're apt to tell the consignment shop the dress costs $1,000 — or more. The higher the selling price of the dress the more money they make.

Consignment Shops and Alterations

Most consignment shops do not employ seamstresses, so it's difficult for them to assess alteration costs. A reasonably priced dress that is a couple of sizes too large can end up costing a fortune in alteration fees, because alterations on a wedding dress are not simple. A gown that is too large must be taken in at the shoulders, the neck, the sleeves, and the front and back bodice, not to mention standard alterations like the hem and the bustle. Many brides who thought they got a bargain at a consignment shop, learn a hard lesson

when it comes to paying exorbitant alteration fees on a gown they thought was "such a deal!"

Bridal Outlets - Beware

Bridal outlets, with their rack after rack of gowns, including discontinued styles, may not be a bargain either. Many times clients call me to check on gowns they find at outlets. In one case, a woman told me that a gown she was considering was $900 marked down to $450. I did some research, discovered the dress was three years old, discontinued and that the outlet had exaggerated the retail price of the gown. This woman was about to pay $450 for a three-year-old dress that had originally retailed for only $600. Needless to say, she did not buy the gown.

Be sure to find out the manufacturer and style number of the gown. Check on the dress to determine how old it is and to get an idea of the original selling price. Then determine if the gown is a good buy.

Outlet Gowns and Dry Cleaning Costs

Hundreds of people try on gowns featured at outlets. If you purchase one, it's advisable to get the dress dry-cleaned. Be aware that this may add $100 or more to the cost of the gown.

Bridal Outlets and "Knock-offs"

BEWARE! Many outlets *knock-off* (copy) wedding gowns. Not long ago, a woman brought her wedding gown to my store to be altered. It was bought at a local "bridal warehouse". The dress was a copy of a Regency gown I had in stock. The major difference between the two dresses was that the Regency was 100-percent silk and the copy was 100-percent polyester. The lace on her

gown was not as fine as the Regency, nor was the workmanship as good. The Regency silk gown was only $100 more than her polyester one.

At another time, a knocked-off warehouse gown was brought to my shop for alterations. The gown was a mermaid style covered in lace and pearls. The pearls were glued onto the gown, and when I started to steam the bodice, they fell off. For that reason, the dress could be neither steamed nor pressed. I didn't tell the bride because I didn't want to upset her, nor did I tell her that I had the original Ilissa gown in stock. For only $75 more, she could have had an original dress with sewn-on pearls.

Another incident occurred when a woman told me she had bought a fabulous gown at an outlet by a famous designer named Lili. She added that the dress had originally cost $1,200, but that she'd only paid $650. At that point, I pulled out my Lili brochure and asked her to show me her dress. It turned out that her gown *retailed* for $650. She had paid full price at an outlet.

A Word of Advice

The stories are endless. Before making a decision on a wedding gown you saw at an outlet, do your homework. Know what the dress originally cost; know the manufacturer and style number. Find out how old the dress is and consider dry-cleaning costs. *Be an educated consumer.*

Outlets and Alterations

The seamstresses that work for outlets in our area are independent contractors who rent space from the outlet. They don't work for the outlet, so it is not responsible if the alterations are botched.

Outlet Gowns are Not Returnable

Gowns purchased at outlets are not returnable for credit, refund or exchange. Buying a gown off-the-rack at an outlet does not mean you can return it, as you can when buying a dress off-the-rack at a department store. This is true even if the gown is dirty or damaged. Once you buy the dress, it's yours. That's why you must be very cautious when shopping for gowns at outlets.

One of my clients who brought her gown to me for alterations said she was high-pressured by the salesperson at an outlet. After she bought it, she cried for days because she realized it wasn't the gown she really wanted — the one she'd dreamed about. When she tried to return it, the manager at the outlet told her to "read the sales slip." It plainly stated that the dress was not returnable for any reason. She spent a fortune redesigning her so-called "bargain" dress into the gown of her dreams.

Bridal Outlets and Consignment Shops - In Summary

The best advice I can give you is to use your head. Shop at reputable bridal shops no matter what your budget. Many stores carry beautiful, new, inexpensive gowns. Ilissa, for example, makes a gorgeous line of very affordable gowns called the "Boutique Collection".

After all is said and done, it might be smarter, less expensive and less aggravating to shop at a reputable, traditional bridal salon. Everyone likes a bargain, but it seems that outlets and consignment shops — while fast becoming synonymous with savings — are also becoming synonymous with heartache. Who needs it?

An elegant brocade Victorian suit — perfect for a second or informal wedding.

Right — *the classic hour-glass figure.* What could be more perfect than the sheath for the bride with perfect proportions. The sheath is becoming almost as traditional as the classic full-skirted wedding gown. Sheaths are particularly flattering for the petite bride, making her appear taller without overpowering her.

Left — *the inverted heart figure.* If you're slim shouldered and lacking in the bust department, this gown may be for you. The full, poufed sleeves give more substance to the upper body, while the sweetheart neckline adds more dimension to the bustline. A basque waistline is most flattering, while a full skirt hides larger hips.

♥ Left —
The heart-shaped figure. If you're full-busted with broad shoulders and slim hips, try to select a gown like the one pictured here with a sweetheart neckline. Inset sleeves also help to lessen the full look of the bust and shoulders. The full skirt adds dimension to a slim hipline.

♥ Right —
The full-heart figure. If you're full-busted and full-hipped, create a small waistline and contoured body with a gown like the one pictured here. An off-the-shoulder portrait collar coupled with a full skirt (that hides larger hips), gives the illusion of a small waist. The basque waistline is also most flattering.

305

Mr. and Mrs. Donald P. Winston
request the honour of your presence
at the marriage of their daughter
Leslie Sue
to
Mr. Mark Lawrence Grenwalt
Sunday, the seventh of September
nineteen hundred and ninety-seven
at twelve noon
First Episcopal Church
1521 Harvey Drive
Concord, New Hampshire

Leslie and Mark

Thank You

Leslie and Mark

Invitations

You can invite guests to your wedding by phone, handwritten note or by printed invitation. Today there are hundreds, even thousands, of invitations to choose from, but did you ever wonder why they come in so many styles, colors and shapes? Because they were designed not only to invite, but to convey a mood, an ambiance for the occasion. Let's say you receive a folded card with cows pictured on the front, strung from one end to the other. Inside there's a message:

"Let's Party Till the Cows Come Home!"

And handwritten inside:

Please celebrate our marriage with us
at a barbeque at the home of
Sarah and Miles Franklin
June 26 — 5:00
222 Candlewood Terrace
Boca Raton
Sue Smith and Don Jones
Regrets only: 864-9865

This invitation reveals many things — who's hosting the party, the date, time and address. But first and foremost *it informs you that this affair is informal.* Formal invitations do not have pictures of cows strung across the front, nor are they handwritten.

People, on the other hand, who receive envelopes made of fine paper with their names and addresses penned in calligraphy, know that someone has gone to a lot of trouble and expense to invite them to a formal affair. They know it before opening the envelope.

Because you want to create the right ambiance for your wedding whether it's formal, semi-formal or informal, it's important to select the right invitations. I can't tell you the number of brides and their mothers who say, "The invitation isn't important, they'll pitch it anyway." Pitch it they might, but the person who got the cow invitation will say, "What a cute idea — this sounds like a fun party!" While the person who received the invitation with the beautiful, elegant envelope will think, "What a sophisticated affair this is going to be!" One person is laying out his tux while the other is polishing his cowboy boots. The invitation said it all.

Hundreds of invitation catalogues are on the market with the cost of invitations running from about one-hundred-fifty dollars per hundred (including the little cards, called enclosures, that accompany the invitations) to thousands of dollars per hundred. Take your time and look hard. It's important to find the right invitation, conveying the right ambiance, at the right price.

Thermography vs. Engraved

Years ago, engraving was the only method of printing. The copy (wording of the invitation) was etched onto a copper plate. The plate was inked and when paper was pressed to it, the copy was transferred to the paper in relief (raised lettering). Small pieces of tissue paper were then placed on the paper to absorb excess ink. The copper plates used for the engraving were given to the bride as a memento (as they are today), and tissue paper is still put over the print on the invitation.

Engraving is expensive. The alternative is thermography, an inexpensive heat-printing process that mixes ink with powder to produce raised lettering. If you run your fingers over an engraved invitation and one printed by thermography, you can't tell the difference — except in your pocketbook. Thermography produces fine-quality, raised lettering, sans the expense.

For formal weddings (with unlimited budgets) engraving is a *must*, although thermography is acceptable for formal and semi-formal weddings.

Paper Content and Weight

Paper may be made from cotton or other fibers. It may be thick or thin depending on its weight; thick paper being more expensive than thin.

Naturally, cotton paper invitations will be more expensive than those printed on pulp paper. Crane, known for the quality of its paper and invitations, is considered among the world's finest.

When to Order Them

You may order your invitations any time after the wedding date is set and the ceremony and reception places are reserved. It's best to order them early when your stress level is low.

If you're thinking of engraved or custom invitations allow two to three months for delivery. Thermographed invitations are usually delivered within two to three weeks. Printed invitations, the kind found at local printing shops, are usually available in days. If you decide to get a "proof" (a sample of the printing), allow an extra 10 days for the order to be completed.

TIP: To save time when you order your invitations, be prepared. Know the correct spelling of names and all middle names of the parties involved. Know the correct names and spelling of the ceremony and reception places and street addresses. Know ceremony and reception times.

When to Send Them

Invitations should be sent to out-of-town guests two months in advance of the *respond date* (usually two to three weeks before the wedding date), and for local guests, two weeks to one month in advance of the respond date.

THE PARTICULARS

Determining The Guest List

Guest lists may pose problems when two families are involved, so let's look at guests in terms of *priority* for both the bride, groom, and their families.

In order of importance:

Priority List I

1. Immediate family — including parents, brothers and sisters, grandparents, step-parents, spouses and dates.
2. Extended family — aunts, uncles, and cousins, including step-relatives, spouses and dates.
3. The bridal party — including dates and spouses, parents of the ringbearer and flower girl, and clergy with spouse or date.

Priority List II

1. Close family friends.
2. Close friends of the bride and groom.
3. Close business associates of the families.
4. Close business associates of the bride and groom.

Priority List III

1. Distant relatives.
2. Distant friends.
3. Casual acquaintances in the community or work place.

The bride and groom should first discuss Priority List I with her family if they're paying for the wedding. Let's assume you've decided to invite 100 to 125 people. You both have large families. By the time you get through List I, 75 people are on it. That leaves 25 invitations (one invitation usually invites two people) that should be divided equally between both families and the bride and groom. These invitations should be sent to the people on Priority List II. People on Priority List III will get announcements.

If the bride has a small family and the groom a large one, things should be divided proportionately. Let's assume you're inviting 150 guests to the wedding. After going through List I, the bride has 20 people on her list, the groom has 40, leaving 90 people to be invited. For these 90, the groom and his family should be given 17 invitations (inviting approximately 34 people), the bride and her family the remaining 27 (inviting approximately 54 people). What's fair is fair.

If the bride and groom's families are equally paying for the wedding, all should be involved in the decision. Meet and go through the lists. If one family lives out of town, call and agree on a total number of guests, then send the Priority Lists with a little note, "We agreed on 150 people. You get 75, we get 75. Here's a few Priority Lists to fill out — it will make the selection easier."

If one family's numbers, however, far outweigh the other's, it's up to that family to pick up the tab for extra guests, especially if the bride's family is paying for the wedding (unless her family is wealthy and doesn't object). Many times the parents of the bride have told me, "We have a small family and a tight circle of friends. Our guest list totaled 25. When my daughter got the list back from her fiancé's family, it had 100 names on it. That just isn't fair."

If the bride and groom had sat down with her parents first to establish parameters, this wouldn't have happened. If the groom's parents had been told they were limited to 25 people, they wouldn't have invited 100. If they insisted, however, on the extra 75 guests then they should pay for them (including food, liquor, extra invitations, centerpieces, etc.).

If the bride and groom are paying for their own wedding, they may decide the guest list. Their priorities may be different than their families'. Maybe their close friends and business associates are more important to them than their out-of-town family whom they see once in a blue moon. In this case, they should tell their parents the number of guests they're permitted to invite and which family members they're *not* inviting. The parents should stick to the numbers, but if they insist on inviting their out-of-town family or exceeding the limit, then they should pay for the extra guests, extra centerpieces, invitations, etc.

The Importance of Announcements

By the time you get to Priority List III, your guest list may be full. You may want to invite distant friends, relatives, casual acquaintances or business associates — but can't. What do you do? Send announcements — those tactful little cards that announce your wedding *without requiring a gift in return.*

It's smart to use your head. Many times friends or relatives on tight budgets can't afford to attend your wedding or send a gift. An announcement lets them know you thought of them. It'll be appreciated.

Printed or handwritten announcements should be sent out the day after the wedding, never before. (See samples in this chapter.)

Invitations and Numbers

Always buy 25 more invitations than you need. Whenever I sell invitations to a client, I ask them to look at the price structure (chart below). 25 invitations cost $73.90 and 100 invitations cost $89.90 *(regular lettering prices)*. If you bought 100 invitations, ran out and had to order 25 more, it would cost you $73.90. Had you ordered 25 additional with the original order for 100, *(Add'l 25s)* it would have only cost $20.30. The extra 25 invitations always come in handy. Many people at the last minute will remember someone they forgot. Also, mistakes are made addressing

---

Refer to this chart when reading this chapter

ITEM DESCRIPTION	PAPER NUMBER	REGULAR LETTERING PRICES					EXCLUSIVE LETTERING PRICES				
		25	50	75	100	Add'l 25s	25	50	75	100	Add'l 25s
INVITATION Prices Include Double Envelopes & Tissues	2R-1W	73.90	79.90	84.90	89.90	20.30	81.90	87.90	92.90	97.90	22.10
RETURN ADDRESS ON ENVELOPE FLAP Raised Printed - Assures Delivery or Return	2R-RAVWJ	14.90	15.90	17.90	19.90	3.10	21.90	22.90	24.90	26.90	3.80
LINED INNER ENVELOPES Select only a lining color listed on this page	Specify Color	4.25	8.50	12.75	17.00	4.25	4.25	8.50	12.75	17.00	4.25
RECEPTION (Folder) No Envelopes - Enclosed with Invitation	2R-1111R	33.90	34.90	35.90	36.90	8.30	37.90	38.90	39.90	40.90	9.30
RESPOND (Folder) Printed Return Envelopes - Give Name & Address	2R-1111E	38.90	40.90	42.90	44.90	10.10	44.90	46.90	48.90	50.90	11.60
INFORMAL PERSONAL NOTE (Folder) Includes Name or Monogram & Single Envelopes	2R-1111N	33.90	34.90	35.90	36.90	8.30	37.90	38.90	39.90	40.90	9.30

All accessory papers will match the sample accessory shown.   When ordering, please specify Lettering Style & Ink Color for each item.

envelopes. If you have extras you needn't worry. If you use a calligrapher you should always order at least 25 extra outside and inside envelopes.

Dates or spouses of members of the bridal party should receive invitations. The clergy, including spouse, should receive an invitation. Make sure these people are on your list.

How many times have I heard, "I need 300 invitations," and my response is, "You're having 600 people at your wedding?" Invitations usually invite couples (Mr. and Mrs. Smith or Ms. Susan Brown and Guest). Based on the 300 figure (actually the total, estimated guest list), you'll need 150 invitations. Next, add the number needed for single guests and for those out-of-town family and guests who *you think aren't coming*. (Be prepared. Don't assume someone isn't coming unless they tell you they aren't. Allow for all contingencies.)

Add your bridal party and clergy, an additional 25 for insurance, and you'll come up with the number of invitations you should need. They're ordered in increments of 25 so round off to the highest number.

How to Price an Invitation - Their Parts and Purpose

Regular lettering costs less than *exclusive* lettering and examples of both styles of print are found at the front of invitation catalogues. The difference between them relates to *type of print* only — not the quality of the print which remains the same for both. (There isn't very much difference in price. If you were on a tight budget ordering 100 invitations including all extra cards, regular lettering, you would only save $29.00.) See chart on preceding page.

RETURN ADDRESS ON ENVELOPE FLAP: The return address of the person hosting the wedding is printed on the outside flap of the invitation envelope. It normally doesn't include the names of the hosts, just the address. (Please see example in this chapter.) This isn't the same as the address that is printed on the respond card envelope. Don't confuse the two.

Many clients skip the flap imprint to save money. If your time is valuable, don't do it. Imagine writing (all invitations must be handwritten, no stick-um labels) your address on 100 envelopes neatly and legibly. It's time consuming, boring, and tiring.

LINED INNER ENVELOPES: Most standard-sized invitations come with two envelopes. The outside envelope has glue on it and may be sealed, the inner one doesn't. The inner envelope also may be lined in pretty, colored paper that costs more. If you're on a tight budget skip the lining.

RECEPTION (Folder): The *reception folder* tells your guests the time, place, and address of your reception. It also should tell them the *type* of reception, "Reception and Dinner," or "Reception and Brunch," or "Cocktail-Hors d'oeuvres Reception." It designates the formality of the wedding with the words "Black Tie" or "Black Tie invited, preferred or optional," printed as *corner-copy* (a notation printed in the lower-left or right-hand corner) on the reception folder. The reception card is enclosed with the invitation.

Skip the reception card if the reception is at the same place as the ceremony. On the invitation at the bottom, centered or as corner-copy, say "Reception immediately following." The invitation company may charge you more for an extra line, although the cost is usually minimal. If you skip the reception card, you may also put "Black Tie" or "Black Tie invited, preferred or optional" on the invitation as corner-copy.

RESPOND (Folder): The *respond card* is sent to your guests with the invitation. It asks them to respond — will they be attending or won't they? It may also ask which choice of entree they'd prefer.

The respond card comes with a printed envelope that the recipient is expected to return to the host. It's up to the host to put stamps on these envelopes. The respond card is enclosed with the invitation.

INFORMAL PERSONAL NOTE (Folder): This is a long name for a simple "thank-you note" but that's what it is. They are printed with the bride's name or the bride and groom's name, come with envelopes and may be used for any occasion once the wedding is over.

If you look at the price list, you'll notice that there's only a dollar difference between 25, 50, 75, and 100. I advise my clients to buy a minimum of 100 informals and always 25 more thank-you notes than the number of invitations purchased. You'll be glad you did.

Those Extra Charges

Standard invitations include black ink. There's an extra charge for colored ink — per item. If you ordered pink ink for your invitations, return address envelope flap, reception card, respond card and informals, you'd pay $32.50 based on a per item charge of $6.50 — for pink ink. You may even have your invitations printed in gold or silver "foil" — which is the real thing. Prices vary,

so check your invitation catalogues for more information.

As mentioned before, you'll pay extra for lined envelopes, exclusive lettering and extra lines. Invitation companies allow a set number of lines on the invitation, reception and respond cards. If you go over the allotted number they charge.

Flexibility

Invitation companies are very flexible. You may write your own copy or add a poem, verse or even your monogram. You may have Hebrew letters printed or embossed in a corner of the invitation, or you may even have it printed in a foreign language — English on one side, for example, French on the other. Your possibilities are endless so be imaginative. Whenever you make changes, there's normally an up-charge. Find out what the cost is and have it written on your receipt.

The Proof

If you're adding a verse or poem to your invitation, extra lines or printing it in a foreign language — get a *proof*. Many people think that a proof is a sample invitation, however, it's only a copy of the printing.

Once you get the proof you can see how the invitation will be printed. Look at the way it's spaced, the style of print and make sure there are no mistakes in spelling, addresses, names or punctuation. If there's an error on the proof and you don't catch it, *you are responsible* — not the store who sold you the invitations.

A proof may cost a little more but it's well worth it. I've found that 90 percent of my clients will change something they don't like after seeing the proof. Invitation companies charge minimal fees to make the changes.

Reviewing the Invitations and Enclosures

The store will type out or write the wording for your invitation and enclosure cards and give it to you to review. Check for all errors, punctuation, spelling and wrong addresses. Make sure names, date, time, place, and address are on the invitation and on the reception card. I once had a bride who left her name and the groom's off the invitation.

Again, if you make a mistake it's your fault. The store will keep a copy of the order faxed or sent to the invitation company. If you didn't catch the error, you must pay to have the invitations reprinted. If the printer, however, made the error, they'll correct it at no charge.

The Custom Invitation

Custom invitations are different from ones produced by standard invitation companies such as Regency or Carlson Craft. A custom invitation means you can mix and match the basic paper stock and colors. You may add or delete extra layers of paper, fabric, even bows or lace (the real thing). Custom invitations are expensive.

Elite and Graphic Imprints, among others, manufacture these spectacular invitations. Printed on fabulous papers in assorted sizes, they range from the sedate to the ultra glitzy. A proof is a must with these invitations. They're too expensive to chance mistakes. You are charged for any changes you make — so get everything in writing.

The Informal Invitation

If you're having an informal wedding, choose informal invitations. You may buy invitations and handwrite them or you may even call your guests by phone. If you're having over 50 people it might be a good idea to have the invitations printed — but they don't have to have raised lettering.

Don't buy a stuffy, formal invitation. Choose a colorful invitation decorated with flowers, for example, or a beach scene. Do something funny like the cow invitation. Let the invitation reflect the mood you want to convey.

The Semi-Formal Invitation

The semi-formal wedding invitation is printed by thermography — engraving isn't necessary. For a semi-formal evening affair you may select a classic, traditional, plain or paneled invitation of white, ivory or ecru paper imprinted with black or grey ink. The envelope lining should be either pearl or white.

Some women waste hours trying to match the color of their invitations to the color of their bridesmaids dresses. One has nothing to do with the other. Remember, invitations must convey the formality and the mood of the wedding.

There's nothing wrong with a little pizazz. Invitations with beautiful embossed flowers with matching inks and liners are very appropriate for morning or afternoon semi-formal weddings. A brightly colored floral invitation would be ideal for an afternoon garden wedding. An invitation with a boat scene would be perfect for a semi-formal wedding on a yacht.

The Formal Invitation

Traditionally, the formal invitation is plain or paneled, ivory, ecru or white. If money is not a concern, engraving is a must. You may, however, prefer custom invitations for the formal wedding. These are big and glitzy, or big and sedate and are printed on fine papers. They're gorgeous and expensive. Those dramatic black-and-white paneled invitations with matching black liners are ideal for a formal black-and-white wedding.

If you're having a formal affair keep it formal. Stay away from cute invitations — no flowers or boats. This invitation must inform your guests that *this* is a formal wedding.

The NITTY-GRITTY

Now that you've selected the invitation, how do you word it? Let's look at a traditional invitation.

If the bride's family is hosting the wedding:

1. *Mr. and Mrs. Russell Hart Smith*
2. *request the honour of your presence*
   (religious ceremony)
3. (or) *request the pleasure of your company*
   (non-religious ceremony)
4. *at the marriage of their daughter*

At Catholic weddings you may say, "at the Nuptial Mass uniting their daughter."

5. *Cynthia Maria*
6. *to*
   ("to" is used for invitations to a ceremony,
   "and" is used for invitations to a reception)
7. *Doctor Michael Winton Jones*
8. *on Saturday, the twentieth of September*
9. *nineteen hundred and ninety-five*
10. *at six o'clock in the evening*
11. *The Windsor Chapel*
12. *Five Northeast Church Street*
13. *Windsor, South Dakota*
    (no zip codes)

The First Line - Who's the Host?

The first line of a traditional invitation tells the recipient who's *hosting* the wedding. It may be the bride's parents, grandparents, a sister, friends of

the couple, or the bride and groom themselves. Years ago, the person hosting the wedding was not necessarily the one who paid for it. Today this isn't always the case. I can't tell you how many fiancés have said, "You and I are throwing the wedding, not your parents." Or the mother of the bride to her protesting daughter, "Your fiancé's parents are not paying for this wedding, and there's no way their names are going on this invitation."

Many times couples paying for their own weddings will use traditional wording (preceding example) not wanting to offend the bride's parents.

Other couples use this wording:

Together with their parents
Marie Ann Mayberry
and
Thomas Wilson Pickett
request the honour of your presence
at their marriage
(or) *to celebrate their marriage*

The wonderful wording of this invitation leaves no one out. Everybody's happy.

Another factor to be considered is the ability of the parents to contribute — they might not be financially able. Many times brides will say, "My mom's widowed and can't help much, but she's my right arm. I don't know what I'd do without her!" In this instance, even though the bride and groom were paying for their own wedding, they included her mother's name on the invitation.

If the bride and groom's parents are hosting the wedding, equally. (The groom's parents names are only mentioned on the invitation if they are the hosts or share the costs equally):

Mr. and Mrs. Russell Smith
(Bride's parents first)
and
Mr. and Mrs. Mark Thompson
request the honour of your presence
to celebrate the marriage of

1. (or) *at the marriage of their children*
Thelma Marie
to
Mark Thomas

If the bride's parents are divorced and they're hosting the wedding:

Mrs. Harriet Alice Snow
(Bride's mother first)
and
Mr. Robert Snow
request the pleasure of your company
at the marriage of their daughter
Julie Jo

If both parents have remarried and are hosting the wedding:

Mr. and Mrs. Charles Robert Clerk
(Bride's mother first and step-father)
and
Mr. and Mrs. Robert Allan Snow
(Bride's father and step-mother)
request the honour of your presence
to celebrate the marriage of
(Not "their" daughter)
Denise Alba

If only one parent has remarried and they're both hosting the wedding:

Mr. and Mrs. Harold James Adams
(Bride's mother, remarried and step-father)
and
Mr. Adam Tolf
(Bride's father, not remarried)
request the honour of your presence
to celebrate the marriage of
Cynthia Jane

Reverse it:
Mrs. Elizabeth Susan Tolf
and
Mr. and Mrs. Adam Tolf
request the honour of your presence
to celebrate the marriage of
Cynthia Jane

How Things Have Changed

Years ago divorce was taboo and divorced parents' names never appeared together on an invitation, no matter how friendly they were. In her book, *Your Wedding How to Plan and Enjoy It*, Marjorie Binford Woods writes of a friendly, divorced couple who planned on sending a joint invitation to their daughter's wedding, "This is not considered good taste...among discerning parents and belongs only in the 'raised-eye-brow department.'" * How things have changed!

If your mother is divorced and remarried and she and your step-father are hosting the wedding:

1. *Mr. and Mrs. Charles Reed Jones, junior*
(Bride's mother remarried and step-father)
2. *request the pleasure of your company*
3. *at the marriage of Mrs. Jones' daughter*
4. *Jill Louise Martin*

Or, to be less formal, line three can read:

* Footnote see page 356.

to celebrate the marriage of

If your father is divorced and remarried, and he and your step-mother are hosting the wedding:

1.　*Mr. and Mrs. Michael Joseph Martin*
　　(Bride's father remarried and step-mother)
2.　　*request the pleasure of your company*
3.　*at the marriage of Mr. Martin's daughter*
4.　　　*Jill Louise*

If you'd like, you may substitute line three with:

to celebrate the marriage of

TIP: Divorce can be very tricky. Often one parent or the other will refuse to contribute in any way, which can cause bitterness and resentment on all sides. It's up to the bride to decide if the non-contributing parent should have a place on the invitation. If you decide to exclude them, you may send them an invitation as you would any other guest.

Many brides don't like to include the names of step-parents on the invitations. However, if either is sharing the cost of your wedding, along with your parents, their name should be included.

If your mother or father is deceased:

Mrs. Robert Adam Tolf
(Husband deceased)
(or) *Mr. Robert Adam Tolf*
(Wife deceased)
request the pleasure of your company
at the marriage of her (his) daughter

(If you're thinking of putting your late parent's name on your invitations, don't. A deceased person's name shouldn't appear on a wedding invitation. Weddings are a time of joy, not of sadness.)

If your mother has remarried after the death of your father:

1.　*Mr. and Mrs. William Robert Hanson*
2.　　*request the honour of your presence*
3.　*at the marriage of Mrs. Hanson's daughter*
4.　　　*Emily Renee Tolf*

Or if that sounds too formal, substitute line three with:

to celebrate the marriage of

Or, if you're very close to your step-father, line three may say:

at the marriage of their daughter

Reverse it. *Your father has remarried after the death of your mother:*

1.　*Mr. and Mrs. Robert Adam Tolf*
2.　　*request the honour of your presence*
3.　*at the marriage of Mr. Tolf's daughter*
4.　　　*Emily Renee*

Or, if that sounds pretentious, substitute line three with:

to celebrate the marriage of

Or, if you're close to your step-mother, line three may say:

at the marriage of their daughter

If you're hosting your own wedding:

Ms. or Miss, or Dr. Susan Margaret Jones
(Bride's name first preceded by title. Dr. may be written out)
and
Mr. Joseph Michael Kent
request the pleasure of your company
at their marriage

If the groom's family is hosting the wedding:

Mr. and Mrs. Joseph Johns Hopkins
request the honour of your presence
at the marriage of
Miss Maybelle Harriet Jones
(Title is used)
to
their son
Harry Steven

If friends are hosting the wedding:

Mr. and Mrs. William Alerton Hunt
request the pleasure of your company
to celebrate the marriage of
Ms., Miss, Dr. Joanna Ann Phillips
(Bride's name first preceded by title. Dr. may be written out)
to
Mr. Mark David Kent

What About a Double Wedding?

If the brides are sisters, a single invitation may be sent:

Mr. and Mrs. Steven Vincent Smith
request the pleasure of your company
at the marriage of their daughters
Susan Linda
(Older bride first)

to
Mr. Mark Casaway
and
Marie Lynette
to
Mr. Dino D'Arcio

If they're not sisters, the families may send single or separate invitations:

Mr. and Mrs. Mark Russell Thompson
(Older bride's parents first)
and
Doctor and Mrs. Frank Jones Alerton
request the honour of your presence
at the marriage of their daughters
Sarah Marie Thompson
(Older bride, include surname)
to
Doctor Michael David Bern
and
Allison Anne Alerton
(Younger bride, include surname)
to
Mr. David Frank Kelly

PUNCTUATION

In the examples I've given, no initials are used. They're not proper on an invitation. Titles that are abbreviated are Mr., Mrs., Ms., and Dr. although Doctor may be written out. Academic doctors shouldn't use the title. If the word "junior" follows a name it may be abbreviated to Jr. If it's written out a small "j" is used. If the host is a high-ranking officer in the military, the name is preceded by his title, "Colonel and Mrs. Armstrong Jones." If the person is clergy, the title should read, "The Reverend and Mrs. Jackson Arnold Smith," or "Rabbi and Mrs. Robert Berns." Most elected officials' names are preceded by their title, "The Honorable Judge and Mrs. Philip Roth Horton." There is no punctuation after the names and only proper nouns and titles are capitalized.

If the woman to be married is a physician, her title should be used if she is issuing the invitation. If she isn't issuing the invitation, she may decide to omit it. The choice is hers. A woman in the military may or may not use her title.

You'll notice in the previous examples that the groom's name is always preceded by a title, Mr. or Doctor. However, the bride's name is never preceded by a title unless she and the groom are hosting their own wedding, or the wedding is hosted by friends or by the groom's parents. Divorced or widowed women should use the name they legally use, that may or may not be their maiden name. In any case, if the name of the bride is different from her host's, her full name should be used:

Mr. and Mrs. Mark Peter Davis
request the pleasure of your company
at the marriage of their daughter
Susan Elen James (or) Susan Davis James

If the Bride or Groom is in the Military

If the bride or groom is an officer in the military, and is a lieutenant or higher, his or her title precedes their name on the invitation (although a woman in the military doesn't have to use her title), with the branch of service on the next line spelled out:

Captain Jones Earl James

(or) Captain Elizabeth Meyers Smith
United States Army

If they're of lesser rank in the military, their title is placed on the second line with their branch of service:

Jones Earl James
(or) Susan Anne Wilson
Lieutenant, junior grade, United States Navy

If they're seamen or petty officers, or non-commissioned officers or privates, their names are placed on one line with their branch of military on the following line. Titles are not used:

Paula Lee James
United States Army

Michael John Smith
United States Navy

The Second Line of the Invitation

The second line states, "request the honour of your presence." Honour is spelled with a "u" the way the British spell it. The phrase, "request the honour of your presence" is used for a religious ceremony. If the ceremony is non-religious or the invitation is to a reception use, "request the pleasure of your company." The word "request" is not capitalized, nor is there any punctuation at the end of the line.

The Date and Year

The date appears on the line after the groom's name. It is written out beginning with the day, date and month of the wedding and may be done two ways:

Saturday, the twentieth of May

(or) *on Saturday, the twentieth of May*

The day is always followed by a comma. It is capitalized as is the month. If you precede the day of the week with the word "on" it is not capitalized, nor is there any punctuation at the end of the line.

The date is followed by the year, although it's not necessary that it be on the invitation. The choice is yours. Most invitation companies, however, include the year in their samples. I also feel the year should be included because most families like to keep invitations as mementos. If you add the year it should be written this way:

nineteen hundred and ninety-eight

Notice the "n" in nineteen is not capitalized, nor is there a hyphen between the words nineteen and hundred. However, the year is hyphenated. There is no punctuation at the end of the line.

The Time

The time of the ceremony should always be written out. For example:

at six o'clock in the evening
at one o'clock in the afternoon
at twelve noon
at half after four o'clock
(never four-thirty)

Because some people can never make it to a wedding on time, brides and their mothers often ask me if they can fudge the time on the invitation, "The wedding is supposed to start at 6:30 —

could we say 6:15?" Quarter hours are not used on invitations. In this case, if you fudged the time you'd have to say "six o'clock" which would be an imposition on your punctual guests. I don't advise it.

The Ceremony Place and Address

The exact name of the ceremony place should be written out — no abbreviations. For example:

Saint Luke Catholic Church
(or) *The Boca Raton Resort and Club*

If you have many out-of-town guests or the place isn't well known it's advisable to add a street address. This follows the name of the place. The number of the street may appear in numerals except for the number "one" which is always written out. If the names of streets are numbers, they should be written out when the number is ten or less. After ten, use numerals. There should never be an abbreviation. Look at the examples below:

One Rockford Place
5 West Tenth Terrace
200 Northeast 48th Avenue

Notice the word "One" is capitalized. In this case it's a proper noun. There's no punctuation at the end of the line.

The city and state follow the street address. Once again notice that there are no abbreviations, for example:

Banff, Alberta
Saint Louis, Missouri
(No zip codes)

R.s.v.p. and Other Little Words on an Invitation

For informal weddings an R.s.v.p. may be printed at the bottom of the invitation in the lower-left or right-hand corner. It may include an address or a phone number where recipients may write or call advising whether or not they plan to attend. Years ago, the R.s.v.p. was used exclusively for formal weddings. People were expected to reply with a handwritten note. There were no respond cards. Unfortunately, our hurried society doesn't allow us the time to sit and write these thoughtful, beautiful notes anymore, and in all my years in this business, I've only sent out two formal wedding invitations with an R.s.v.p.

If you must send a formal invitation with an R.s.v.p., I'd suggest you print a phone number including area code rather than an address. I think people are more likely to call than to write. Don't forget to turn on your answering machine.

If your reception is in the same place as your ceremony, you should in the lower, left-hand corner of your invitation, or centered at the bottom, in smaller type size, add:

Reception immediately following

This will save you the cost of a reception card — there'll be a small fee for the additional line.

If you do not have a reception card, it's proper to print: "Black Tie" or "Black Tie invited, preferred" or "Black Tie optional" in the lower right or left-hand corner of the invitation in smaller type size.

Addressing the Envelope Flap

You must put the host's name and address (or just the address) on the back flap of the invitation. Initials are not used.

House numbers are written in numerals except for the number "one" which is written out. Apartment numbers, rural route numbers and box numbers also are written as numbers. Street numbers are also written as numbers except for the number "one". If the name of the street is numerical, it's written out only if it's the number ten or less. There are no abbreviations, except for titles. Look at the examples below:

Mr. and Mrs. James Francis Scott
One Melroad Place
Fort Wayne, Indiana 63457

(or) 5467 Northwest Tenth Terrace
Pittsburgh, Pennsylvania 43654

(or) Dr. and Mrs. James Clarke
Rural Route 5
Lackland, Maine 54321

(or) 3245 Southeast 51st Street
Apartment 543
New York, New York 10018

(or) Post Office Box 1234
Rye, New York 23456

The Outside Envelope - Write Your Guests' Names Correctly

It is very considerate and proper to correctly write the names of your guests. Look at the examples below:

Mr. and Mrs. William Russell Smythe

No initials, but you may skip the middle name as in the following examples:

Mr. and Mrs. William Smythe and Family

("and Family" only if entire family is invited)

If specific children of Mr. and Mrs. Smythe are invited, their names will go on the inside envelope only. If you have a large-card invitation or custom invitation with only one envelope, the names of the children will follow beneath the parents' names on the outside envelope:

Mr. and Mrs. William Smythe
Caroline and Henry
(Girl's name first)

Many invitation books say that children living at home over the age of 18 should have their own invitations. I disagree, unless you permit them to bring a guest. If you do, send them an invitation.

If your guest is permitted to bring a date and your invitation only has an outside envelope, take the time to learn the date's name and put it on the outside envelope under your guest's:

Ms. Cynthia Harper
Mr. Joel Henderson
(Woman's name first)

If you do not have the time or cannot find out the name of the guest's date you may write "and Guest" on the outside envelope of the invitation.

For an engaged couple living together, write the envelope this way:

Doctor Joanne Stewart
Mr. Jack Sloan
(Woman's name always comes first)
(Doctor may be written out)

For those in the military, clergy or those with Jr. following their name, or elected officials, follow the rules under Punctuation.

The Address on the Outside Envelope
Follow the examples below:

One Long Island Center

(One is always written out, numerals may be used for numbers higher than the number one.)

20 Northeast Tenth Way

(No abbreviations, N.E. or S.W., for example, if street name is ten or under, write it out.)

Apartment 205
(or) *Rural Route 6*
(or) *Post Office Box 9*

The words "Apartment," "Rural Route," and "Post Office Box" are all written out. The numbers, however, may be written numerically. Names of cities and states may not be abbreviated.

Saint Louis, Missouri 34567

The Inner Envelope
The inner envelope specifically designates who is invited to the wedding. Unlike the outside envelope, you don't use first names but you do use titles. You do, however, use first names of close relatives in conjunction with their titles, for example, Aunt Martha and Uncle Jim (the woman's name always comes first). Children's names are listed on a line beneath their parents, girls' names before boys'. Look at the following examples:

1. Eric and Susan have two kids, Elaine and Michael. Elaine is 18, Michael is two. She's invited, he isn't. What do you do? On the outside envelope you write:

Mr. and Mrs Eric Johnson

And on the inside envelope you write:

Mr. and Mrs. Johnson and Elaine

This tells Eric and Susan that little Michael is not invited. This also tells them Elaine is not permitted to bring a guest. (If you wanted her to bring a guest, you would have sent her a separate invitation.)

2. You're inviting your grandparents. The outside envelope will say:

Mr. and Mrs. Michael Kent Jones

The inside envelope will say:

Grandma Josie and Grandpa Mike

(This familiarity is only taken with close relatives — and the woman's name always comes first.)

3. You're inviting a single person and want them to bring a guest, but know they're not dating anyone. The outside envelope will read:

Doctor Joanna Barton Elias

The inside envelope will read:

Doctor Elias and Guest

If you didn't want them to bring a guest, the inside envelope will read:

Doctor Elias

4. You're inviting an engaged couple or couple who live together. (In this situation, always make it a point to find out the name of the fiancé or roommate if you don't know their name.) The outside envelope is addressed to the person you know:

Ms. Renee Barton
(or) *Mr. Steven Freifeld*

The inner envelope will say:

Ms. Barton
Mr. James
(Ms. Barton's fiancé or roommate)

(or) *Ms. Casperski*
(Mr. Freifeld's fiancée or roommate)
(Woman's name first)

Mr. Freifeld

If your invitation doesn't come with an inside envelope, write the outside envelope as you would the inside — include first names.

The Reception Card

The reception card tells your guests the *type* of reception you're having, the time, where you're having it and the address. It also designates the formality of the affair. Once again, everything is written out and the same rules apply as those for addressing the outside envelope. Look at the following examples of respond cards:

Reception and Dinner
(Both in caps)
immediately following ceremony
Boca Pointe Country Club
7144 Boca Pointe Drive
Boca Raton, Florida

(or) *Reception and Brunch*
at one o'clock in the afternoon
The Embassy Club
One Norwalk Lane
Chestnut Hills, Georgia

(or) *Luncheon*
at twelve noon
Buckingham Palace
London, England

It's not necessary to put a street address on the reception card if the place is well known — like Buckingham Palace. There is no punctuation at the end of the lines and no zip codes are used.

A word about "Black Tie" or the words "Black Tie invited,""Black Tie optional" or "Black Tie preferred". The most formal weddings will be "Black Tie" only, and this must appear on the reception card.

Many brides who don't like to obligate their guests to wear a tux or to rent one for their formal weddings will put "Black Tie optional, preferred or invited" on their reception card. This means that male guests may choose, or not choose to wear a tux — but whatever they decide they must wear formal garb, dark suit and tie. This also means the ladies must be dressed formally.

"Black Tie invited", "preferred" or "optional" may also appear on the reception card for a semi-formal, evening affair. This tells the guests they're going to a function where everyone is expected to dress appropriately, although the men aren't *required* to wear formal attire.

In our relaxed society, I've attended beautiful semi-formal and even formal weddings where some guests looked like they were going to a hoe-down. I think formal weddings should be "Black Tie". But if you don't want to obligate your guests, or if you're planning a semi-formal evening affair, put "Black Tie invited, preferred or optional" on your reception card. You'll be glad you did, and so will the guest who might have come improperly dressed.

The Respond Card

The *respond card* is sent with the invitation. It includes a self-addressed, stamped envelope (stamp provided by the host). Guests should mark the respond card and return it to the host. Respond cards follow different formats:

1. You may send a respond card like the example below which mixes an old tradition with the new.

Kindly respond on or before May twelfth

This respond card asks the guest to reply by a certain date, and gives them space to handwrite their reply.

In those not-so-long-ago days, when formal invitations were sent with R.s.v.p.s and respond cards were considered in poor taste, the recipient was expected to answer the invitation with a handwritten reply. These became beautiful mementos of the wedding for the bride.

When you got an invitation to a formal wedding, you pulled out your finest note paper and fountain pen and you wrote:

Mr. and Mrs. James Smith, Jr.
accept with pleasure the invitation of Mr. and Mrs.
Jones on Friday, the twenty-fifth of March

(or) *Mr. and Mrs. James Smith, Jr.*
regret that they are unable to accept the invitation of
Mr. and Mrs. James on
Friday, the twenty-fifth of March

Be warned, however, that many people don't know what to do with this type of respond card. I've had clients tell me that people wrote in the word "YES" or "NO", others just wrote in numbers. If you want to send this type of respond card follow the TIP at the end of this sub-heading.

2. In this example, "Number of Persons" is written on the respond card. For some reason those

three words act as a signal — the guests think they've got the green light to invite as many people as they please. One of my clients told me a guest filled in the number "8" — only two people had been invited to the wedding.

The favour of a reply is requested
before the twentieth of May

_____

will _____ *attend*

---

3. In the preceding example, if the guests aren't coming, they'll write their name on the line and the word "not" in the space between the words "will" and "attend". If they are attending, they'll write their name on the line and leave the space between "will" and "attend" blank.

4. Below is the respond card I prefer. The guests write their name on the line and check off "Accepts" or "Regrets". If only one member of the party is attending (the husband, for example), he will write in *Mr. James Woods* and check "Accepts".

Kindly respond on or before
December 10, 1996

M_____

Number of Persons: _____

The Wedding of Kathy and Mike
Please reply on or before
March fifth

M_____

_____ *Accepts*

_____ *Regrets*

---

5. If you're offering a choice of entree it should be included on the respond card.

The favour of a reply is requested
before June fifteenth

*M*_____

_____ *Accepts*　　_____ *Regrets*

Please select one entree for each person attending:
_____ *Chicken Francaise* _____ *Beef Wellington*

What date goes on the respond card?

Normally, caterers want a final head-count 72 hours in advance. Calculate the respond date this way: Let's say the wedding date is June 26th and for your own peace of mind, you'd like a final head-count the week before, which is June 19th. You must, however, allow a week for "stragglers" (those people who don't bother to respond). It's up to you to call these people because you can't take the chance they'll show up at the reception. This makes your respond date June 12th or about two weeks before the wedding date.

You shouldn't send invitations out months before the wedding. Your guests might lose them and forget about it. If you get more "regrets" than anticipated, you may send invitations to others on your Priority Lists who had to be skipped. It's proper for guests to receive an invitation up to two weeks before the respond date.

The Respond Card Envelope

The address of the persons hosting the wedding is normally printed on this envelope because the respond cards will be returned to them. If the host lives out of town, it's not unusual to use the bride's name and address, *not* the bride and groom's. And don't forget to put a stamp on them.

TIP: Number each guest on your list. Then on the back of each respond card envelope, in the lower right or left hand corner, put the guest's number. If they forgot to put their name on the respond card, you'll know who they are and can call them.

INFORMAL PERSONAL NOTE (FOLDER)

Informals are thank-you notes that match your invitations and should be purchased with them. They're inexpensive compared to the "six packs" you buy at a drug store. Years ago, they were only in the bride's name since she was the one who sent the notes, but today more and more grooms are getting involved. Both names may be used or a monogram combining the bride's and groom's initials.

Here are some samples:

Mr. and Mrs. Thomas Albert Jones

(or) *Denise and Albert Jones*

For those women keeping their maiden names:

Denise and Albert

(or) *Denise Lynn Roberts*
Thomas Albert Jones

Some couples omit their names and choose a monogram. They come in many different type styles and designs. In the following example, the middle initial represents the couple's surname.

The initial to the left of the middle represents the bride's first name. The initial to the right of the middle represents the groom's first name. In the example below, the couple's name is Hoffer — the bride's name is Katherine, the groom's name is Robert.

KHR

Rules for Thank-You Notes

NEVER send a note with "THANK YOU" printed on the outside or a verse printed on the inside of the card. *You must send a handwritten thank-you note to every person who sent you a gift* including your mother, mother-in-law, or maid of honor, no matter how many times you may have personally thanked them. Each note must be *sent within three weeks of receiving the gift,* whether you received it before the wedding or on your wedding day.

Gifts are normally sent to the bride before the wedding. It's smart, therefore, to order some additional informals printed in the bride's name only, or with her monogram so that she may begin sending thank-you notes as needed.

As the gifts arrive, log them in a notebook with remarks like the example below:

Name:	Date Received:	Gift:	Remarks:
Aunt Rose	5/20	Waterford Vase	Gorgeous
Sue Hasting	5/25	Toaster	Not Again
Fran Berry	5/30	12 Napkin Rings	Great!

Once a week, take the time to write your thank-you notes. After they're written, cross the recipient's name off the list. This way you won't get bogged down and your guests will appreciate your prompt, courteous reply.

There's nothing worse for a person to send a gift a week or two after receiving an invitation — and not receive a thank-you note or a thank-you photo until three months after the wedding. This is rude and inexcusable. Thank-you photos are rarely ready within three weeks of the wedding which is why I strongly object to them.

What Should You Write?

Address the person(s) who sent the gift:

Dear Sue and Bob:

You should mention who received the gift:

John and I would like to thank you for the lovely toaster.

You should tell them why you like it and how you're going to use it:

It's really a super model — good for any size slice of bread. John and I like to bake our own and now we can cut big slices and toast them!

Thank them again, add the proper salutation, depending on your familiarity with them, "Yours truly" or "Love" and sign it with your name only if the gift is sent before the wedding, and both names if it's sent after the wedding.

Yours truly,
Betty and John

If you receive cash, say thanks for the lovely check, and tell them how you intend to spend it. "We're saving for a new car — now we're going to be able to buy it a lot sooner than we expected."

TIP: To save money, if you bought expensive custom or engraved invitations, buy less expensive informals since it's not essential that the thank-you notes match the invitations.

ALL THOSE OTHER CARDS

Believe it or not, you can put more cards in an invitation than reception and respond cards. Here are some others with an explanation:

1. Maps — If you send formal or semi-formal invitations, it's very tacky to include mimeographed or hand drawn maps. Most invitation companies offer "Direction and Map Cards". They may be either thermographed or engraved to match your invitation.

2. Within-the-Ribbon or Pew Cards — These are small cards that are engraved or printed with the words "Within the Ribbon." These are included with the invitations that are mailed to close family members or special friends. Guests bring them to the ceremony and hand them to an usher who will seat them at the front in specially designated pews or chairs.

3. At-Home Cards — These cards are included with the invitation informing the recipient of the new address of the bride and groom. It also tells the recipient if the bride is keeping her name. For example:

Dr. Marie Allen
Mr. Frank Pierson
after June twenty-fourth
21454 Northeast 51st Terrace
Apartment 231
New York, New York 34321

How to Recall an Invitation

If the wedding is cancelled or postponed, you may call your guests or send out handwritten notes or printed cards. Unlike most invitation books, I don't believe an explanation is necessary.

If you handwrite a note in the case of a *postponement*, it might say:

Dear Sue and Tom:
Sorry to tell you that our wedding had to be postponed until next April. You'll receive another invitation later. In the meantime, thanks for the lovely toaster. Bill and I are putting our gifts away until the wedding takes place.
Love, Denise

In the case of a *break-up*:

Dear Sue and Tom:
Sorry to inform you that Bill's and my wedding won't be taking place. Included with this note is the wonderful toaster you sent us. Thanks once again.
Love, Denise

If the wedding is cancelled, return all gifts within six weeks along with a personal note.

If the wedding is temporarily postponed and there are too many guests to write to, printed cards should be sent by the hosts.

Mr. and Mrs. John Smith
announce that the marriage of their daughter
Deborah Lynn
to
Donald Hudson Jones

has been postponed from
July twenty-eighth
to
September twenty-third
at twelve noon
Saint Mark Roman Catholic Church
201 Pavilion Terrace
Wilton Mannors, Alabama

If the wedding has been indefinitely postponed or there is a break-up, add either of these phrases after the groom's name:

has been indefinitely postponed

(or) *will not take place*

A wedding may be cancelled due to unforeseen circumstances, a fiancé in the military being called for an emergency or a death in the immediate family. In either case, a larger wedding may be cancelled in favor of one including only members of the immediate families. If this happens, invitations must be cancelled and gifts returned. Notes or printed cards should be sent to guests as soon as possible and should be worded like this:

Mrs. Thomas Ellis Carpenter
regrets to inform you
that the invitations to her daughter's wedding
Friday, the twenty-sixth of December
must be recalled

Announcements

Announcements are mailed directly after the wedding, never before, informing those distant friends, relatives or casual acquaintances of your marriage. They may be sent from parents or close relatives who hosted your wedding, or from the bride and groom themselves. They are purchased from invitation companies. Select a small card (there's not much wording on an announcement) that may be decorative or plain, and word them as follows:

If you hosted your own wedding and wish to send announcements yourselves:

Miss Susan Lynn Smith
and
Mr. Mark Sutton
have the pleasure of
announcing their marriage
Saturday, the twenty-fifth of June
nineteen hundred and ninety-six
Honolulu, Hawaii

Titles are used. There is no punctuation except a comma separating the day from the date and a comma after Honolulu. Titles and proper nouns are capitalized. There are no abbreviations.

If your parents wish to send announcements:

Mr. and Mrs. Michael Johns Scott
have the honour of announcing
the marriage of their daughter
Cynthia Jane
to
Doctor John Smith
Saturday, the fifth of May
nineteen hundred and ninety-seven
Wilmont, Kentucky

If both sets of parents hosted the wedding and wish to send them:

Mr. and Mrs. James Russell Tone
(Bride's parents first)
and
Mr. and Mrs. Michael David Jones
have the pleasure to announce
the marriage of their children
Margo Elaine
and
David Elliott
Friday, the sixth of October
Boca Raton, Florida

How to Stuff Them

Place a stamp on the respond card envelope, mark the guest's number in one of the corners, insert the respond card face up in the envelope, close the flap but don't seal it. Place any other cards with the type facing up (maps, within-the-ribbon cards) over the open end of the respond card envelope, top with the reception card, again with type facing up. Place all in the fold of the invitation with the type facing up. Close the invitation, place the tissue over the print and insert the package into the inner envelope, facing up (the type and tissue are visible as you close the flap). Make sure the name on the inner envelope matches the name on the outer envelope. Place the inner envelope in the outer envelope in reverse so the name on the inner envelope is visible when inserted. Seal, stamp and mail. When the recipient opens the envelope, he'll see his name first on the inner envelope.

If your invitation is a single card (no fold), the tissue is placed over the type and the remaining cards placed over the tissue, always face up and in the same order as above. Most large, single-card invitations don't have inner envelopes and everything is placed in the outer envelope face up.

A Word About Type Styles and Type Size

There are many styles of print featured in invitation catalogues. For formal invitations, scripts are considered the most elegant and there are many types of scripts that you can choose from. These shouldn't have too many curlicues and should be easy to read. No matter what style of print you select, it should be legible and readable.

If you feel the size of the lettering on the sample invitation is too small or too large, you may have it enlarged or reduced. Before you do, however, get a proof to see if you like the change in type size.

Calligraphy

Calligraphy is beautiful, handwritten lettering which is done by an expert — a calligrapher. The calligrapher will write the names and addresses of your guests on the outer envelope, and their names on the inner envelopes of your invitations. It's elegant and expensive.

If money is no object and you're sending a formal invitation, calligraphy is a must. However, it's perfectly acceptable to address your own invitations providing you have neat, pleasing handwriting.

Calligraphy can now be done on a computer. This may be just as expensive, however, as the handwritten ones — and in my opinion, they look a little too perfect. Check the prices of both before you choose.

The Big or Custom Invitations, Weigh Them Before You Send Them

If you have oversized invitations or custom invitations, go to the post office and have then weighed before you mail them. They often require more postage.

How to Write a Place-Card

Place-cards are those little folded cards that designate where the guests are to sit. They may be plain or decorative and may be purchased through invitation companies. They come with the bride and groom's names and wedding date printed on them. Also, they are printed with blank lines so you may write the guests' names and table numbers. Look at the following example:

Susan and Mark
December 12, 1999

Mr. and Mrs. John Jones

Table Number: 4

Other Essentials That May Be Purchased Through Invitation Companies

All the following items purchased from invitation companies may be personalized with the bride and groom's name and wedding date, and decorated with wedding motifs:

1. Shower invitations.
2. Matches.
3. Napkins — (beverage-size napkins should be used for the cocktail hour, and when the cake is served.)
4. Wedding Reception Scrolls — a little "thank you" for the guests, placed at each place setting, with a cute verse, thanking them for attending.
5. Wedding Programs — a personalized memento of the wedding, listing the events of the ceremony and the participants.
6. Personalized toasting goblets.
7. Personalized cake servers and knives.
8. Personalized cake bags — if guests want to take their cake home.
9. Flower-girl baskets and ringbearer pillows.
10. Personalized garters.
11. Personalized wedding books, such as guest books and albums.
12. Personalized plumed pens that guests use to sign the guest book.
13. Ribbons with the bride and groom's name printed on them, used for favors.
14. Bird seed to throw at the couple instead of rice.
15. Personalized cocktail stirrers.
16. Unity candles.

And Finally

This invitation was brought to me from South Africa by one of my brides-to-be. I thought you might get a kick out of it.

Mr. and Mrs. James Frank Smith
long suffering parents of Susan
their second daughter
(thank goodness they only have two!)
have great pleasure and relief
in announcing
that they are finally off-loading her onto
Mr. David Michael Kent
the pleasure of your company is requested
at their marriage
on Saturday, the fifteenth of June
nineteen hundred and ninety-eight
at six o'clock in the evening
The Bickford Mansion
Happy Days, South Africa

Mr. and Mrs. Stewart John Colbert
request the honour of your presence
at the marriage of their daughter
Donna Elena
to
Mr. Evan Michael Clinton
Saturday, the twenty-second of July
nineteen hundred and ninety-five
at five o'clock
United Congregational Church
325 Park Avenue
New York, New York

Transportation

Today, wedding transportation can be fun as well as practical. I recall a wedding where the bride, her parents, grandparents, and female attendants arrived at the church in an old-fashioned trolley car. After the ceremony, the entire bridal party, both sets of parents, grandparents, and the bride and groom hopped the trolley car for the ride to the reception.

At another wedding the bride and groom had a handsome horse-and-buggy waiting to take them to the reception. I'll never forget how radiant that couple looked. They stopped traffic as they made their way through town. And then there's the classic Rolls Royce or the stretch limousine, the choice of most brides and grooms. Today, most couples rent transportation for their weddings. It's an elegant, safe, and fun way to travel.

The Goals of Rented Transportation

The purpose of rented transportation is to take the bride and her father (or parents) to the ceremony, and the bride and groom from the wedding to the reception. If funds are unlimited, a fleet of transportation may be rented to take both sets of parents and the bridal party to the ceremony, and afterward, to the reception. For more information, see Ceremonies chapter.

All those who ride in rented transportation should either make arrangements to leave their cars at the reception site or arrange for transportation to take them home.

How to Find Rented Transportation

Referral is the key to finding good rented transportation. Ask recently married friends, relatives and business associates whom they used and if they had complaints. Too many times I've heard, "The limo didn't show up," or "It was the wrong one!" Don't let yourself in for this kind of aggravation. Consult the appendix for more information.

When and How to Reserve

Reserve rented transportation four months ahead. If your wedding date falls in late May or June — prom months — you should reserve it once your wedding date is set and the reception place is booked. Don't delay, or you may have a hard time reserving the kind of transportation you want.

When you call transportation companies, monitor their "response time" — the time it takes them to return your call. If they return it promptly, make an appointment with the manager or owner — not a driver. Go to their place of business and look at the vehicle(s) they offer for weddings. Make sure they're in good condition and that they're clean inside and out, with a working stereo. You should also meet with the drivers who will be chauffeuring you on your wedding day.

You will be expected to reserve your vehicle(s) with a deposit. Be sure to put it on a credit card to protect yourself in case the company goes out of business.

Discussing Details

Licensing for transportation companies can be strict. They normally have to be licensed by the state and the city or town where they do business. They must be fully insured, and their drivers must be licensed and insured, also. Check that the transportation company and its drivers meet all state and local requirements and are insured — before you do business with them. Find out about your liability and the company's — what are your responsibilities and theirs if there is an accident, or if damage is done to the vehicle? According to Wayne Smith, President of the National Limousine Association, it's advisable to ask if they have insurance protection through the ICC (Interstate Commerce Commission). It would be advisable to hire a company that does.

Discuss your wedding with the owner or manager in terms of the size of the car(s) needed and the number of cars necessary to accommodate your party. This should go in the contract.

The driver(s) should dress formally, either in a tux, uniform, or dark business suit with a tie. You should also discuss what food and beverages are to be included — some companies, for example, will throw in a bottle of champagne, although you may have to pay for hors d'oeuvres. Be aware, however, that some states do not permit liquor in cars, even though you're *not* driving.

The number and types of vehicles used determines the price. A Rolls Royce is more expensive than a stretch limo, for example, and a horse-and-buggy may be more expensive than either one. A fleet of limos is naturally going to be more expensive than using just one or two cars.

Most rented transportation is charged by the hour, but there's usually a minimum. So be sure to ask. Also ask if taxes and tip are included.

Include These Items in Your Contract

— The date, place, and time of the ceremony and reception, including the addresses and phone numbers of the ceremony and reception sites.

— If vehicles are rented to pick up the bride, parents, groom, and bridal party, list the time and place(s) they are to be picked up, including phone numbers and addresses.

— List the license plate numbers of all vehicles to be used, when you reserve transportation. That way you'll make sure you get the same vehicles.

— Stipulate their liability policy for both accidents and damages. The contract should cover your responsibilities and their cancellation policy.

— List food and beverages that are included.

— Specify the dress of the driver(s) —uniform, business suit, tux, etc.

— The rate charged, including tax, the minimum fee and tip policy.

— The amount of the deposit paid and the balance due (put deposits on a credit card).

And Finally - the Follow Up

On the day before the wedding, make sure you call the transportation company to find out if you're on the schedule. Ask how many vehicles have been rented, the time they're to pick everyone up, and the addresses of where they're to go. Let them tell you, that way you'll know if their information is correct. This should ensure that everything runs smoothly.

White Tie for a formal evening wedding.

Formal Wear

It's critical to understand a little about the tuxedo business before you begin to shop, because a little knowledge of this business will have a direct bearing on *where* and *how* your future groom decides to rent formal wear.

Disasters do happen. The groom goes to pick up his tux only to find it's the wrong color or size. The store forgets an usher's shoes, or the studs for his tuxedo shirt, or there's no tux for the father of the bride.

Calamities like these shouldn't happen before a wedding and will not happen to educated consumers. The old adage, "an ounce of prevention is worth a pound of cure," doubly applies when shopping for formal wear.

Most large, national formal-wear businesses operate from central locations where they stock jackets, ties, vests, cummerbunds, pants, shoes and accessories. From the central location, they operate satellite stores where customers shop for formal wear. After a customer selects a tux, it's ordered from the central location, perhaps hundreds of miles away.

Other formal-wear companies keep only samples on hand, but operate by renting tuxedos from large wholesalers, companies who lease the tuxedos to them. The shop calls in the customers' measurements to the wholesaler, who alters the formal wear before it's sent to the store. Many bridal stores and dry cleaners who rent formal wear operate this way.

Other tuxedo businesses keep stock on the premises at all times. This includes standard, classic black-and-grey tuxedos, strollers, etc., and accessories — shirts, shoes, ties, cummerbunds and vests in all colors and sizes. These stores may also rent from wholesalers if they don't carry a particular tux you're looking for.

What to Look for

A good, well-run, formal-wear business will have a tailor on the premises. If a customer comes to pick up a tuxedo or cutaway, for example, and the pants haven't been hemmed or there's a rip in the sleeve, a tailor can fix it immediately. If there's no tailor, all the customer can do is complain — hardly a satisfactory solution to the problem.

That's why it's a *must* that a formal-wear shop have a tailor on the premises.

Ordering formal wear from stores that don't keep stock *on the premises* or have a tailor may be asking for trouble. If an incorrect order is placed with the central location or the wholesaler — and the customer comes in two days before the wedding to pick up the *wrong* tuxedo — there won't be any way to exchange it. This also applies if the wrong size shoes or accessories were sent, or they overlooked a hole in the seat of the pants. Deal with a formal-wear shop that can address these problems on the spot.

Many brides and grooms also like to order "specialty" tuxedos featured in bridal magazines. Most of the time, these are ordered from wholesalers. If your bridal party isn't local or the groomsmen can't get to the store by the Wednesday before the wedding to try them on (so there's time to get replacements if something's wrong), don't risk it. If you do decide to take the chance, however, order them from a store that carries stock, just in case.

Mr. Robert Haber, owner of Tuxedo Junction, a fully-stocked, formal-wear shop in Boca Raton, Florida says, "If a bride and groom go to a store that carries stock and has a tailor on the premises, they shouldn't experience problems. It's very important, however, that they know these things *before* they decide to rent formal wear for the most important day of their lives. By asking the right questions they can avoid disaster."

When and How to Shop - Ask the Right Questions

Shop for formal wear four months before the wedding and reserve it at least one month before. Make sure that all formal wear for the bridal party — shirts to shoes — is ordered from the same shop. This will ensure uniformity for all members of the bridal party.

When you go to a formal-wear shop ask these important questions:

— Do you have stock on the premises, including jackets, pants, ties, shirts, shoes, cummerbunds, vests, studs, cufflinks, and suspenders?

— If you don't have stock on the premises, how far away is your source?

— Do you have a tailor on the premises?

— May we try on the formal wear when we come to pick it up?

If the store answers "no" to any of these questions, or doesn't have a local source providing them with formal wear, find another shop. If they answer the questions satisfactorily, however, you shouldn't experience problems. Now to the fitting.

Proper Fit

When men go to a formal-wear shop to be measured, they should try on different jackets and pants to see how they fit. A good formal-wear shop won't rely solely on measurements to determine the correct fit.

It's common courtesy among formal-wear shops to measure men who'll be participants in out-of-town weddings. The formal-wear store renting the garments will give "measurement cards" to the groom, who will send them to the members of his out-of-town bridal party. The out-of-towners must be measured by a local tuxedo shop and send the cards back to the groom's shop. To avoid problems, tell your groomsmen *not* to measure themselves. It's smart to have out-of-town members of the bridal party try on a few jackets and pants when being measured, so the store can best advise them on the size they should order.

The white dinner jacket for a summer wedding.

The classic tuxedo for formal and semi-formal evening weddings.

The classic stroller is perfect for semi-formal day weddings.

This modern rendition of the cutaway is the choice of many sophisticated grooms for semi-formal day weddings.

A measurement alone should not be trusted in case it was done incorrectly. Trying on the clothes to help determine correct size will cut the chance of mistakes occurring when the tuxedos are ordered by another shop.

Advise your out-of-town bridal party members to be courteous when they go to be measured. The shop makes no money taking measurements. If the store is busy, they should come back at another time, especially if they'd like to try on a few jackets and pants.

What the Tuxedo Rental Includes

The rental includes the jacket, pants, shirt, cummerbund or vest, tie, studs, cufflinks, and suspenders. Shoes are usually extra. A free tux is normally given to the groom, provided there are a substantial number of men in the bridal party, usually five or more.

Deposits, Insurance, and Security Deposits

When the groom and his bridal party reserve tuxes or formal wear, a deposit will be required. Out-of-town members of the bridal party may be asked to send a deposit with their measurements. The balance is due when the formal wear is picked up before the wedding (along with a security deposit, which is refunded when the tuxes, etc, are returned to the store the Monday after the wedding).

It's advisable that the groom and groomsmen take insurance when renting formal wear. The cost is minimal and a tuxedo can be expensive to replace.

The Final Fitting - Rules to Follow

THE GROOM AND ATTENDANTS MUST TRY ON ALL FORMAL WEAR WHEN THEY GO TO PICK IT UP. This means the complete outfit including jacket, shirt, pants, tie, vest, shoes, cufflinks, studs, and suspenders. Men should try on the garments the Wednesday before the wedding if possible. This will give the store time to get a replacement or make alterations if something's wrong.

To avoid problems, try to get all out-of-town members of the bridal party into the formal-wear shop as soon as they arrive.

Be Aware - "Shop-at-Home" Services

Shop-at-home formal-wear services have sprung up around the country. The bridal party goes to the house of the groom or one of the groomsmen, where a fitter comes and measures them for tuxes. The tuxes are then dropped off before the wedding. The only advantage is the price, which may be less than shopping at a formal-wear shop.

The disadvantages are too numerous to mention. There's no stock on hand in case something goes wrong. There's no tailor to do alterations and there's no shop to call if there are problems. The groom and the groomsmen are on their own — not a comforting thought when facing a wedding. My advice is to go to a reputable shop. It's worth a few extra dollars for peace of mind.

What the Groom and Groomsmen Should Wear

At 99 percent of the weddings I attend, no matter where they're held or what time of day, the groom and the groomsmen are dressed in tuxedos. In one of my old bridal books the author writes, "A tuxedo before 6 o'clock..? Never!"* Times have changed, but tuxedos shouldn't be your *only* choice. You do have other options available.

* Footnote see page 356.

The Informal Day or Evening Wedding

Dress for informal weddings is governed by the ceremony place. If the ceremony is held in church or temple, the groom and best man should wear suits — dark in winter, light in summer. If the wedding is held in a club or hotel, for example, suits should also be worn.

If the wedding is on a beach or in a park, you wouldn't expect the groom or best man to wear a suit. They should wear whatever the wedding and ensuing party require.

Strollers and Cutaways for Semi-Formal Day Weddings

Know what strollers and cutaways are? They're types of formal wear for morning or afternoon semi-formal weddings and they're striking! The stroller resembles a suit coat and comes in black or grey, or may be a subtle pinstripe. The stroller is classically worn with a white or ivory wing-tipped shirt and ascot (which is a scarf folded to look like a wide tie), or it's worn with a four-in-hand tie (that looks just like the one your future husband or father wears to work everyday), or a turned-down collar (which looks like a button-down shirt without the buttons). The tie or ascot may be a subtle print in the same color as the stroller or a solid color. A vest is always worn with the stroller, which may be the same color or a solid, complementary color. The pants that match are usually grey or black striped, but may also be a solid color.

The cutaway coat hits about mid-thigh and tapers back from the waist. It comes in the same colors as the stroller and is worn with vest, wing-tipped or turned-down white or ivory shirt, and ascot or four-in-hand tie. The colors are either grey, black, or pinstriped with matching or coordinating accessories, just like the stroller.

The groom may distinguish himself with a different color tie or by a different boutonniere. The ringbearer and fathers of the bride and groom should be dressed as the groomsmen.

Strollers and cutaways are *elegant.* There's no other way to describe them and they're perfect for morning and afternoon weddings. Why brides insist on tuxedos with cummerbunds that match the bridesmaids dresses is beyond me. Tuxedos are not for morning or afternoon weddings and cummerbunds that match dresses are for proms.

What could be more elegant than men in cutaways with vests and ascots? They are proper, traditional, and in this day and age *different.*

Suits and the Semi-Formal Day Wedding

There's no reason why the groom and groomsmen can't wear dark business suits at a semi-formal day wedding. It's perfectly correct. Shirts should be white or ivory with matching, colored ties in subtle stripes (or compatible ties — not stripes and plaids). In summer, they may wear white or ivory jackets with dark pants, white or ivory shirts and matched ties. The groom should distinguish himself with a different boutonniere. The fathers of the bride and groom, and the ringbearer should be dressed like the groomsmen.

The Semi-Formal Wedding After Five - "Black Tie" or "Dinner Jackets"

For semi-formal weddings after five, the groom and groomsmen should wear black or dark grey tuxedos with matching pants, cummerbunds or vests. Their shirts may be wing-tipped or turned down, either white or ivory to match the bride's gown, and a bow tie is worn. They may wear either vests or cummerbunds to match their jackets. At no time are the cummerbunds to match the bridesmaids dresses.

The groom may dress differently than other groomsmen but *HE MAY NOT WEAR TAILS!* He may wear a black vest instead of a cummerbund, or the color of his tie may be different, or his boutonniere. Other than that, the bridal party should be identical. The fathers of the bride and groom should match the groomsmen in dress, as should the ringbearer.

A dazzling alternative is the white dinner jacket, worn with navy or black pants, which may be worn in tropical climates or in summer. White shirts are worn with navy or black cummerbunds and matching bow ties. Navy or black pants are worn with black shoes and socks.

Today, tuxedos are being made in many different colors, and although grey and black are classic, and what I recommend — ties, vests, and cummerbunds are also being made in elegant prints and plaids that look beautiful with tuxedos or white dinner jackets. These are appropriate for semi-formal weddings only.

THE FORMAL WEDDING

"Black Tie" After Five

The majority of formal weddings will be *Black Tie*. The groom and groomsmen wear black tuxedos with white or ivory shirts to match the color of the bride's gown. The shirts are wing-tipped or turned down, and bow ties are worn. They may wear matching black ties, cummerbunds or vests. Black pants, socks and shoes are worn. The fathers of the bride and groom should dress like the groomsmen, as should the ringbearer. The groom may wear a vest instead of a cummerbund, or his bow tie may be a different color, or he may wear a different boutonniere.

In summer or tropical climates, white dinner jackets are also appropriate.

"White Tie" After Six

Ever hear of *White Tie?* It's reserved for the most elaborate, formal weddings held in the evening. The groom and groomsmen wear black tails with white pique vests or cummerbunds and white piqué shirts and ties. They wear fancy studs and cufflinks and their shoes are black patent leather. The groom distinguishes himself with different shirt studs, or a special boutonniere.

A Word of Advice

Today it seems that anything goes in formal wear, and for that reason I can only advise you on the guidelines and what's appropriate for your wedding type. If you decide to break the rules — wear tails at 10 a.m. — do so because you *want* to break the rules, not because you don't know what the rules are.

In Conclusion

Be a smart shopper to guarantee a successful day. Ask the right questions and shop at reputable, fully stocked, formal-wear stores. Make sure a tailor is on the premises.

Coordinate your groom's formal wear to your wedding "type" and the time of day of your ceremony. Don't let your groom overdress. Make sure his formal wear and that of the groomsmen blend beautifully and harmoniously with the total look of your wedding.